MADISON

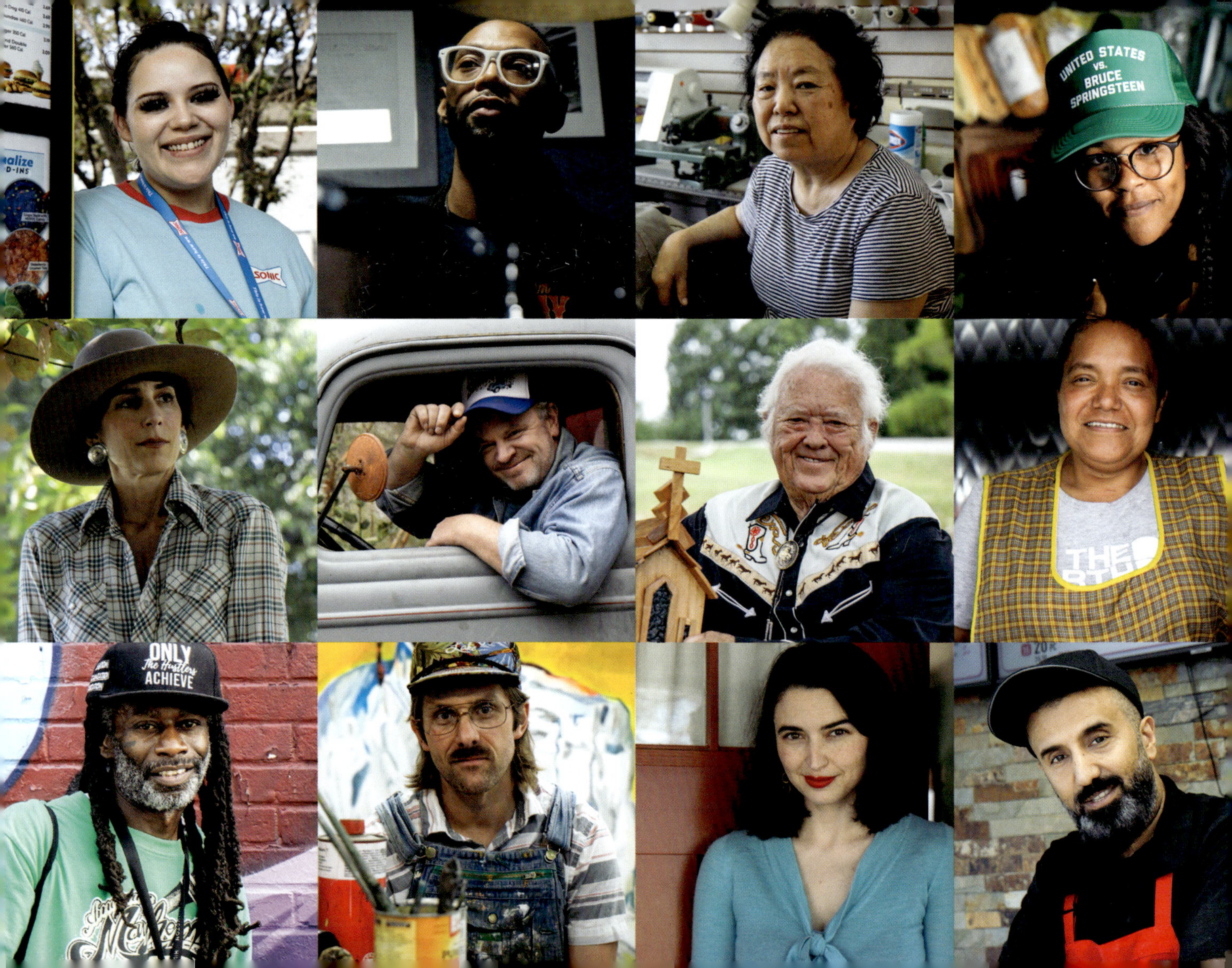
SONIC
UNITED STATES
vs.
BRUCE
SPRINGSTEEN
ONLY
The Hustlers
ACHIEVE

MADISON

Portraits of Our Neighbors

LAURA JO AMARAL
STACIE HUCKEBA

VANDERBILT UNIVERSITY PRESS | NASHVILLE, TENNESSEE

Published 2025

Library of Congress Cataloging-in-Publication Data on file

Library of Congress Control Number: 2025945488

ISBN: 978-0-8265-0826-3 (hardcover)

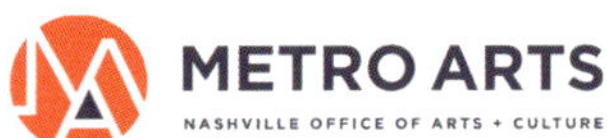

This publication was made possible with the support of a 2024 Thrive Grant through Metro Arts: Nashville Office of Arts + Culture

PRINTED IN CANADA

For my daughters.

Laura

For my neighbors;
past, present, and future

Stacie

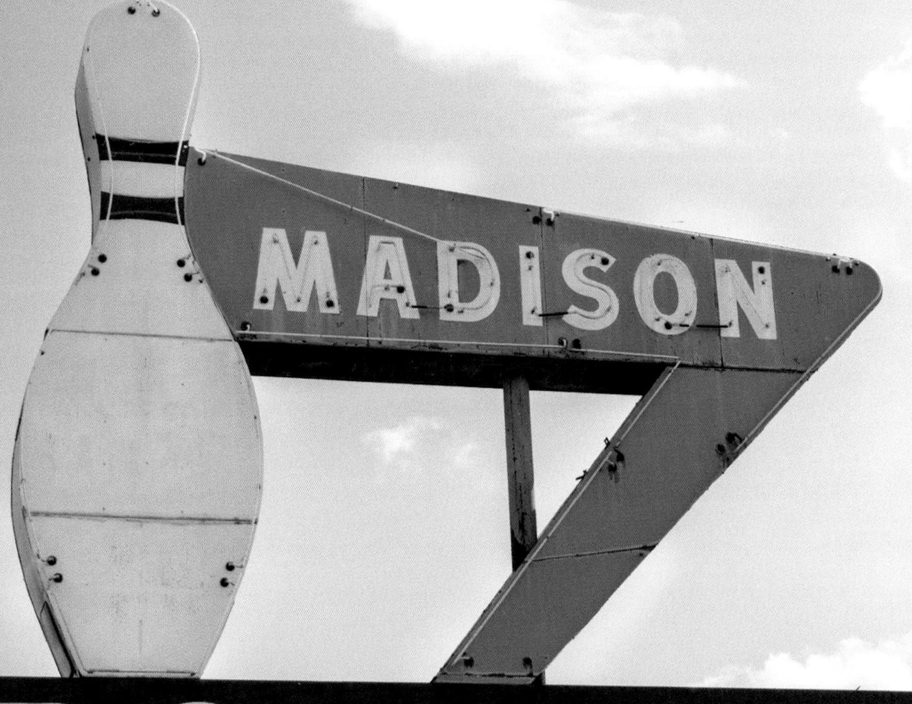
MADISON
BOWLING

Contents

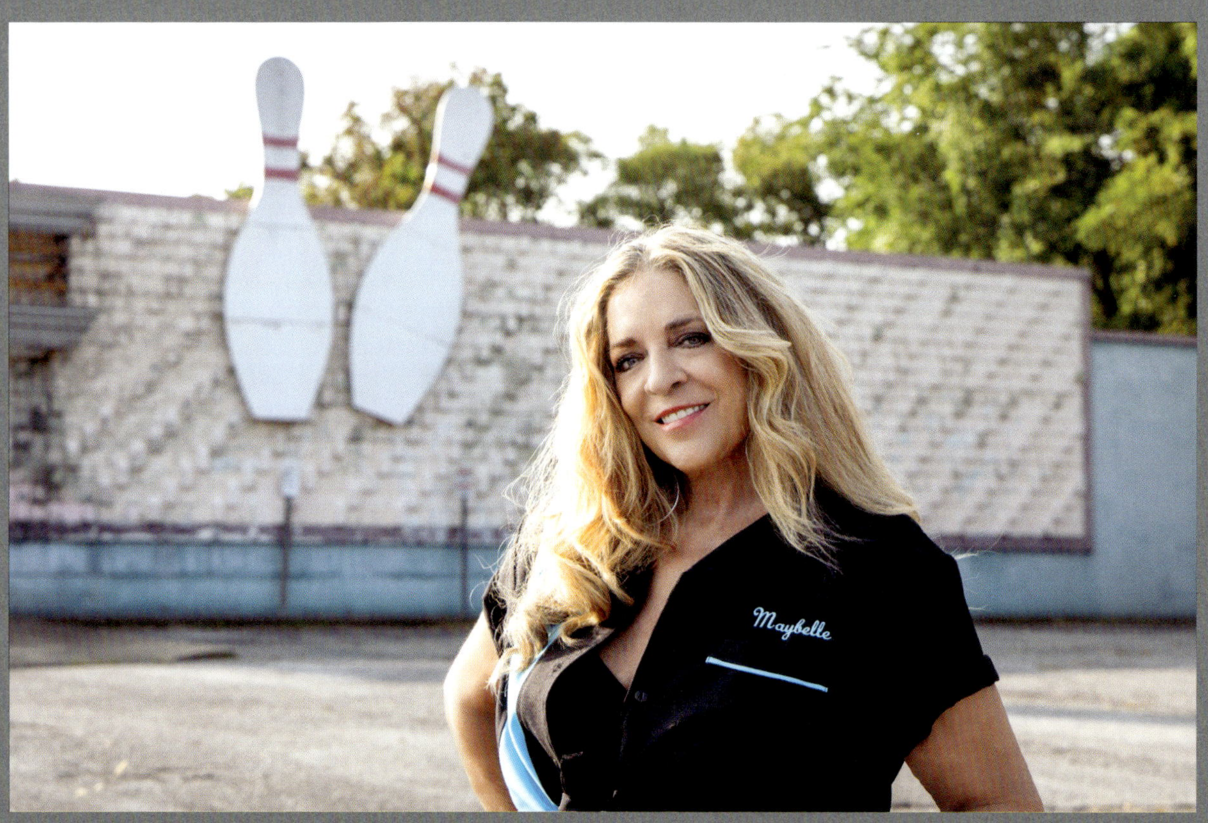

Singer-songwriter **Carlene Carter**

FOREWORD

Carlene Carter

MADISON IS WHERE I WAS BORN AND LIVED over several different time frames in my life. In the late fifties and early sixties, Madison had fewer than four thousand residents. It's seen a lot of growth, but back then it seemed all too perfect for a little girl like me!

Fence rows of honeysuckle lined the property I called home. A creek to wade in ran through the middle of our farm. Dogwoods, huge oaks, and cedar trees were all around our town. It was beautiful and green and people in Madison seemed happy to have found this sweet spot to plant roots.

Probably the reason my family all ended up living here!

My daddy, Carl Smith, purchased this slice of country when he married my momma, June Carter, in 1951. Soon all the Carter sisters and my grandparents became homeowners here, all within just minutes of each other.

And they weren't the only musicians and songwriters in our neighborhood. Our Madison house was filled with music in a big way.

Picking parties brought out guitars and incredible songs sung by Patsy Cline, Harlan Howard, Loretta Lynn, George Morgan, Felice and Boudleaux Bryant, Louise and Earl Scruggs, and my favorite, Brenda Lee. And they were just a portion of that seemingly endless list of music-making friends and neighbors. Music was always a large part of life in Madison. A tradition that carries on today.

People say home is where your heart is. When I think of home it's Madison. They also say you can't go back home again. Well that's not true because I keep coming back.

My kids spent a large part of their lives in the Madison house I grew up in, the same Madison house where my grandparents, Ezra and Mother Maybelle Carter, lived happily and passed peacefully.

My memories, old as they might be, are fresh every time I drive down a street I once walked to school on or rode bikes down with friends. I love it here and can only wish for kids growing up now to have half the good times I had and memories I still cherish of our Madison!

Love this life!!

Carlene Carter

“Madison, Tennessee”

John Hartford

[VERSE 1]
I ain’t got ten dollars
Just these dirty clothes
And the rags I borrowed somewhere
To wipe my bloodshot nose
Left eye someone punched it
So now I barely see
To find my way back to my home in
Madison, Tennessee

[CHORUS]
Madison’s a good old place
If banjo music is your taste
Been living here, since ’63
In Madison, Tennessee

[VERSE 2]
I haven’t got a lot to say
I’ve got some kind of low
And I can hear those horns a honkin’
Out on Gallatin Road
Put my finger on a map
Who knows where I might be
To find my way back to my home
In Madison, Tennessee

[CHORUS]
Madison’s a good old place
If fiddle music is your taste
Been living here, since ’63
In Madison, Tennessee

[VERSE 3]
Out behind the fire hall
Under a full moon
Fiddlers and banjo pickers
Crammed inside a room
Playing songs made popular
Back in 1923
Raising the roof in a little white house
In Madison, Tennessee

[CHORUS]
Madison’s a good old place
If country music is your taste
Been living here, since ’63
In Madison, Tennessee

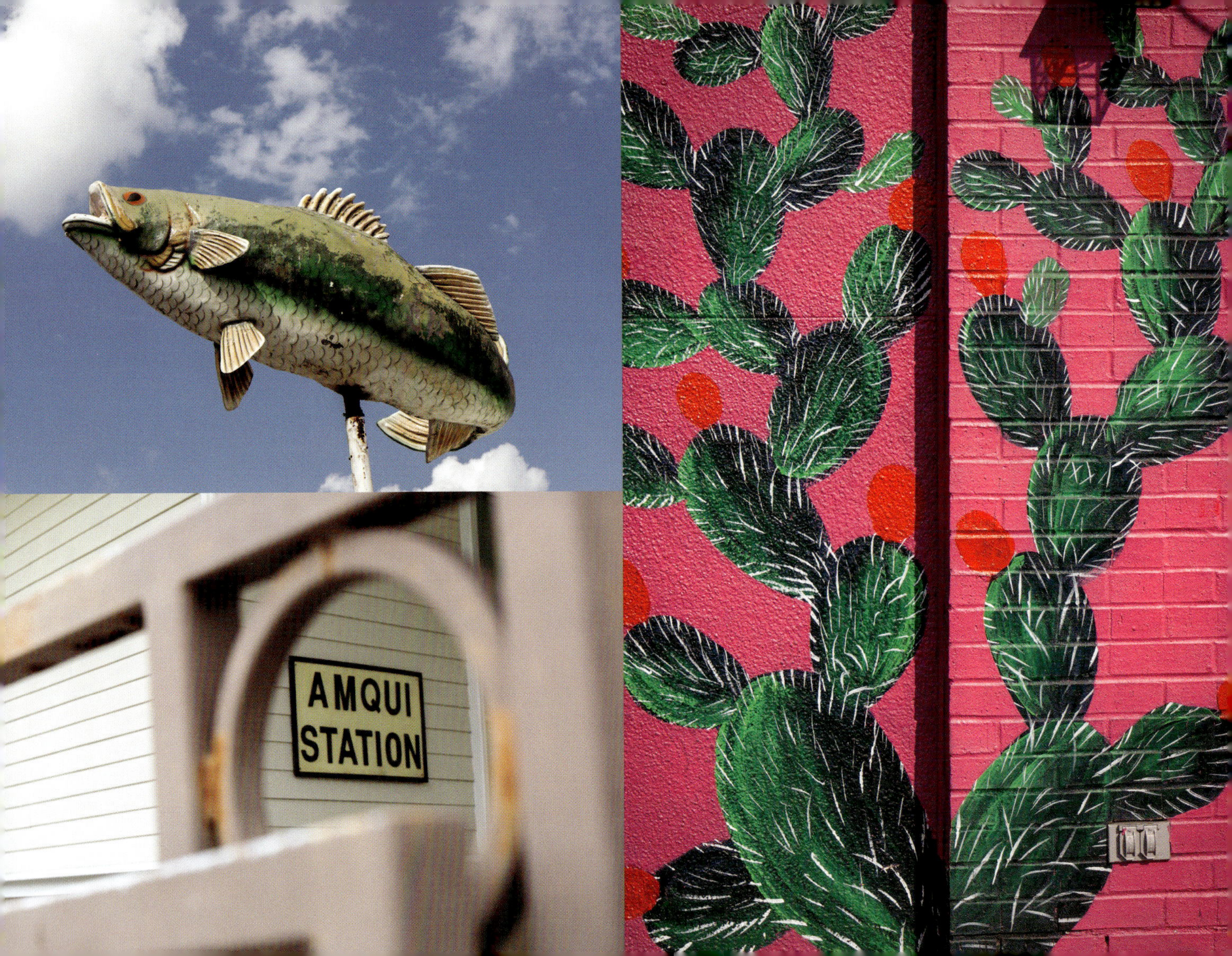
AMQUI
STATION

INTRODUCTION

Early one morning in January 2023, I was driving through Madison on Gallatin Pike when I noticed the familiar old sign at Nashville Clock was covered by a banner announcing a new business: Buzz Doctor 2.0 Vape Shop "Coming Soon." I parked my car to take a quick photo with my phone. Nashville Clock had a national reputation for highly specialized clock repairs often with a long waiting list, and it was definitely a stand out as a "mom and pop" business along that stretch of road. I later read on their website that the retail space had become unviable and they had relocated to focus on repairs and restoration.

Documenting Madison in a creative way had always been a fuzzy idea to me, but driving along Gallatin that morning, the idea for this book actually took shape. I wanted to capture my Madison neighbors for generations to come and to create a photography art book of my neighborhood now.

I reached out to my friend and fellow Madisonian, photographer Stacie Huckeba. She has a background in legacy projects, so she not only understands but is passionate about the significance and importance of the preservation of history. She had just wrapped up a tenure with Dolly Parton, photographing her entire wardrobe archive and serving as the director of photography for her *New York Times*-best-selling book *Dolly Parton, Behind the Seams, My Life in Rhinestones*, and now she was looking for a new personal project.

Our first brainstorming session over breakfast at Madtown Coffee proved fruitful. A diverse list of potential subjects quickly materialized and we imagined photographing them in their current homes and work spaces. Our focus would be on musicians, artists, retailers, farmers, clergy, and other colorful characters who make Madison such a distinctive place to call home.

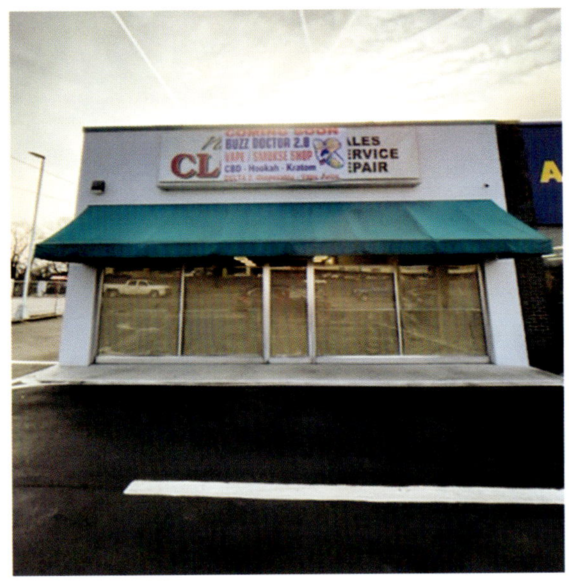

Without a plan regarding funding or logistics, we seized on our enthusiasm and began making calls that very day. Within a week we were out and about in Madison capturing our subjects and documenting their stories. A few months later, we found and applied for a Thrive grant through Metro Arts / Nashville Office of Art + Culture and were honored to be chosen as one of the recipients of that funding in 2024.

We spent more than a year traversing our neighborhood and meeting with our neighbors, and we were inspired to find that all of our participants not only supported what we were doing but appreciated the spirit of community behind it and were excited to be featured both as individuals and for the preservation of our collective history.

Madison has been a part of the Nashville landscape for over one hundred years and has been reinvented many times over. It was once considered a suburb of Nashville and was home to many major country stars. At that time, Madison Square was a thriving retail destination. Now it's home to more small and independently owned stores and businesses, several owned by people of immigrant status, and its residents are more likely to be your typical next-door neighbor than Kitty Wells, Bill Monroe, John Hartford, or June Carter. There is a certain beauty that lies in this incarnation, as there is in the nostalgia from the past.

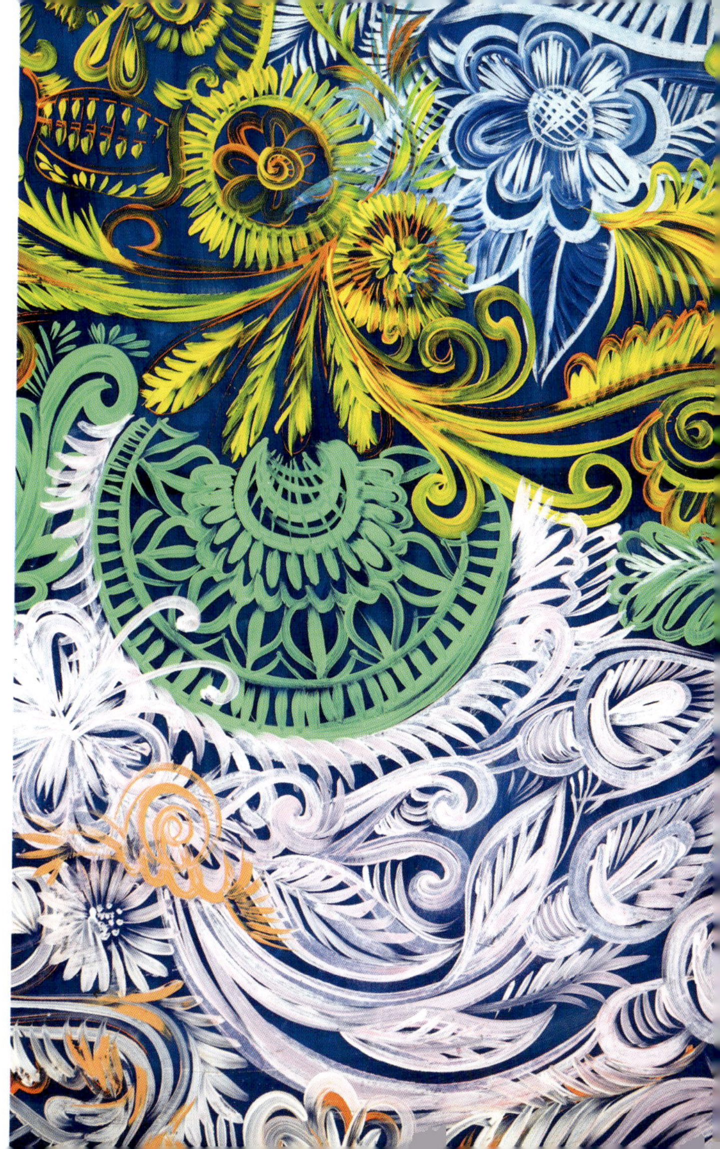

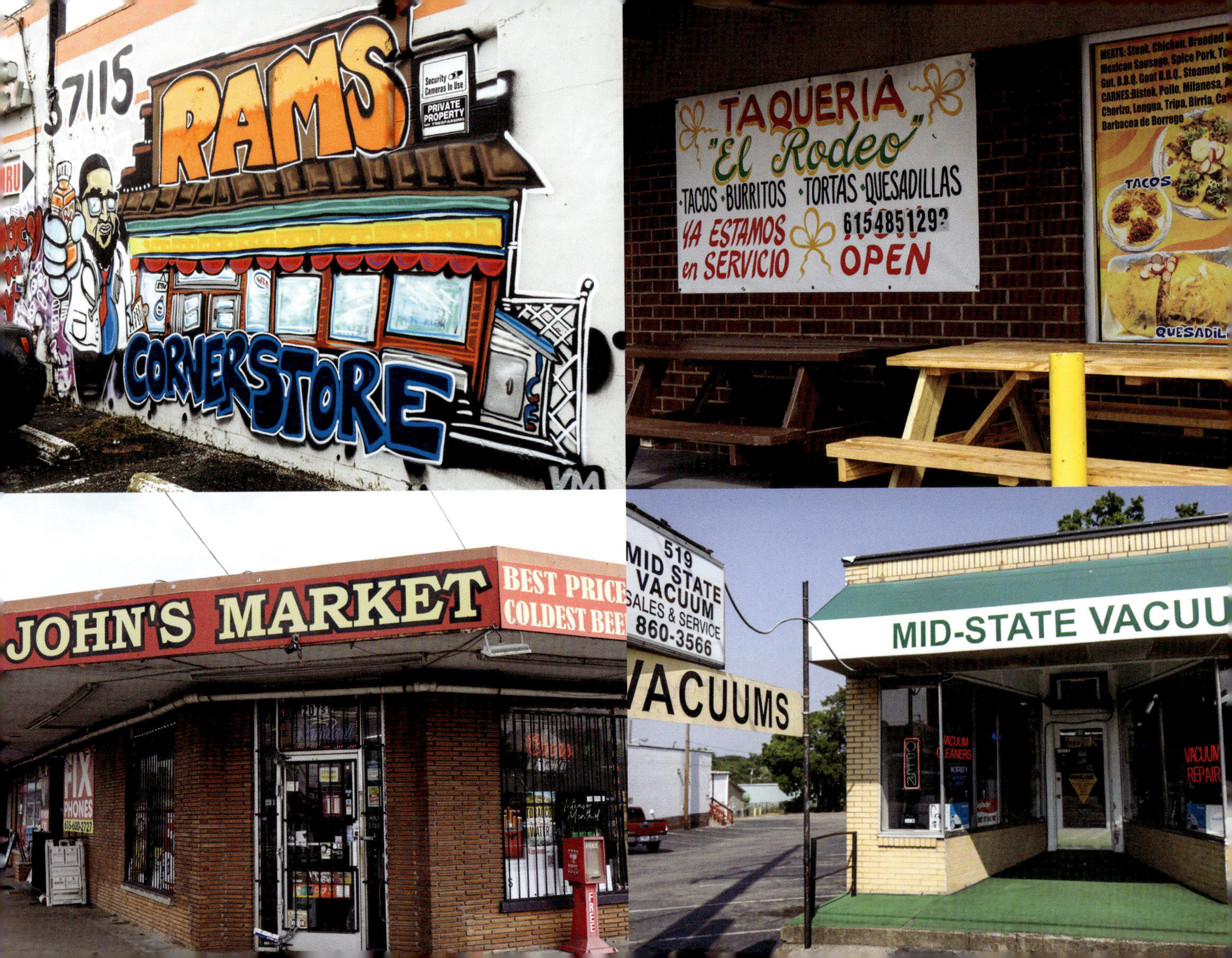
RAMS
Security Cameras In Use
PRIVATE PROPERTY
CORNERSTORE
TAQUERIA
"El Rodeo"
•TACOS •BURRITOS •TORTAS •QUESADILLAS
YA ESTAMOS en SERVICIO
OPEN
TACOS
JOHN'S MARKET
FIX PHONES
519
MID STATE VACUUM
SALES & SERVICE
860-3566
VACUUMS
VACUUM CLEANERS
OPEN
VACUUM REPAIR
FREE

All of Nashville is undergoing major change and Madison is no exception. New businesses and buildings pop up every day and while we accept and even welcome change, we are very much aware of the impact that all of this major development will have on the livelihoods and addresses of the residents who populate this charismatic neighborhood. Change is evident even in this collection. Since we began this project, some of these businesses have closed, some of our participants have relocated, a few people have started new jobs, and sadly, one has passed away. That very change is why we started this book in the first place, and we feel blessed that we had the opportunity to include them when we did.

We are proud to say that we live in Madison and are very charmed and inspired by our neighbors and our neighborhood. We are grateful to everyone who was open to being a part of this book and revealing a little bit about themselves, their lives, their art, their work, and their spaces. Our main goal was to celebrate and uplift our neighbors in these beautiful portraits, and we hope that this book will inspire you to see your own neighbors in their best light, too.

PORTRAITS

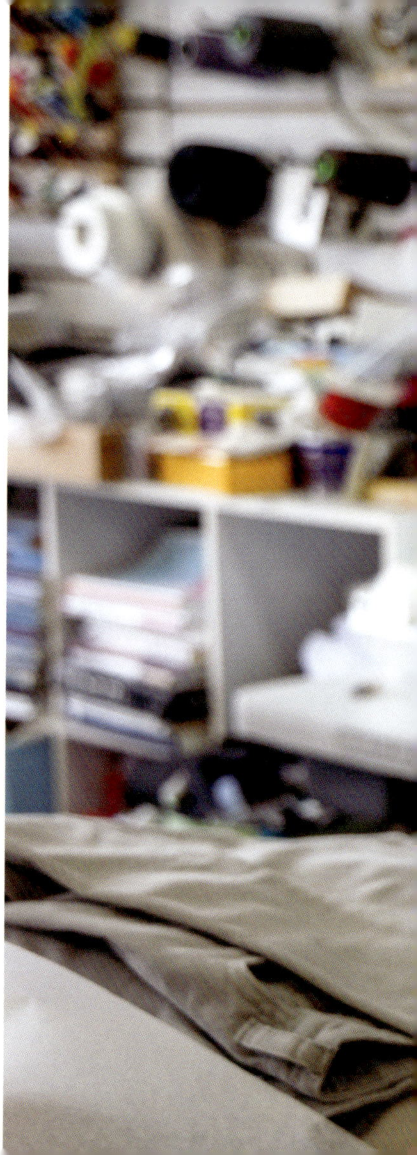

Jenny Lee, owner of Madison Alterations, sits inside her shop. She recounts serving many country stars throughout her twenty-five-plus years of business.

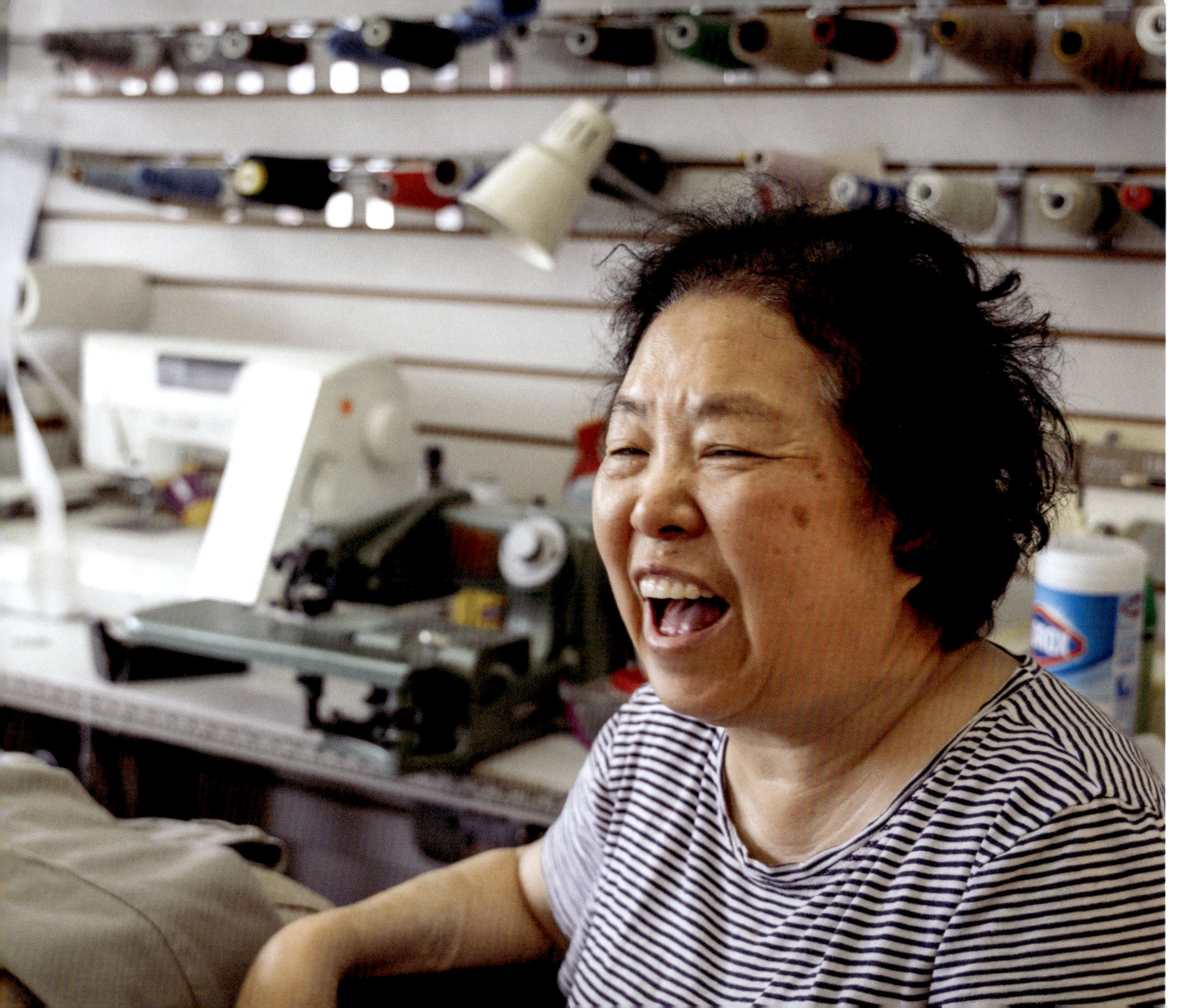

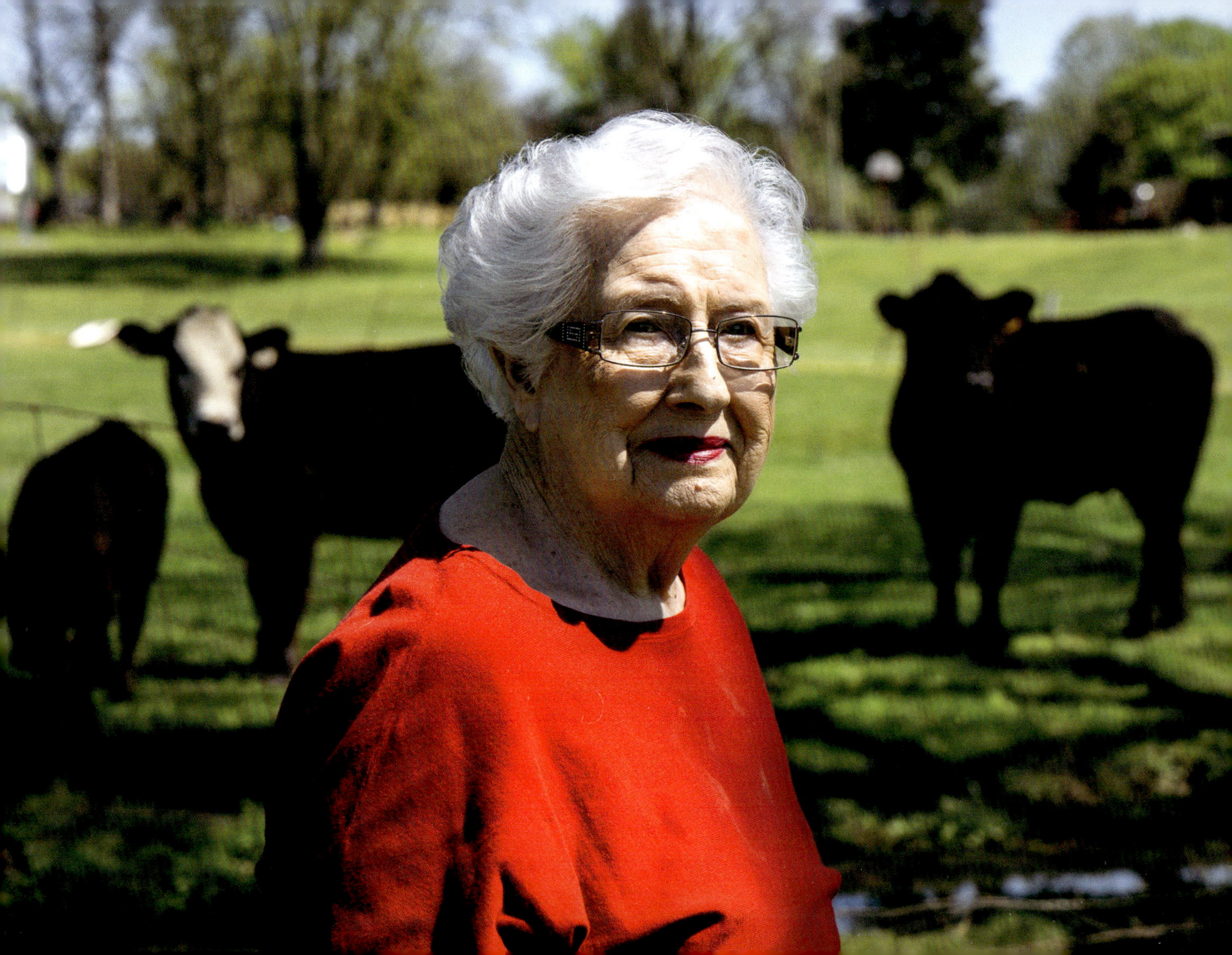

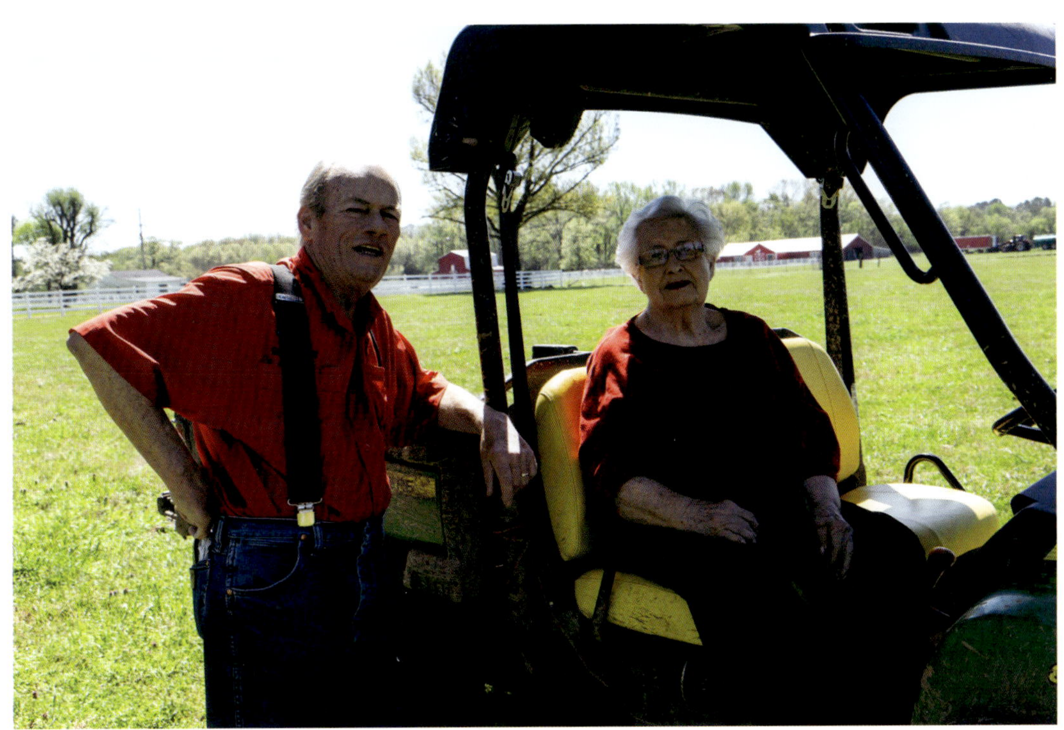

Ms. Juanita Howell and Gwynn Howell, her late son, check on their herd of cattle at their family farm in lower Neelys Bend. The nearly one-hundred-year-old matriarch still takes an interest in the daily operations at the fourth-generation cattle farm.

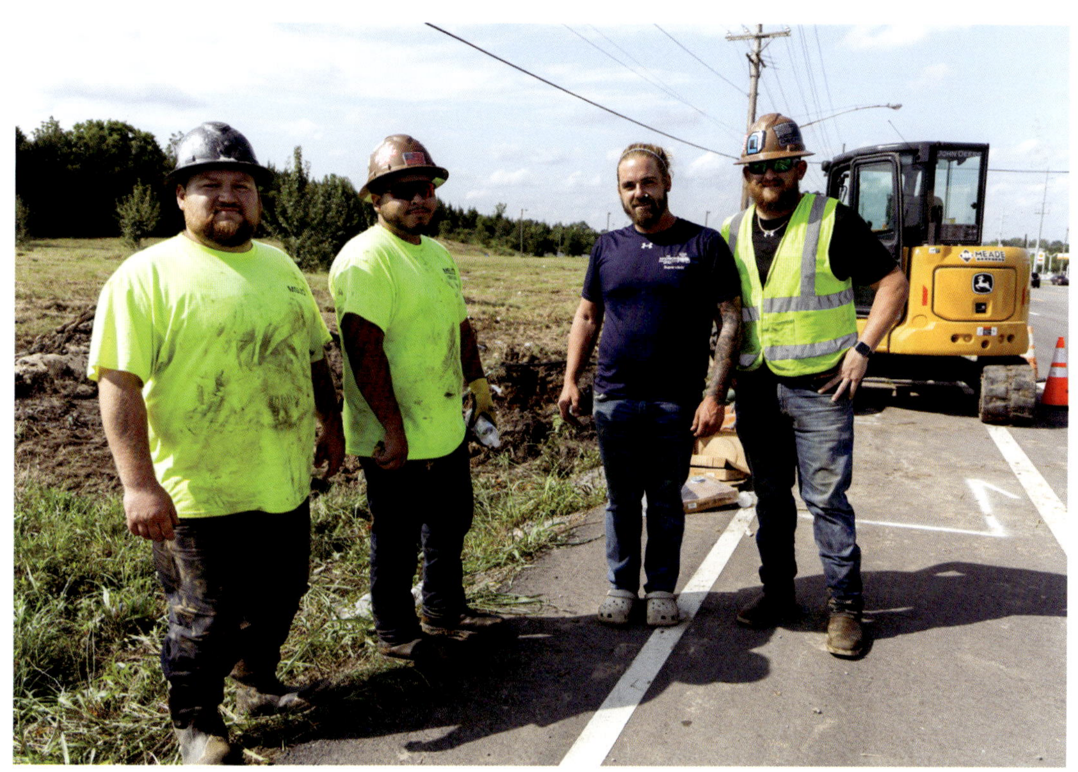

Madison Suburban Utility District

water employees pose after making a repair in Rivergate.

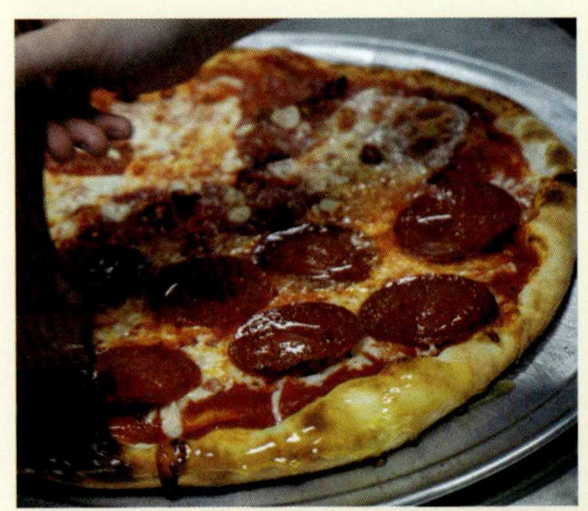

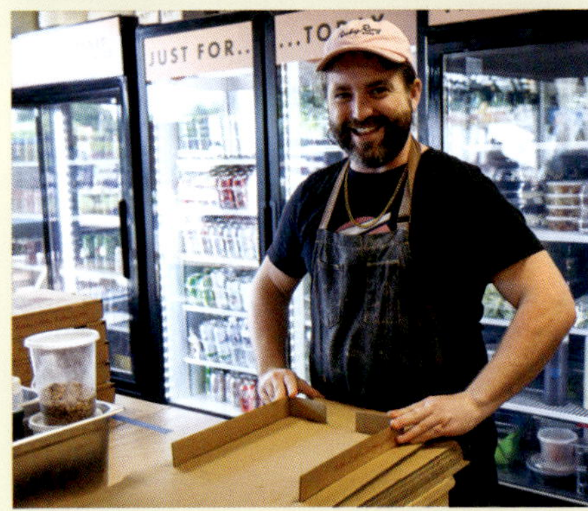
JUST FOR...

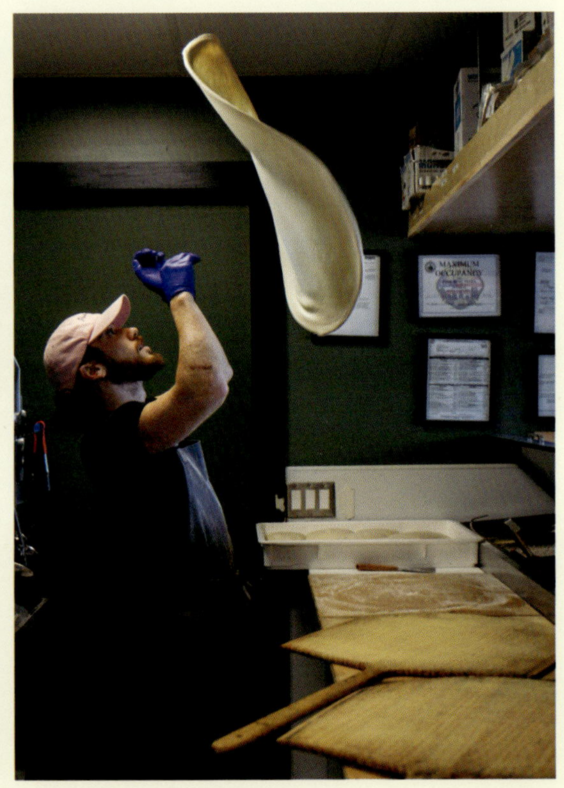
MAXIMUM OCCUPANCY

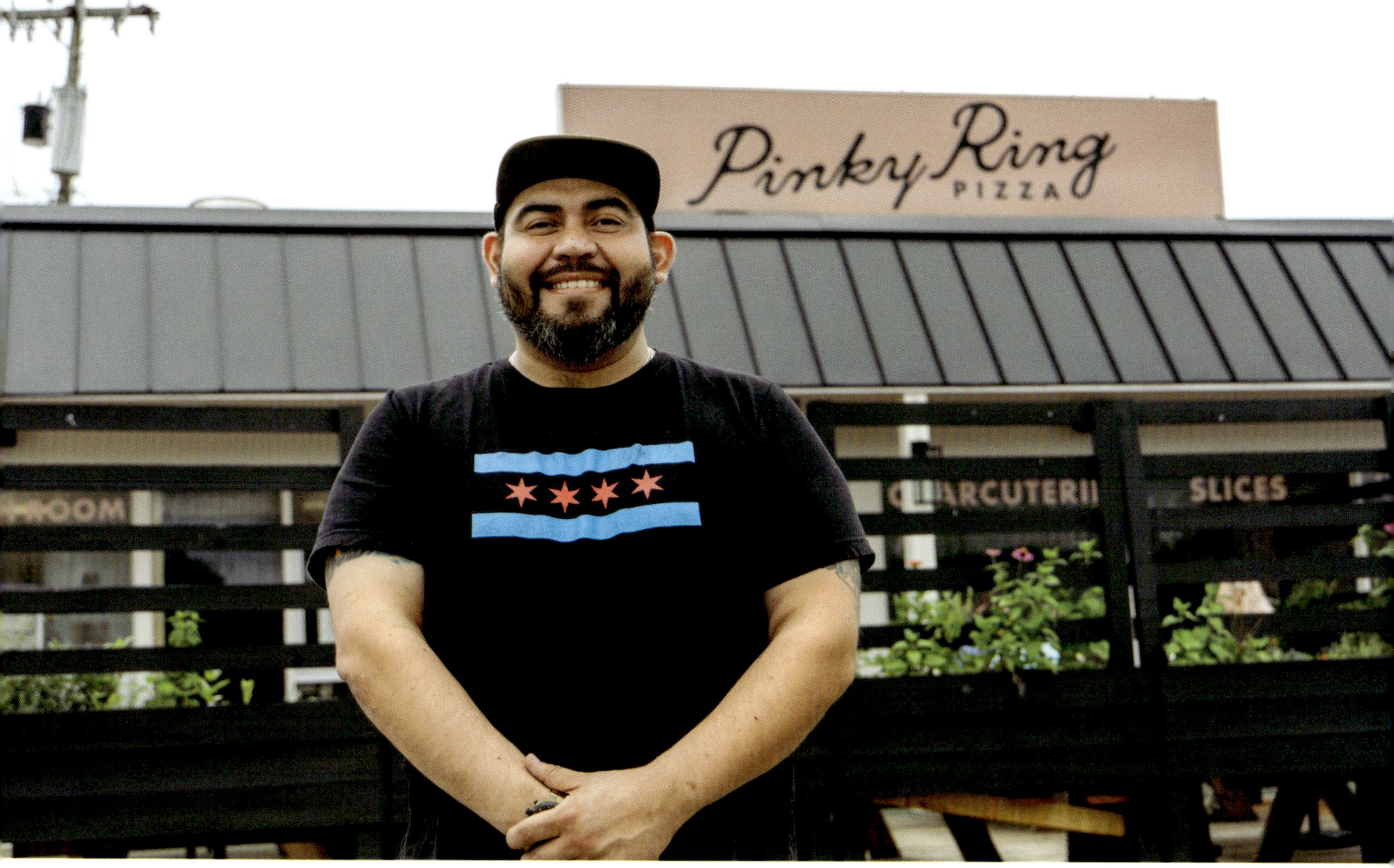

Don Hernandez, owner of Pinky Ring Pizza, stands outside the restaurant. The New York–style pizzeria quickly became a neighborhood favorite.

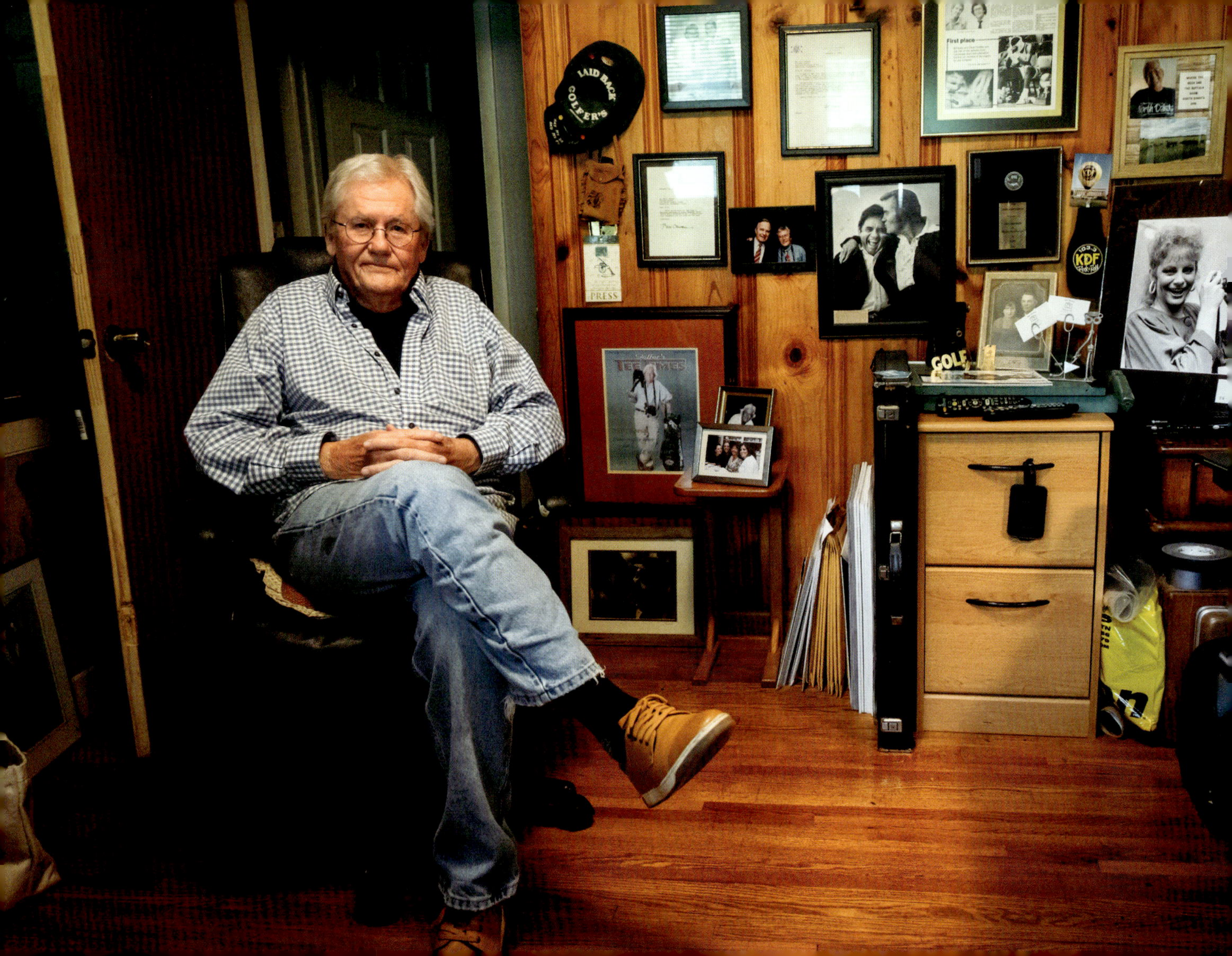
LAID BACK
GOLFER'S
PRESS
First place
KDF
GOLF

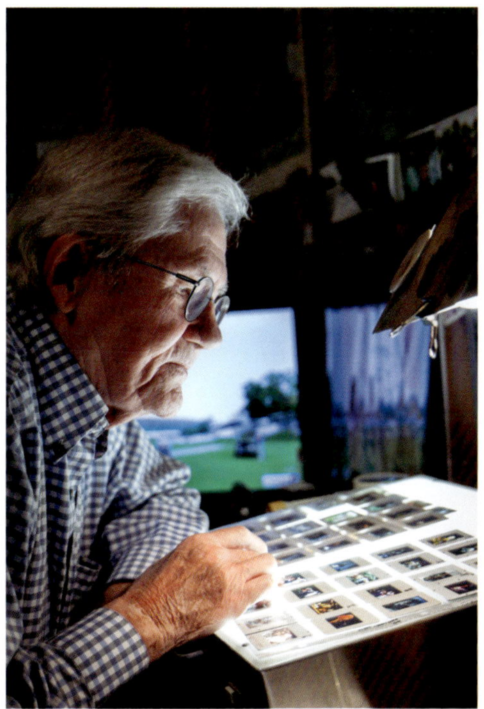

Bill Thorup, retired entertainment photographer and photojournalist, in his home studio looking at photo slides from his days working as Johnny Cash's personal photographer.

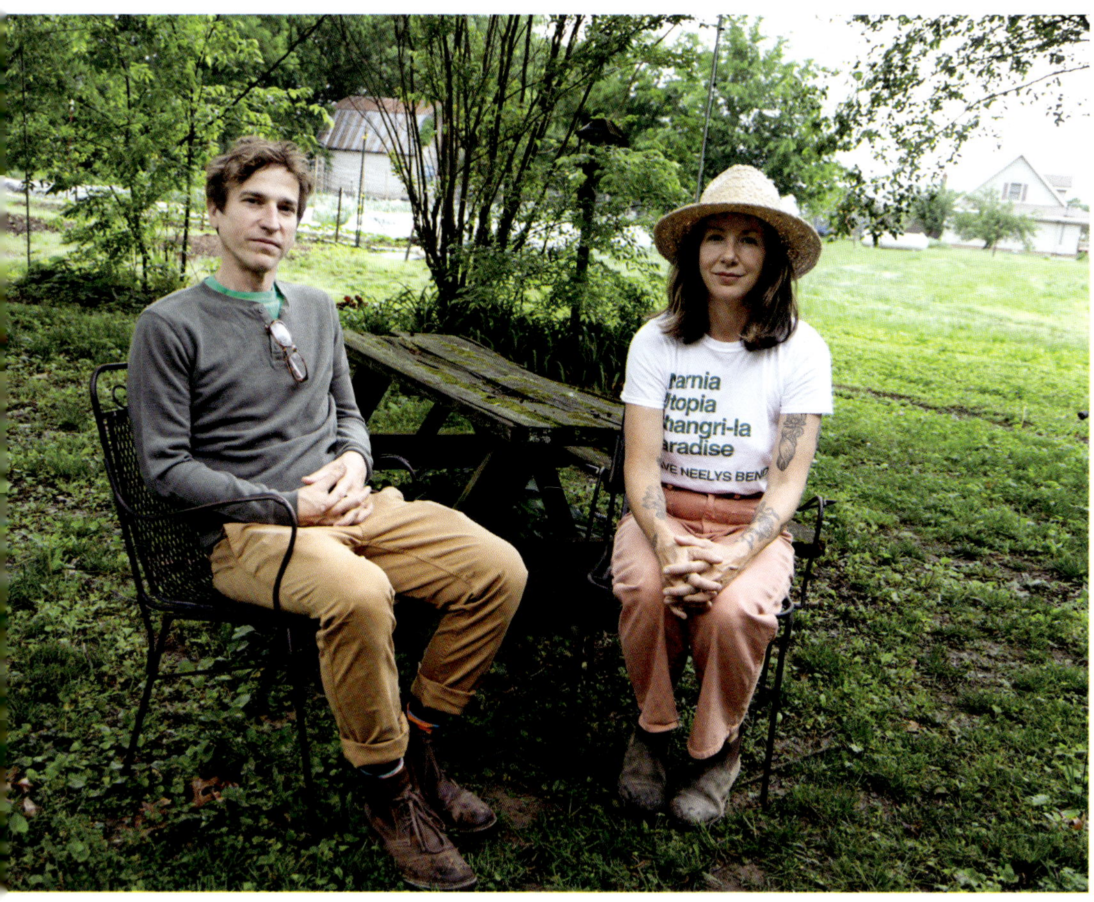

Michael and Tonya Bradford, of Una Acre Farm in Neelys Bend, sit at the picnic table where they first dreamed of starting their farm. They sell their produce through a CSA (community-supported agriculture) and local farmers markets.

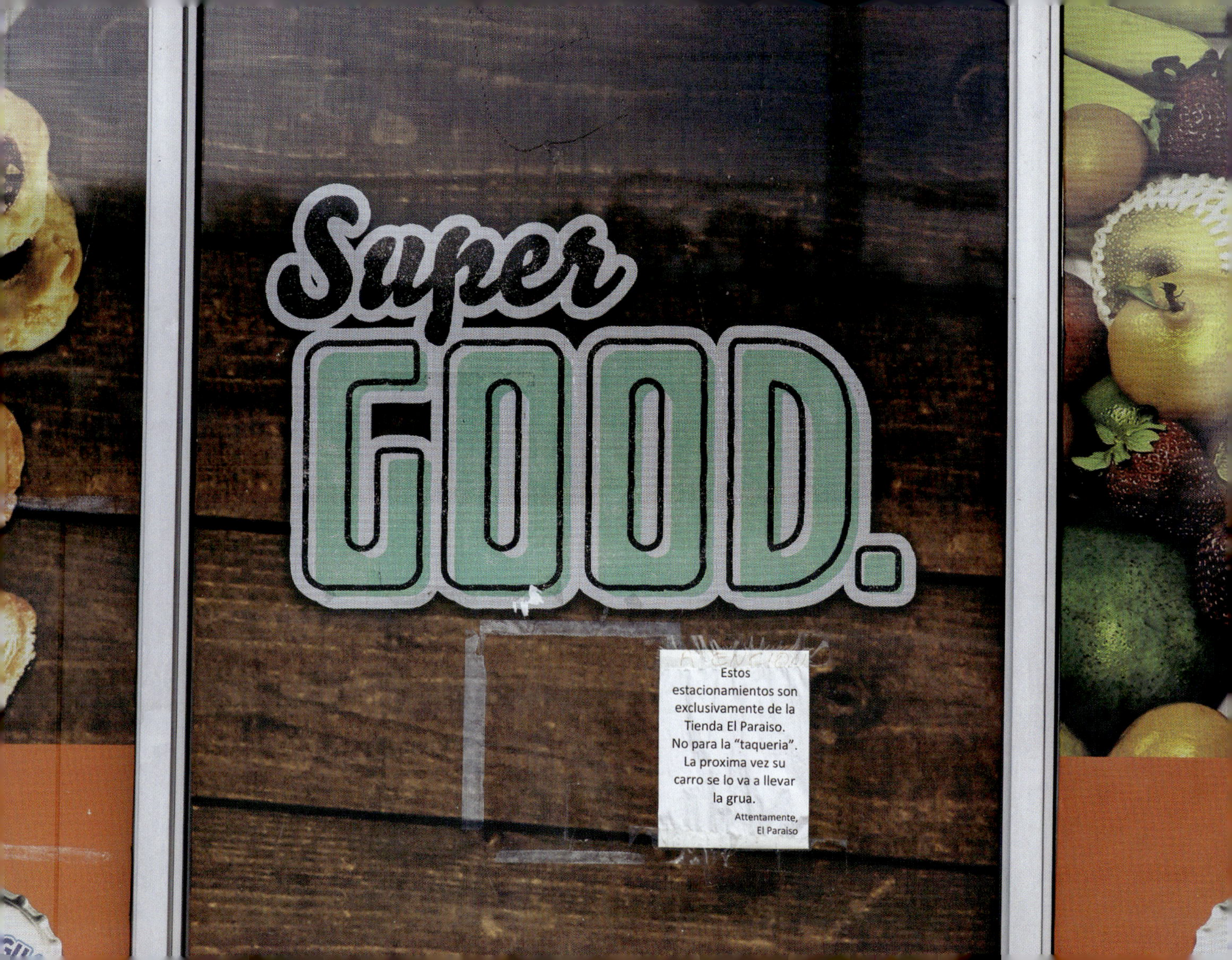

Super

GOOD.

Estos
estacionamientos son
exclusivamente de la
Tienda El Paraiso.
No para la "taqueria".
La proxima vez su
carro se lo va a llevar
la grua.

Attentamente,
El Paraiso

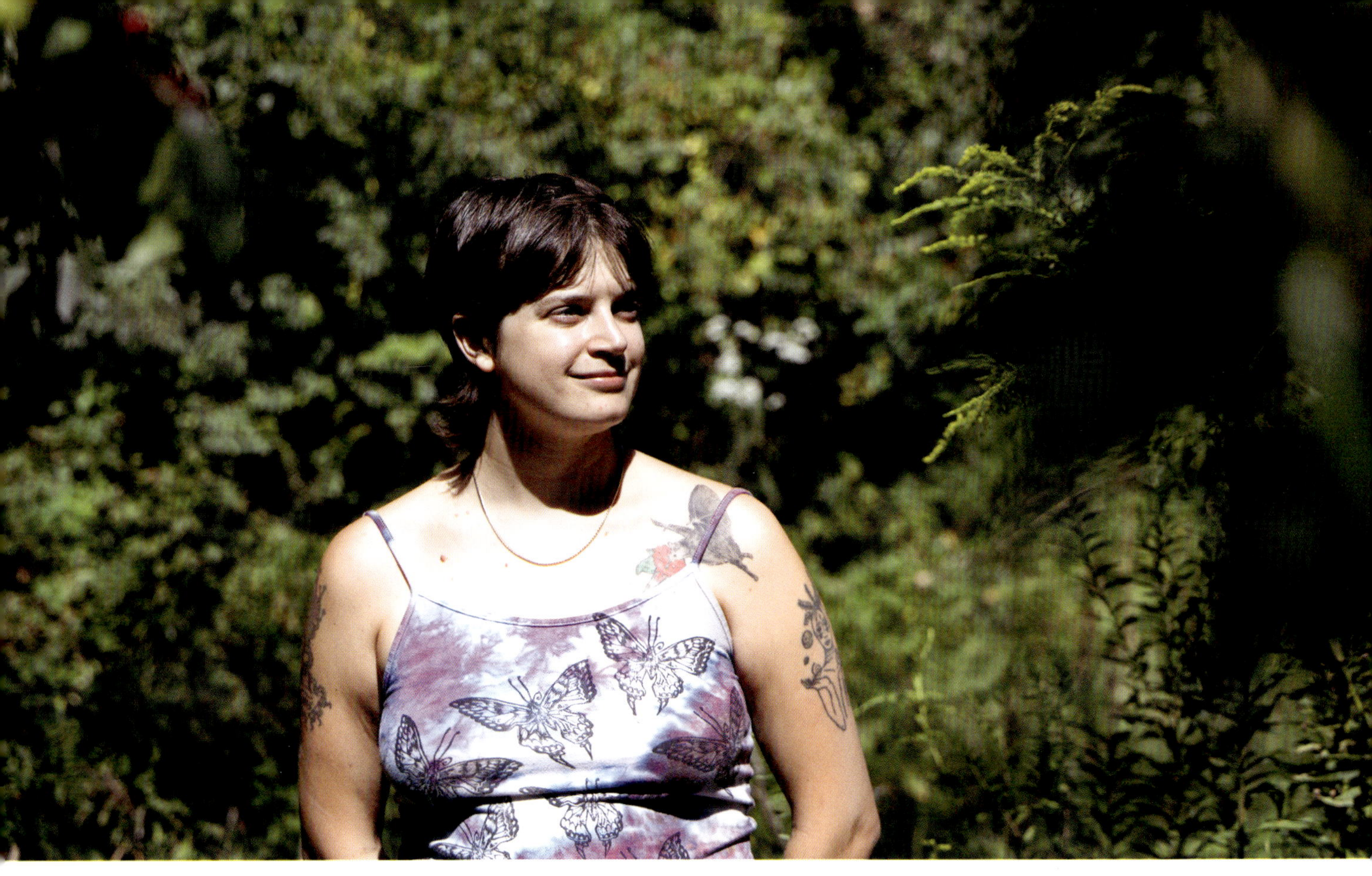

Robyn Robichaud, owner of Plant Portals, stands in their backyard. The community herbalist, forager and gardener makes herbal tinctures and potions and offers herbal consultations.

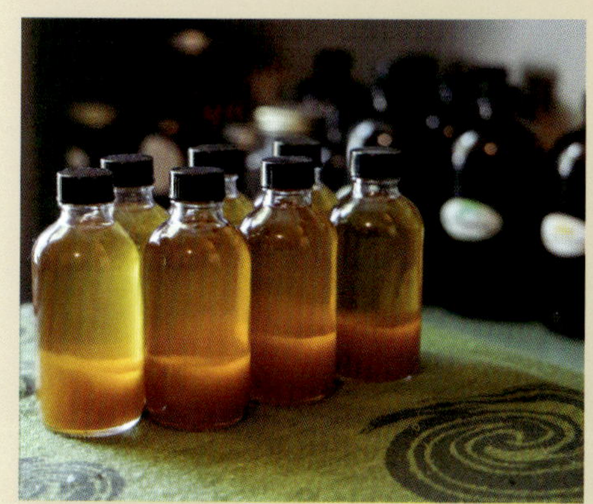

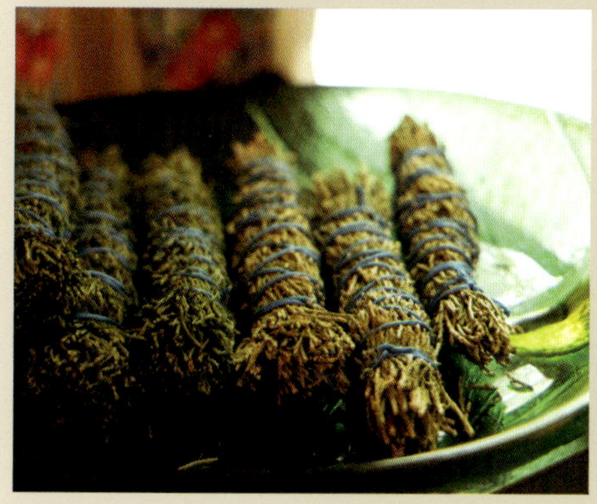

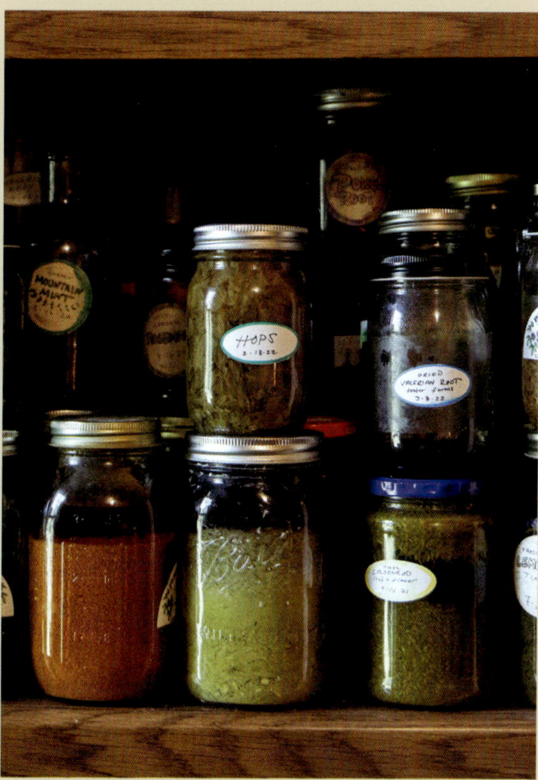

HOPS
DRIED
VALERIAN ROOT

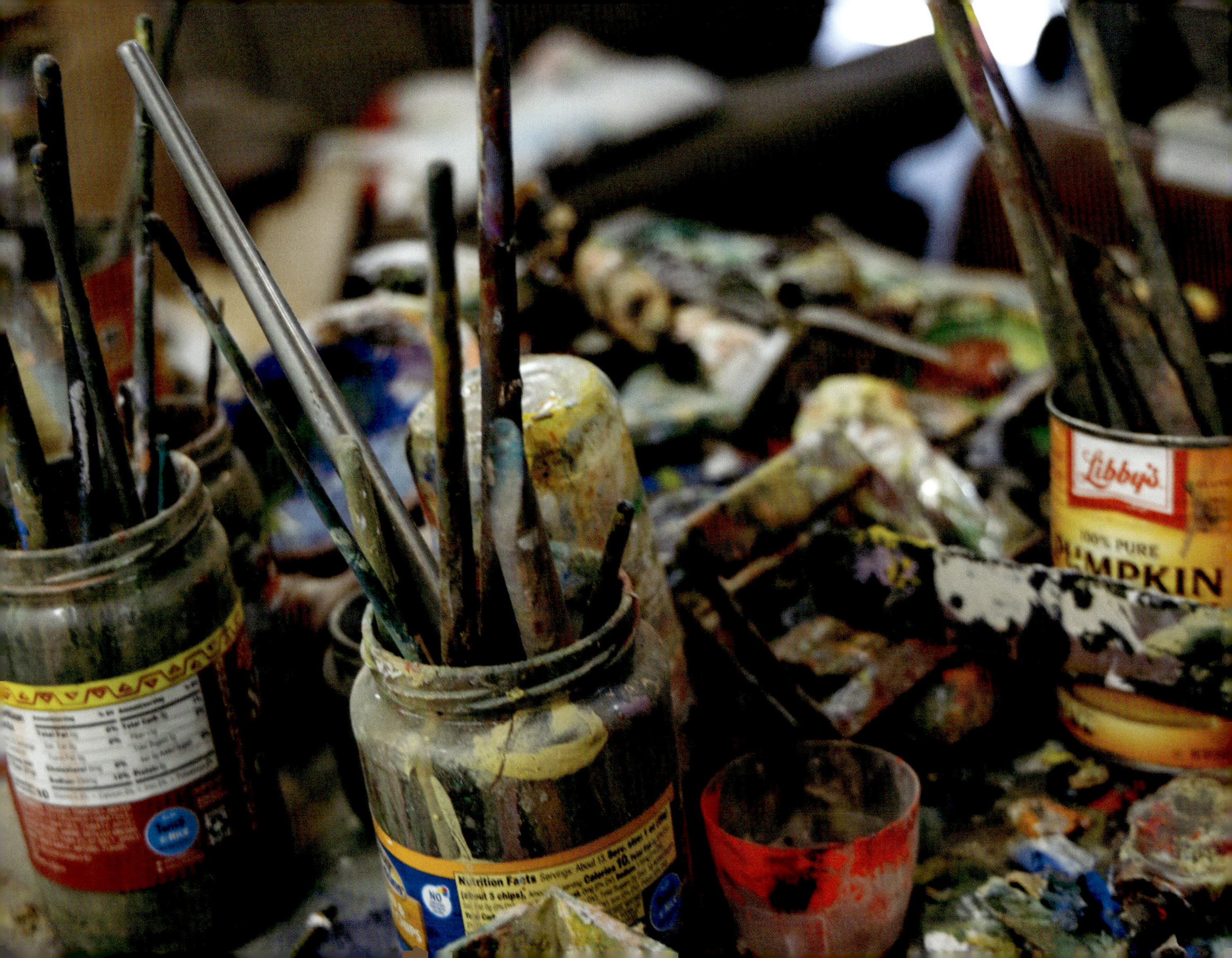
Libby's
100% PURE
Nutrition Facts

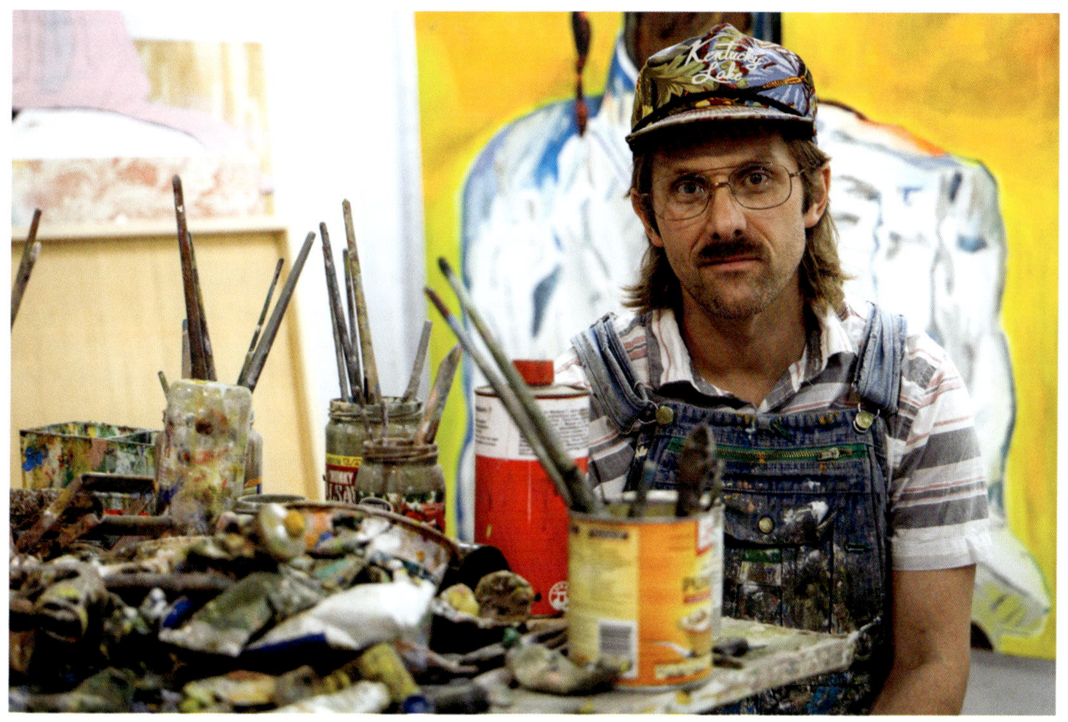

John Paul Kesling paints in his backyard studio. The Kentucky-born artist settled in Madison after many years in New York City. His work is featured in galleries all over the country.

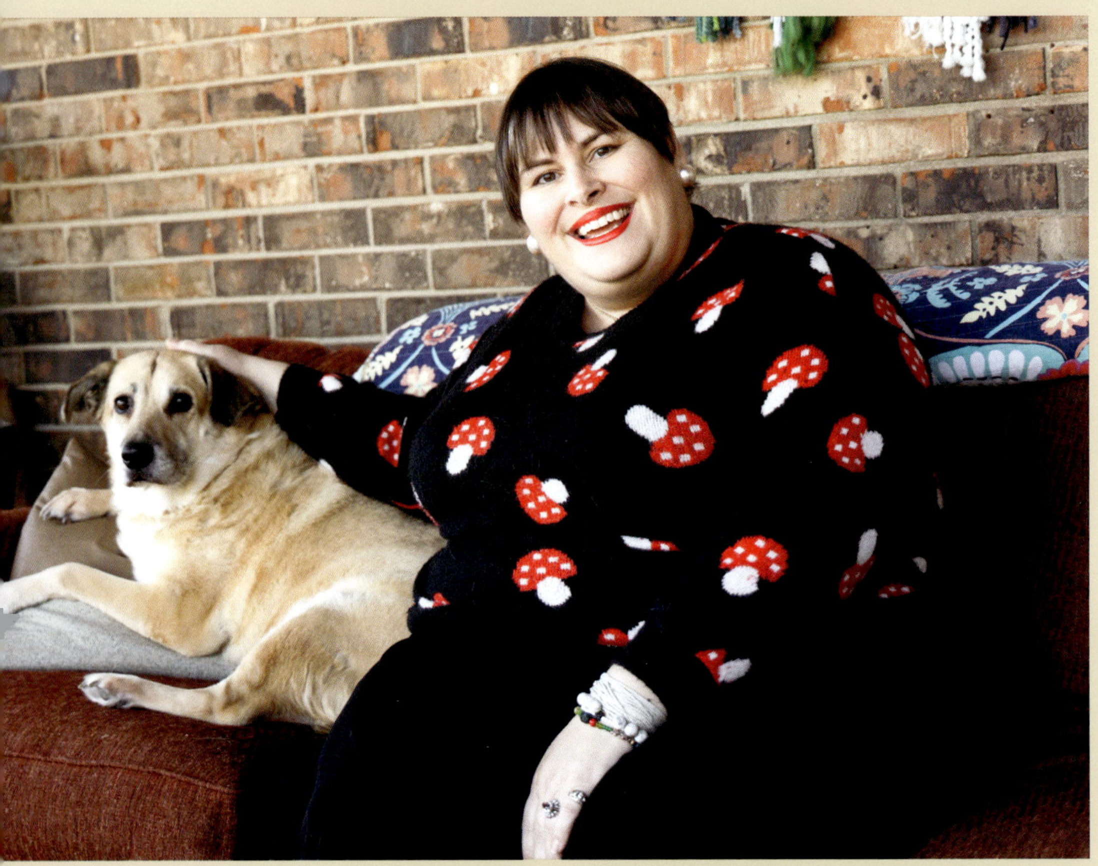

Sonia Fernandez Le Blanc, sixth-generation Nashvillian, storyteller, writer, social anarchist, and owner of Revolutions Imaginarium, sits in her sunroom outside her home with her dog, Macaroni.

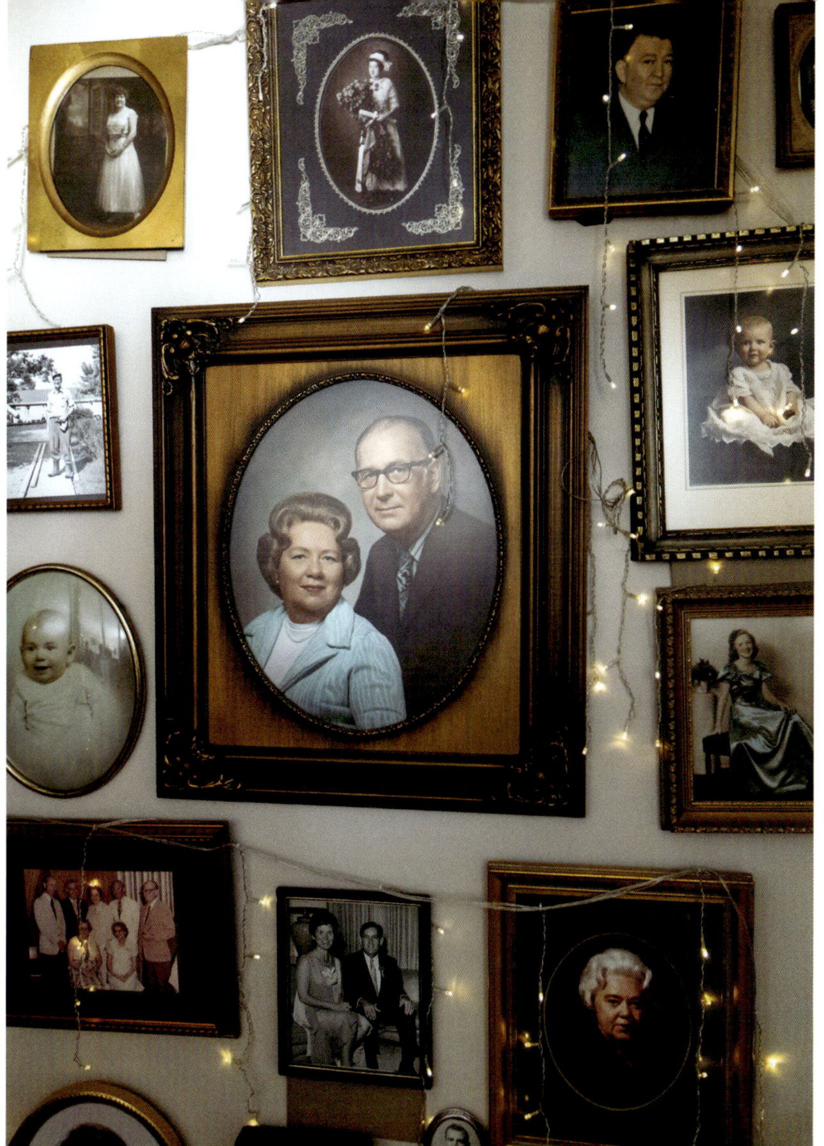

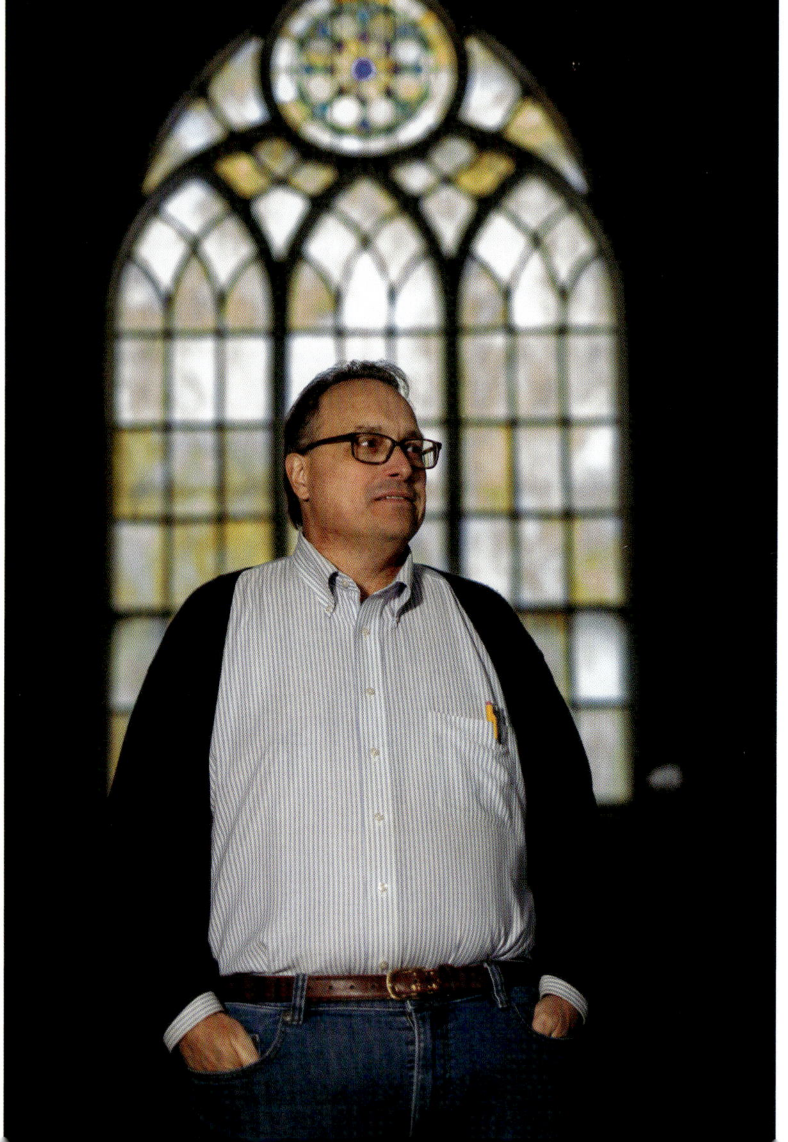

Rev. Jay Voorhees, pastor of City Road Chapel United Methodist Church, in the historic chapel. The church is on the front lines of homeless outreach.

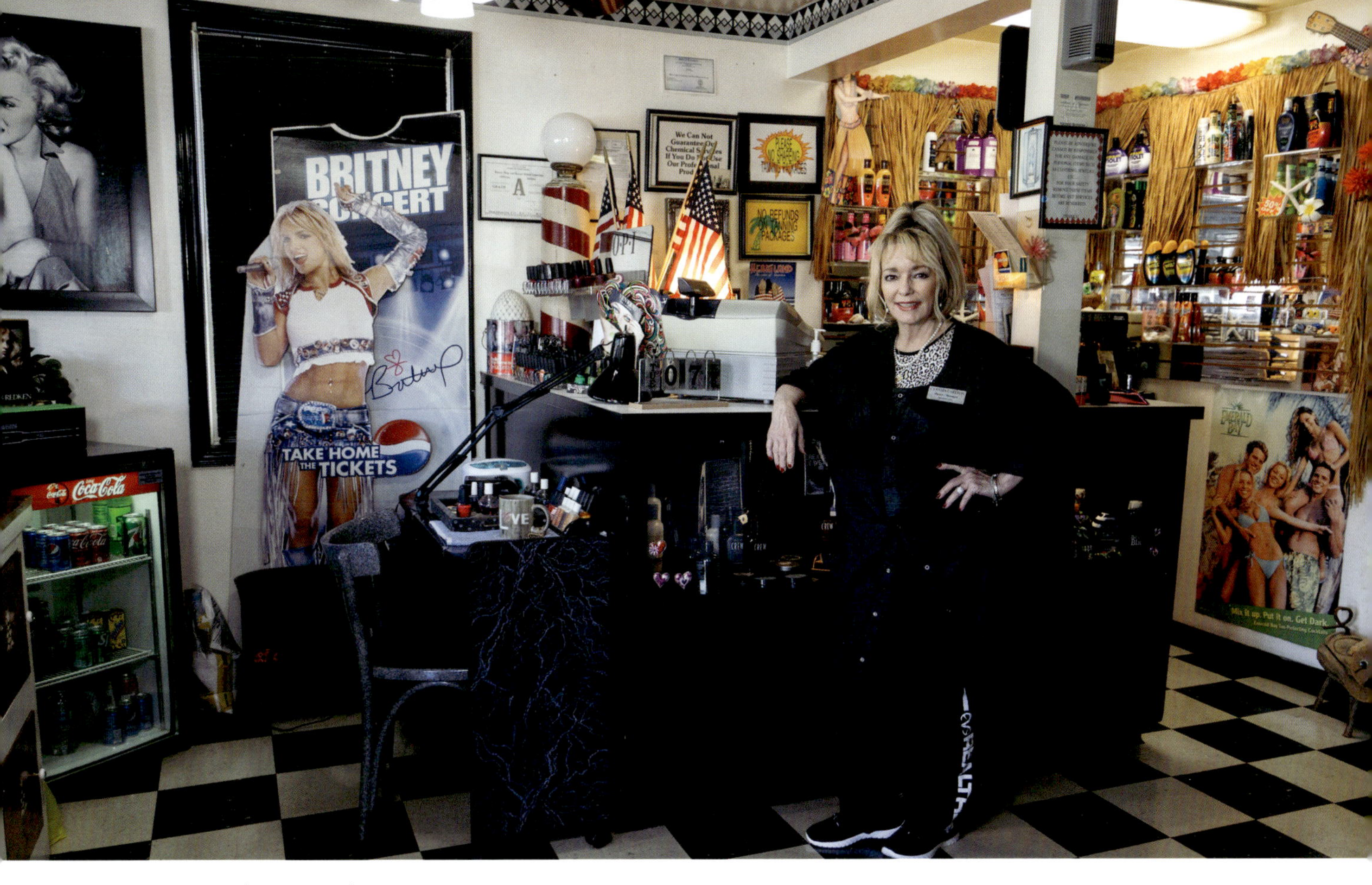

Cynthia Carlton, owner of Neelys Bend Haircutters, inside her hair and tanning salon.

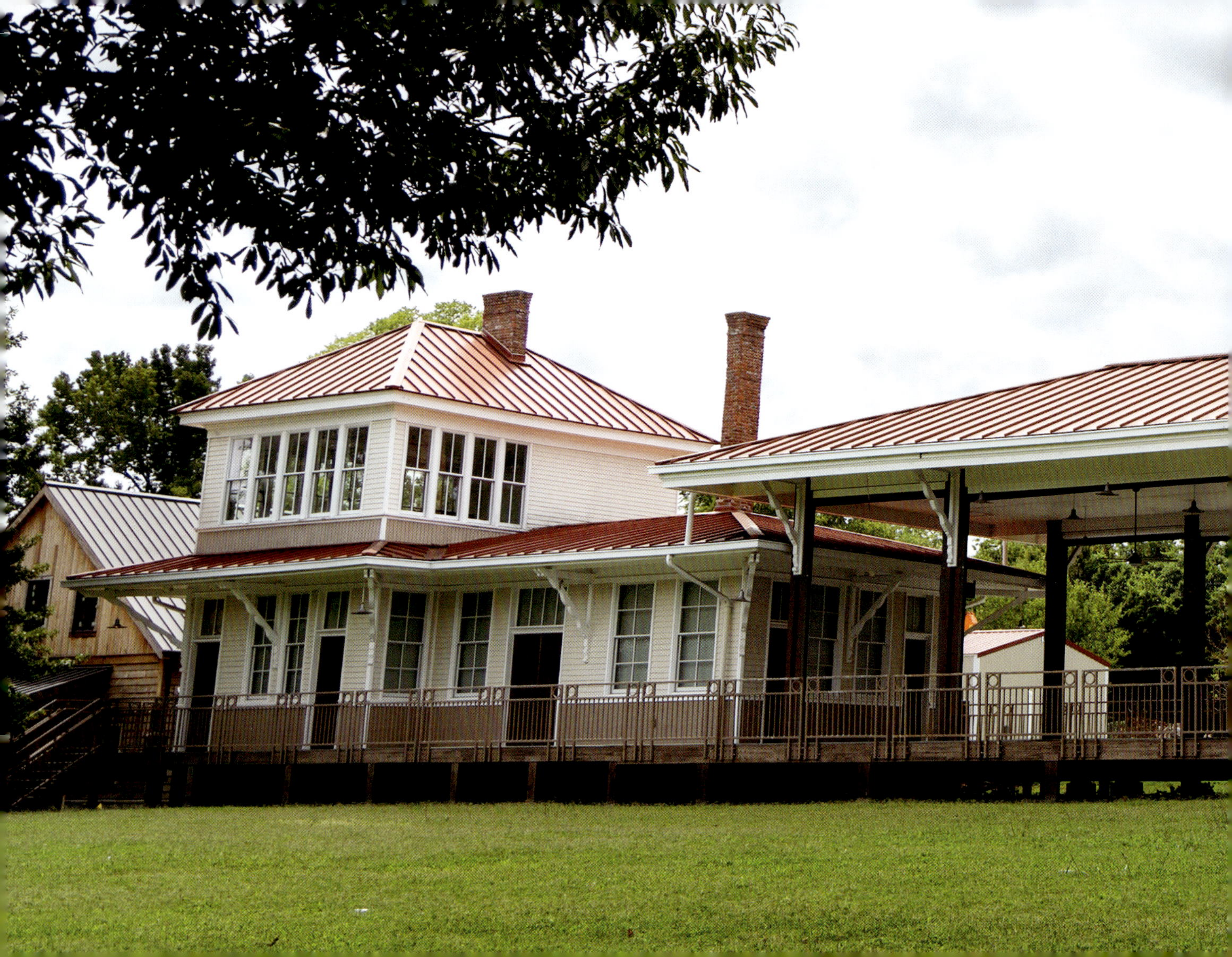

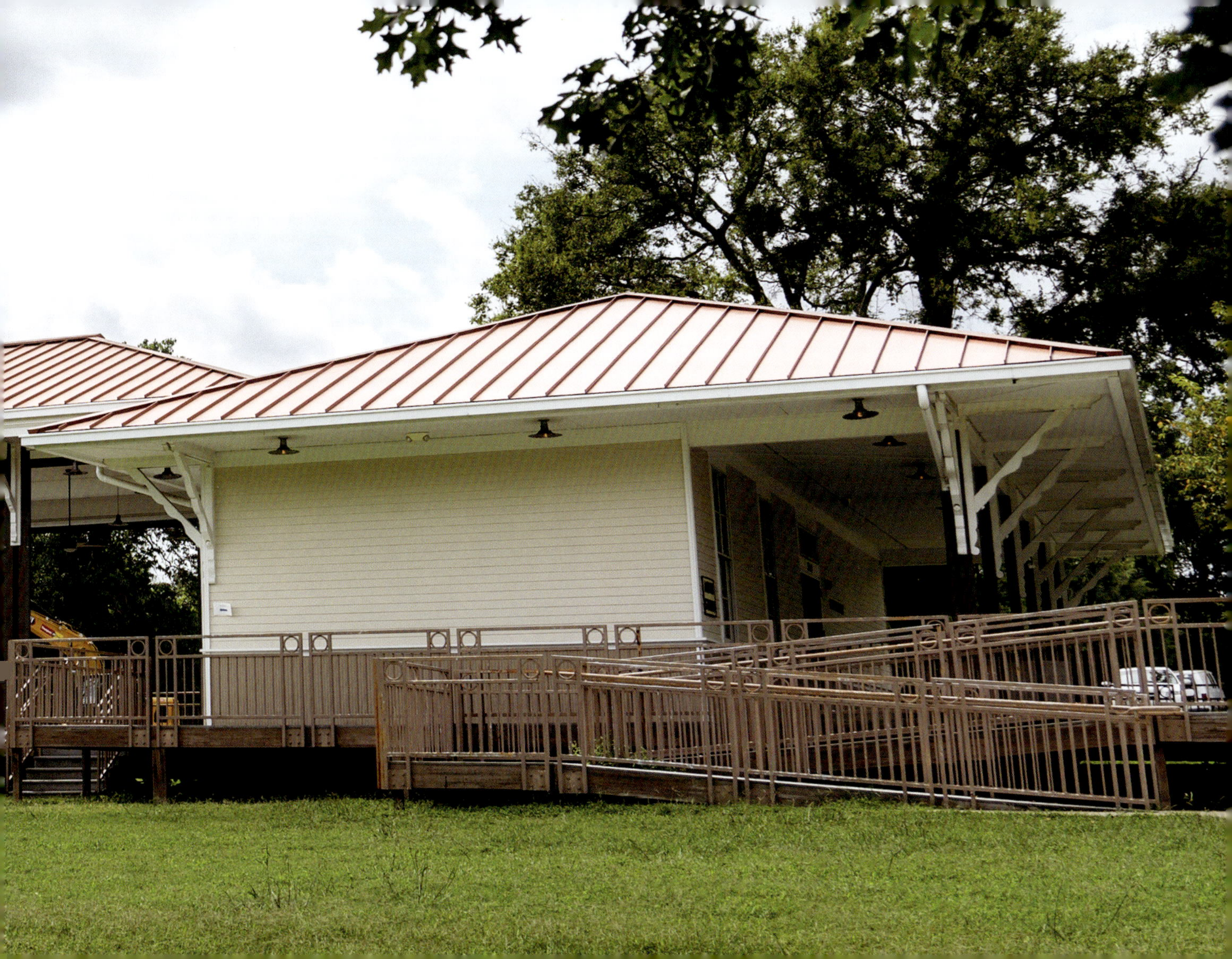

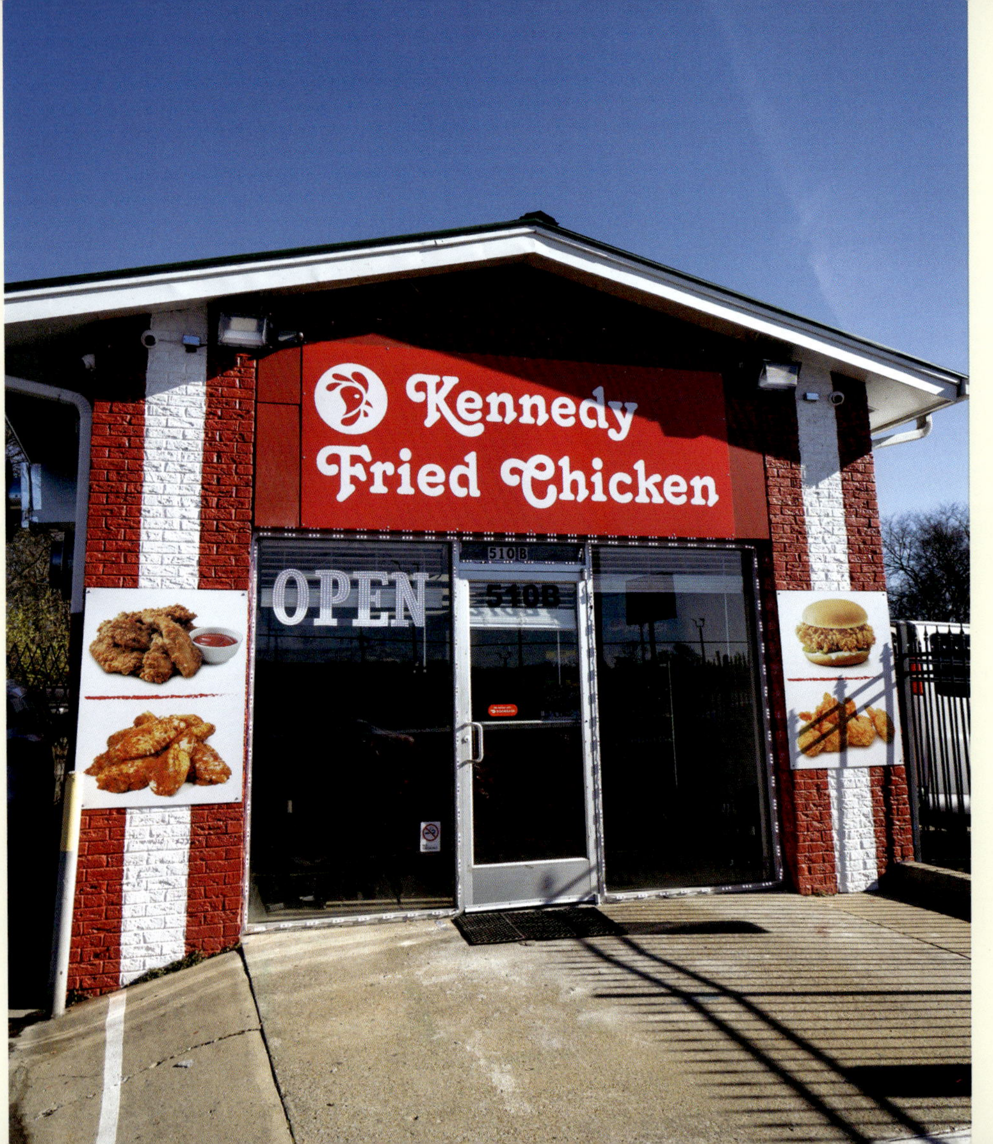

Amran Nasser,
NYC transplant
and owner of Kennedy
Fried Chicken.

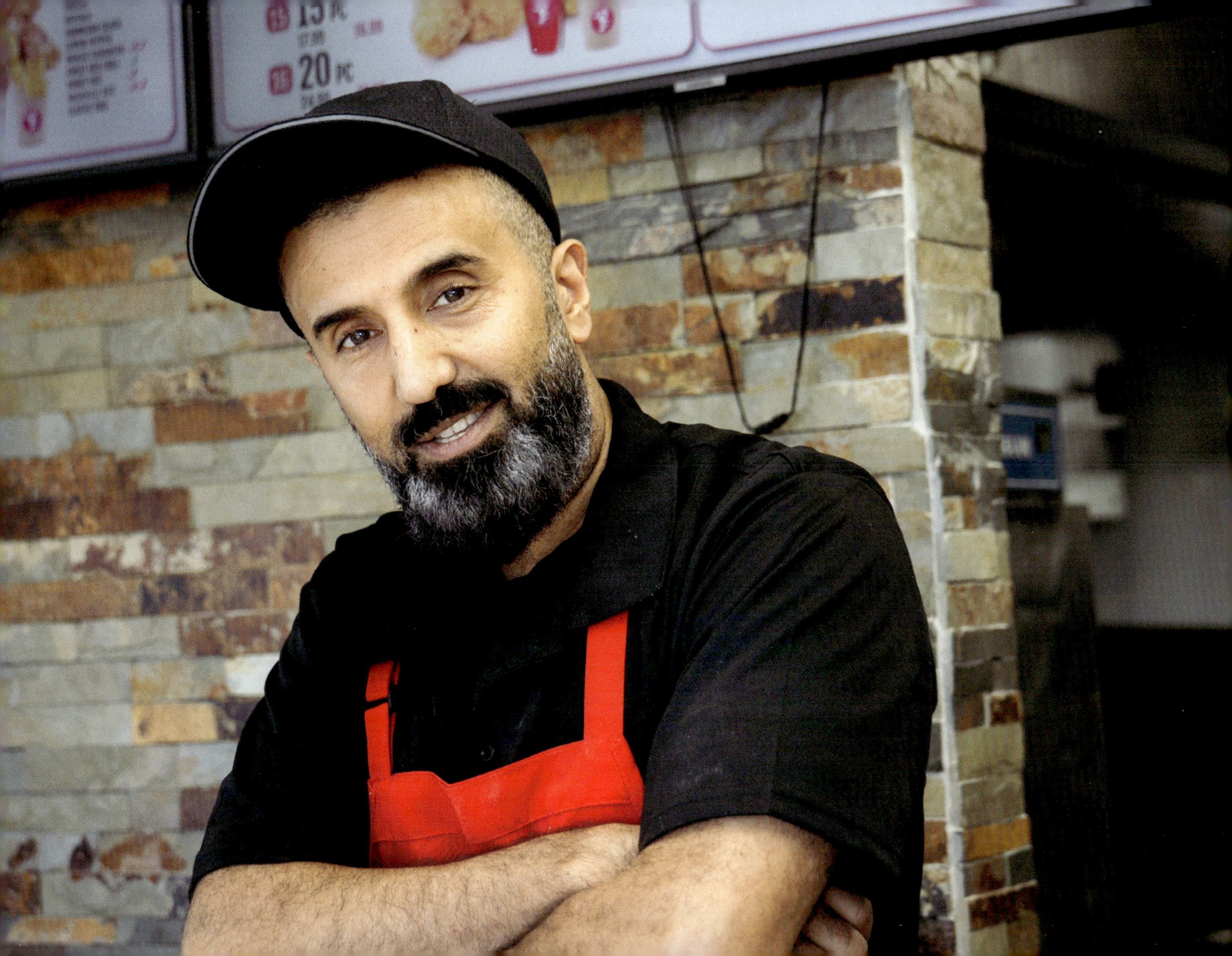

20 PC

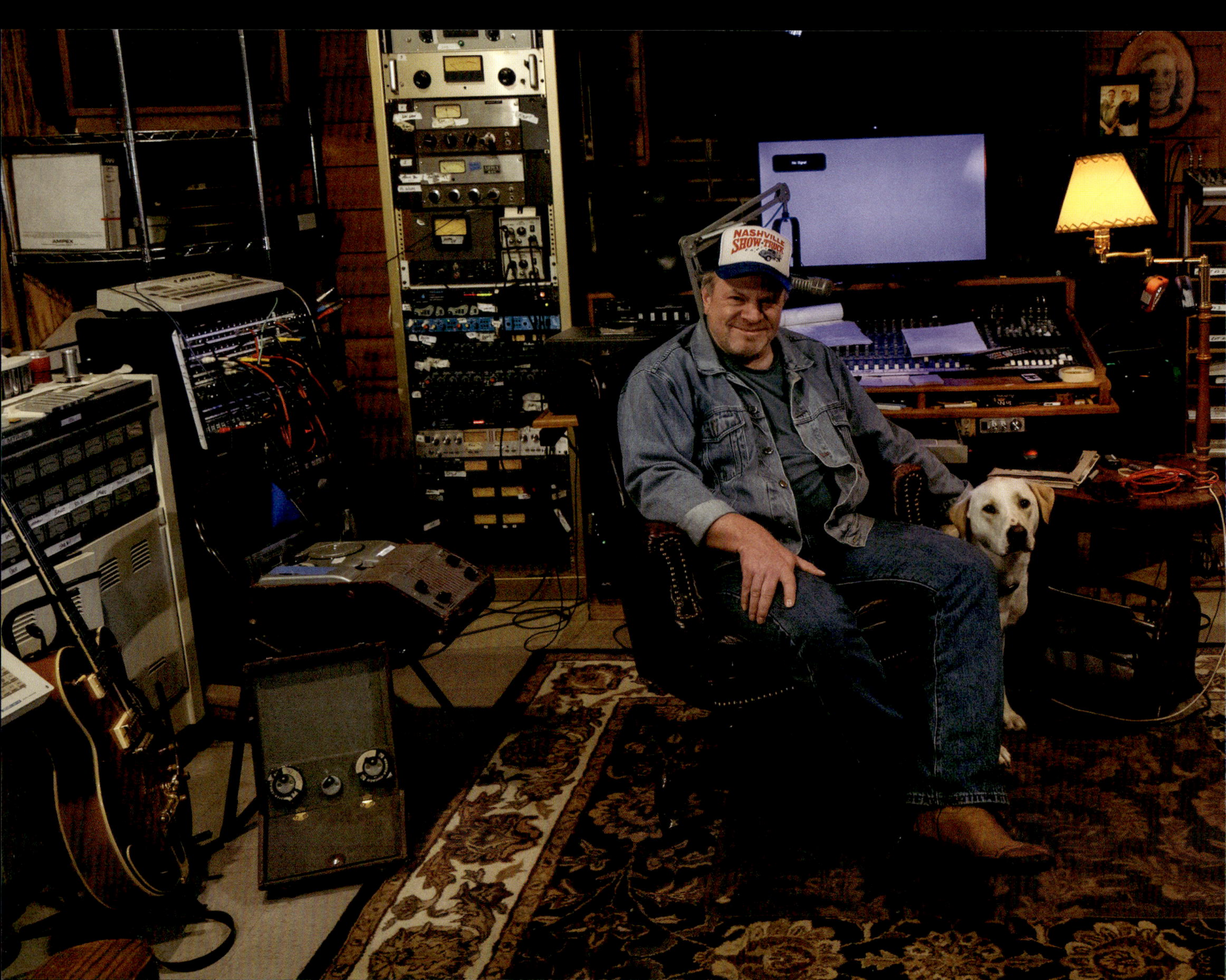
NASHVILLE
SHOW-TRUCK

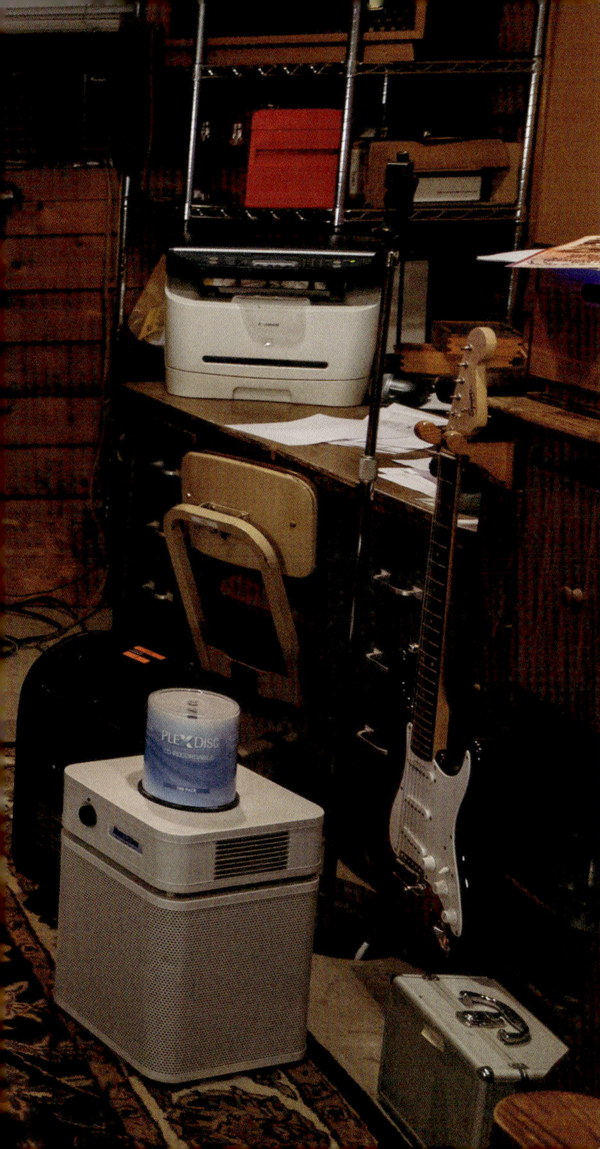

Mark Thornton,

multitalented guitar player, producer, and engineer, inside his studio with his dog, Butter Bean. Thornton was a member of Jerry Reed's band for more than ten years and is now the owner of Sidekick Sound Studio and Nashville Show Truck.

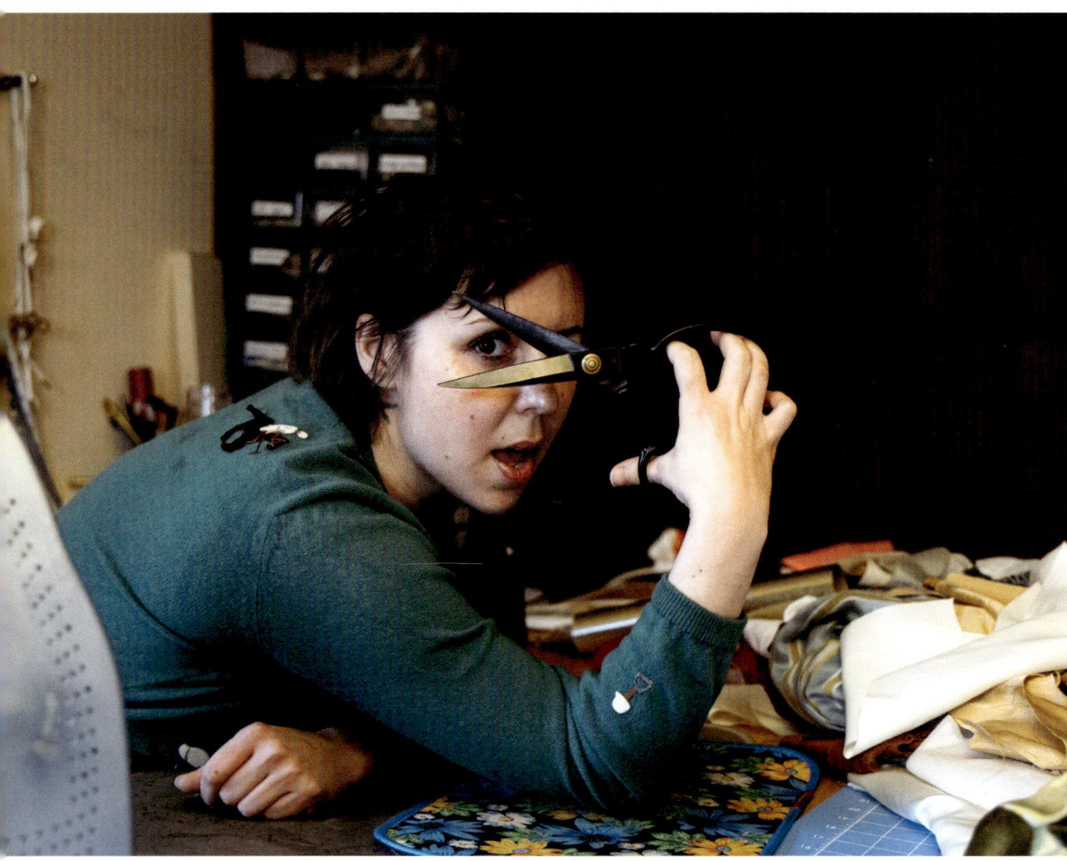

Cybelle Elena, interdisciplinary artist and clothing and costume designer, works inside her home studio.

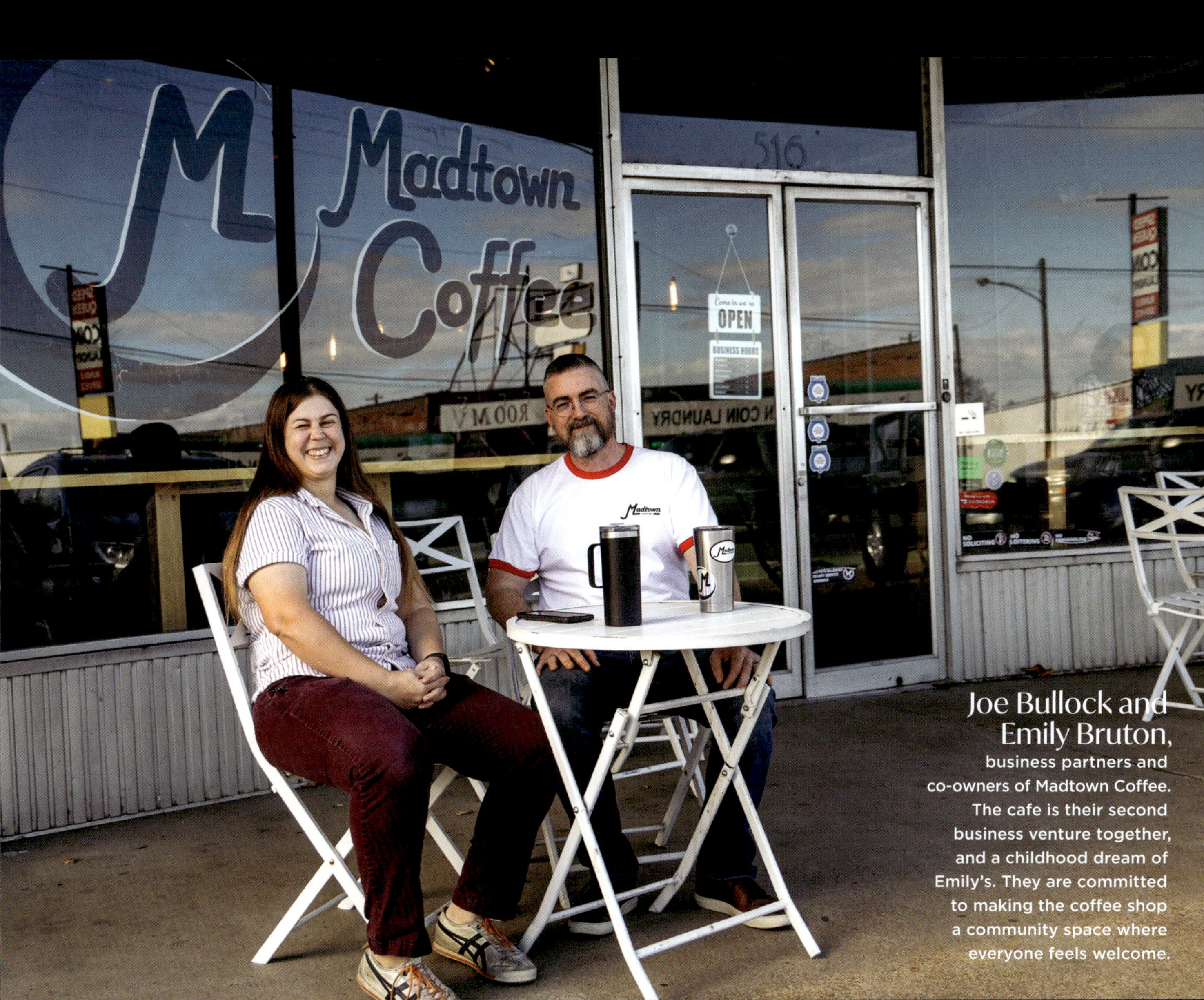

Joe Bullock and Emily Bruton, business partners and co-owners of Madtown Coffee. The cafe is their second business venture together, and a childhood dream of Emily's. They are committed to making the coffee shop a community space where everyone feels welcome.

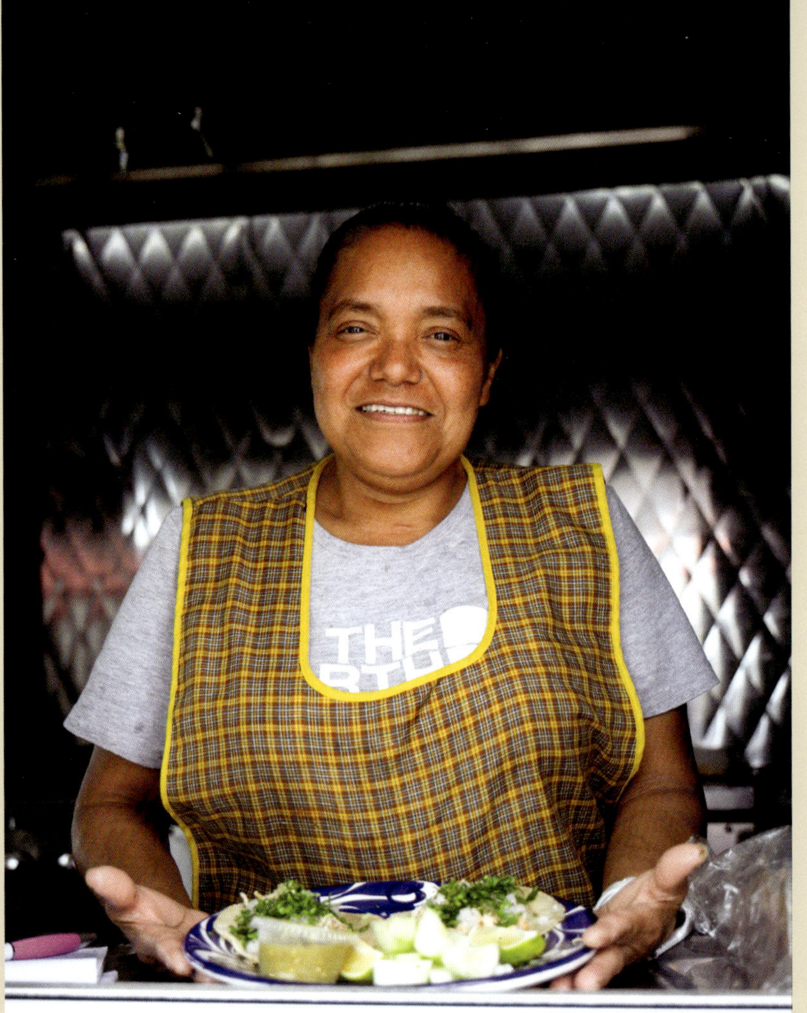

A cheerful employee at Shermay Tacos serves up lunch at the roadside taqueria.

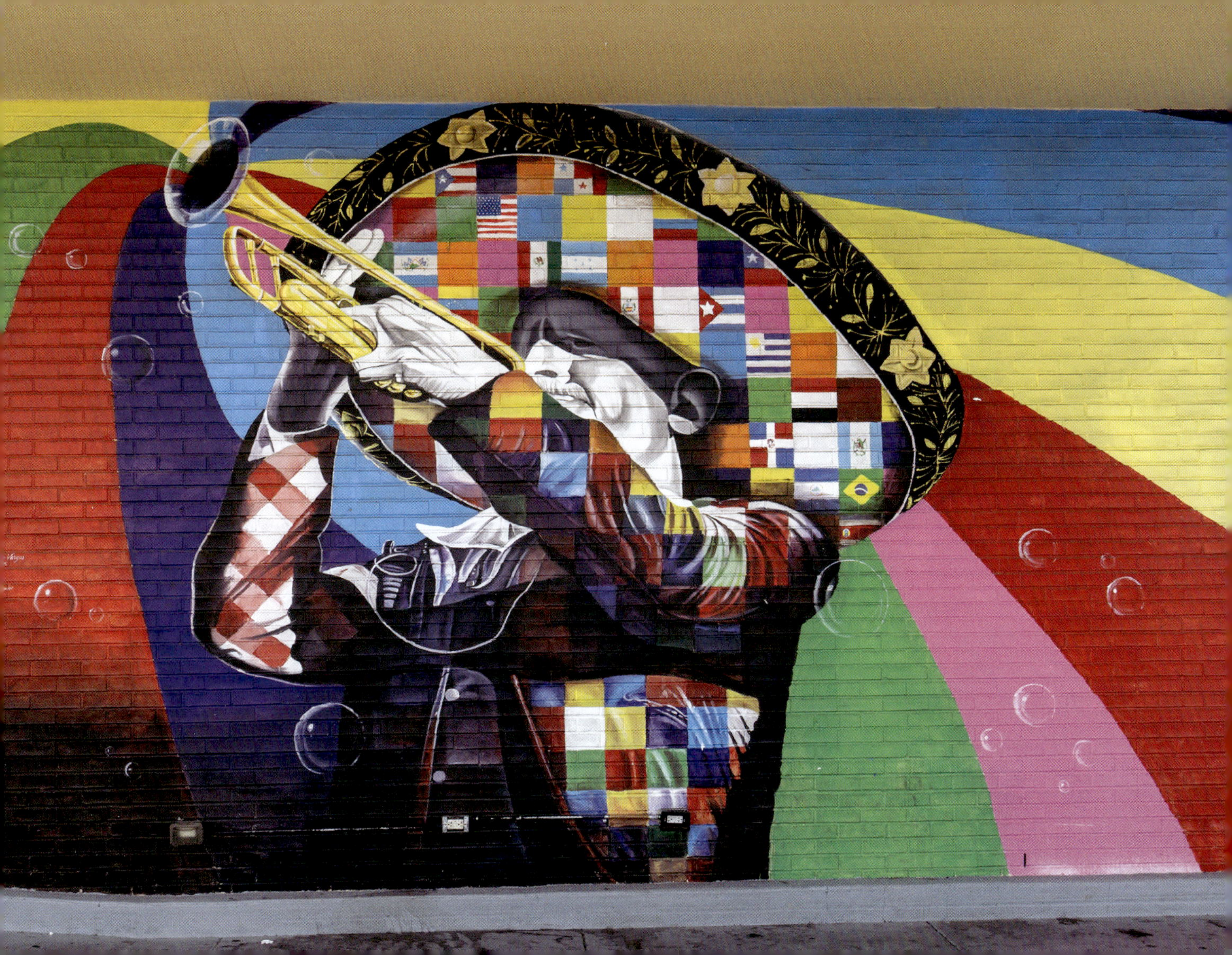

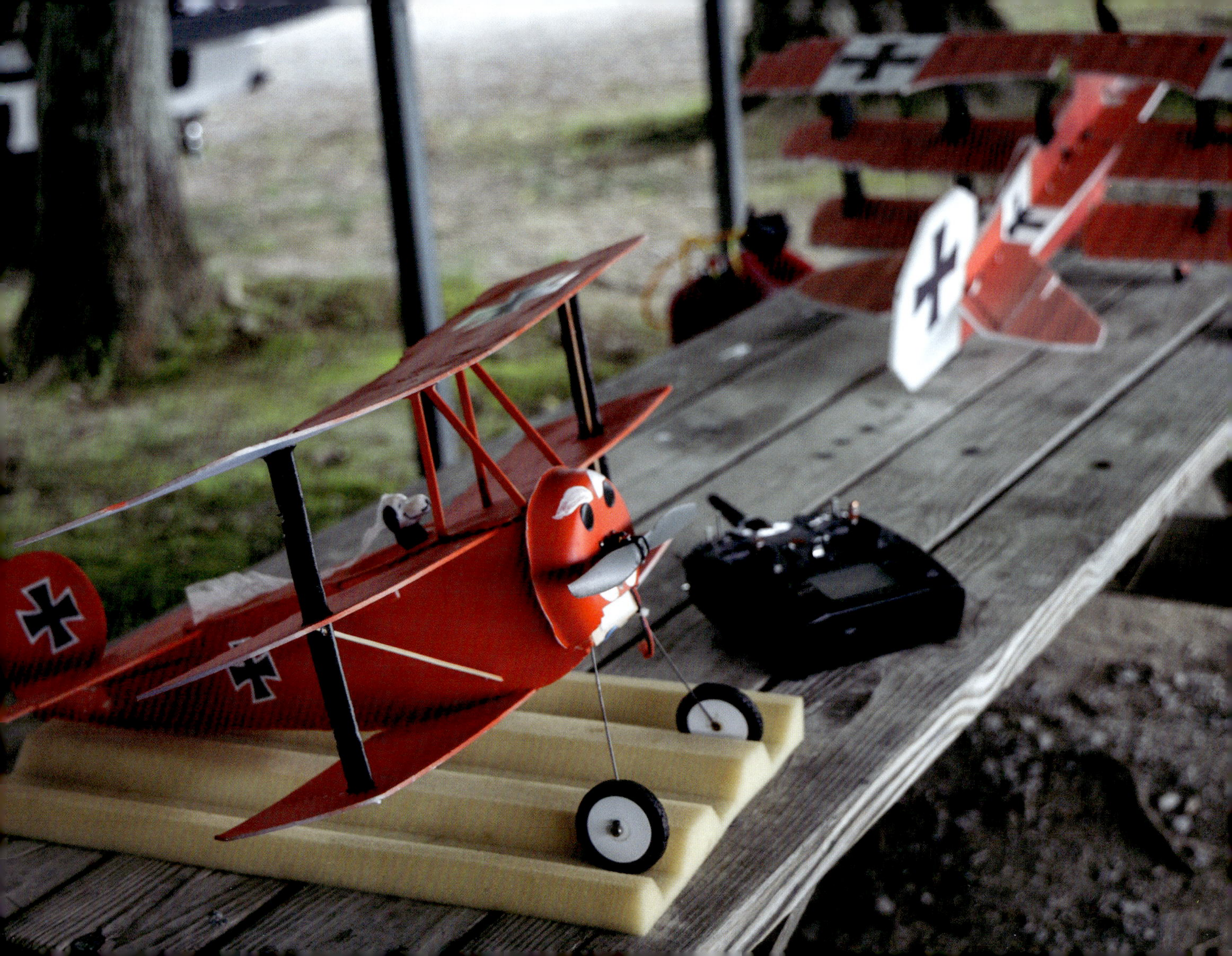

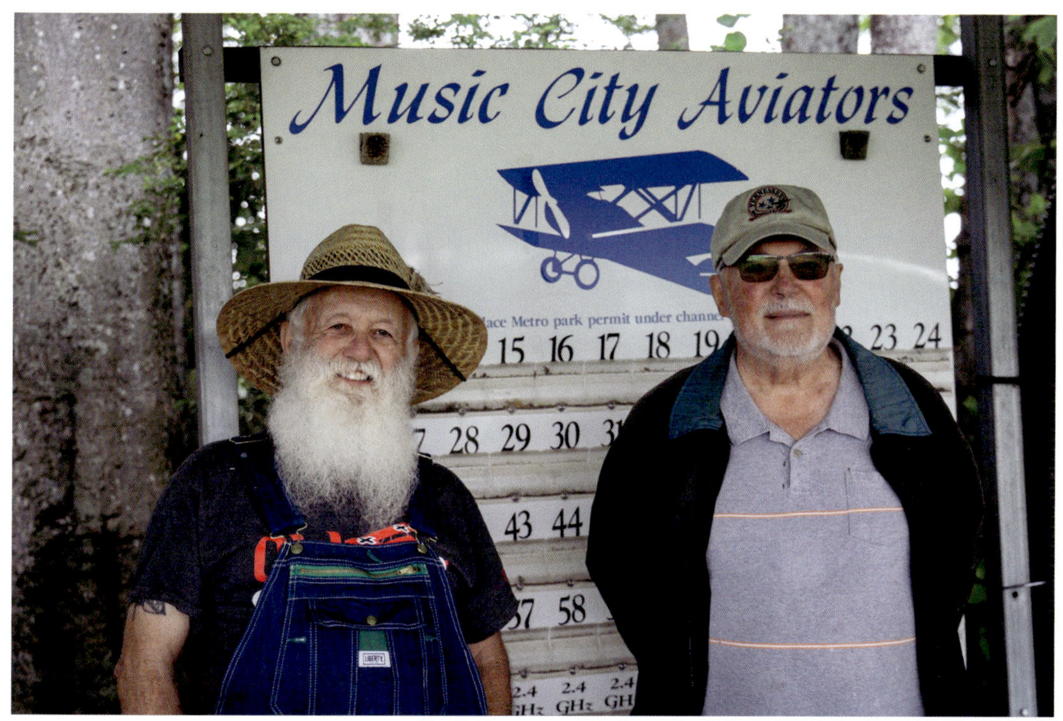

Model-airplane enthusiasts **Don Clark and Dick Tonan** of Music City Aviators fly their planes in the airfield at Peeler Park.

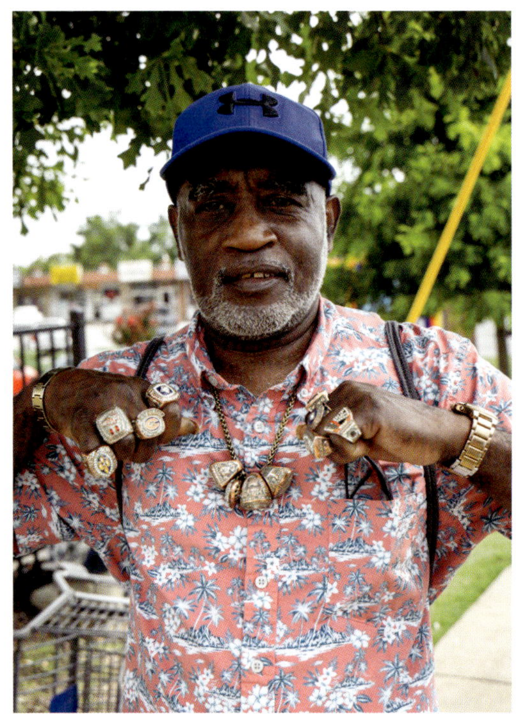

“Superbowl” proudly displays his jewelry.

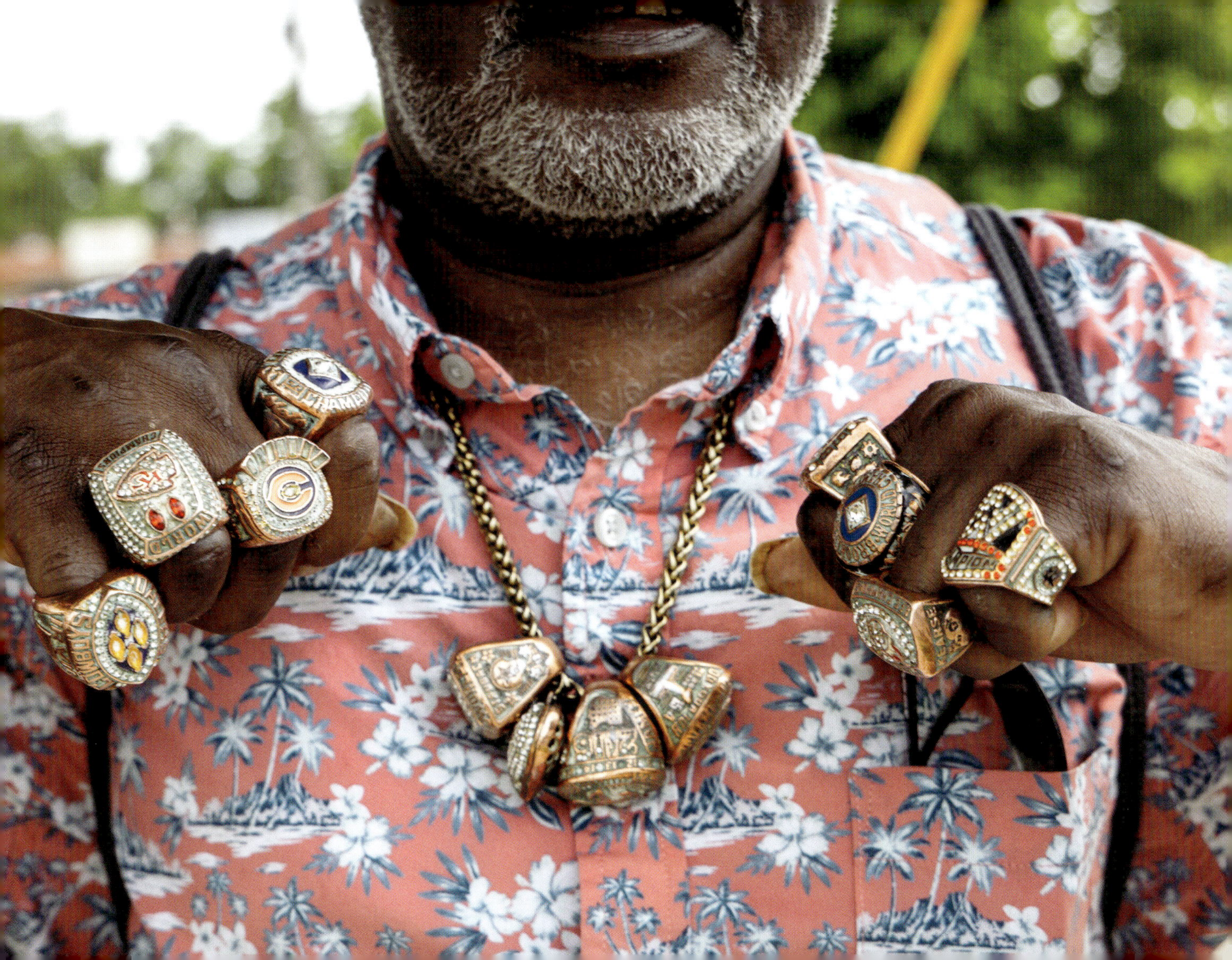

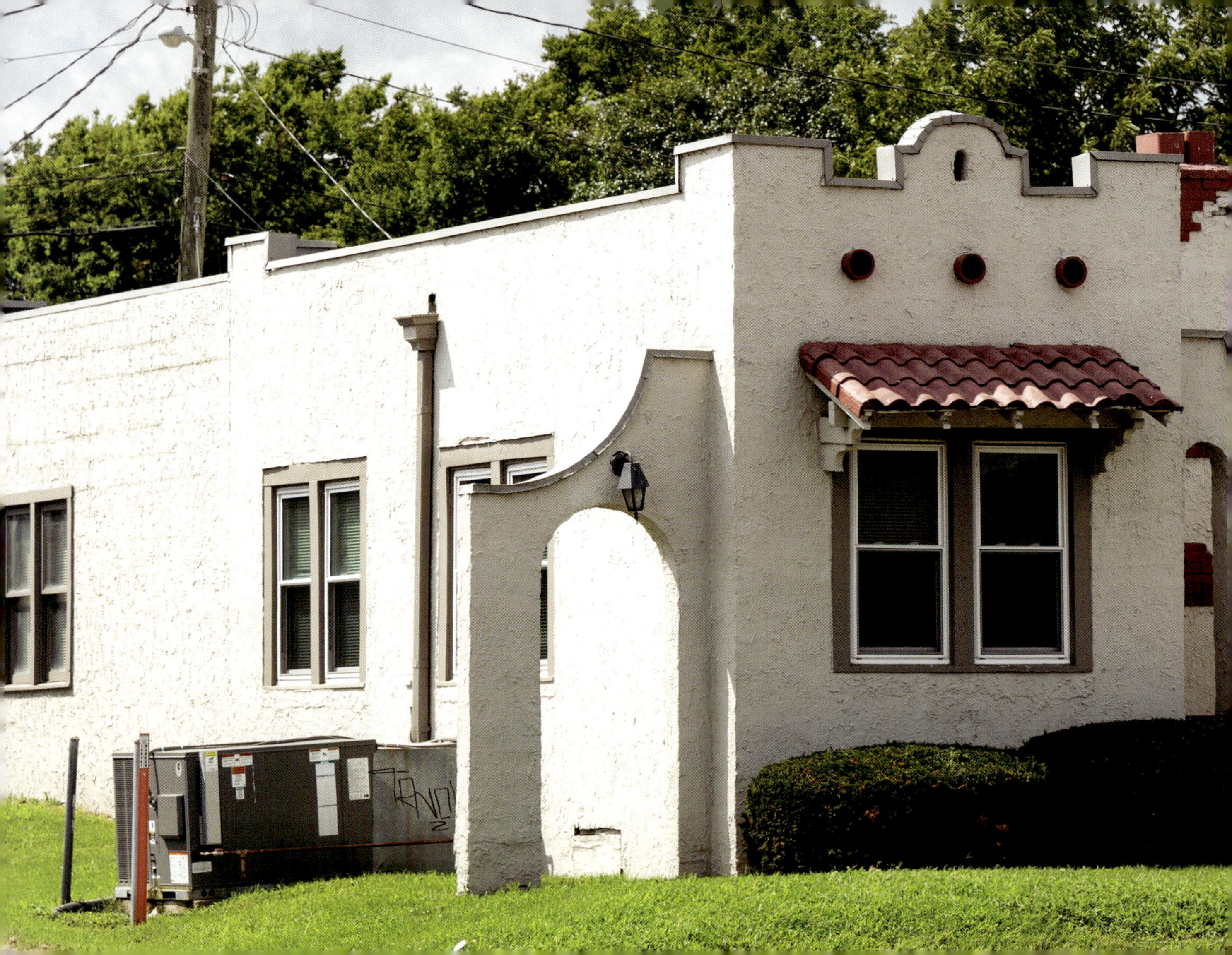

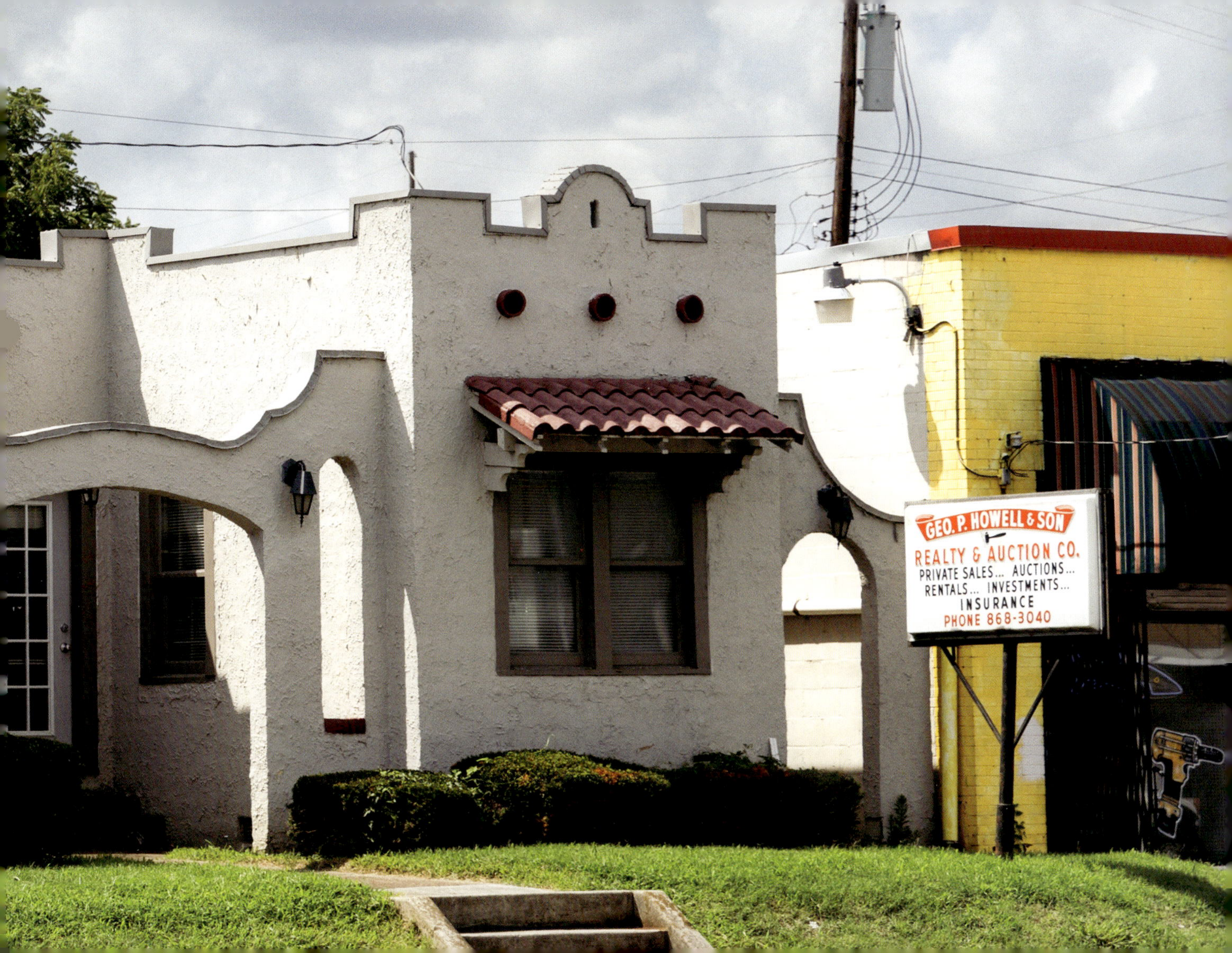
GEO. P. HOWELL & SON
REALTY & AUCTION CO.
PRIVATE SALES... AUCTIONS...
RENTALS... INVESTMENTS...
INSURANCE
PHONE 868-3040

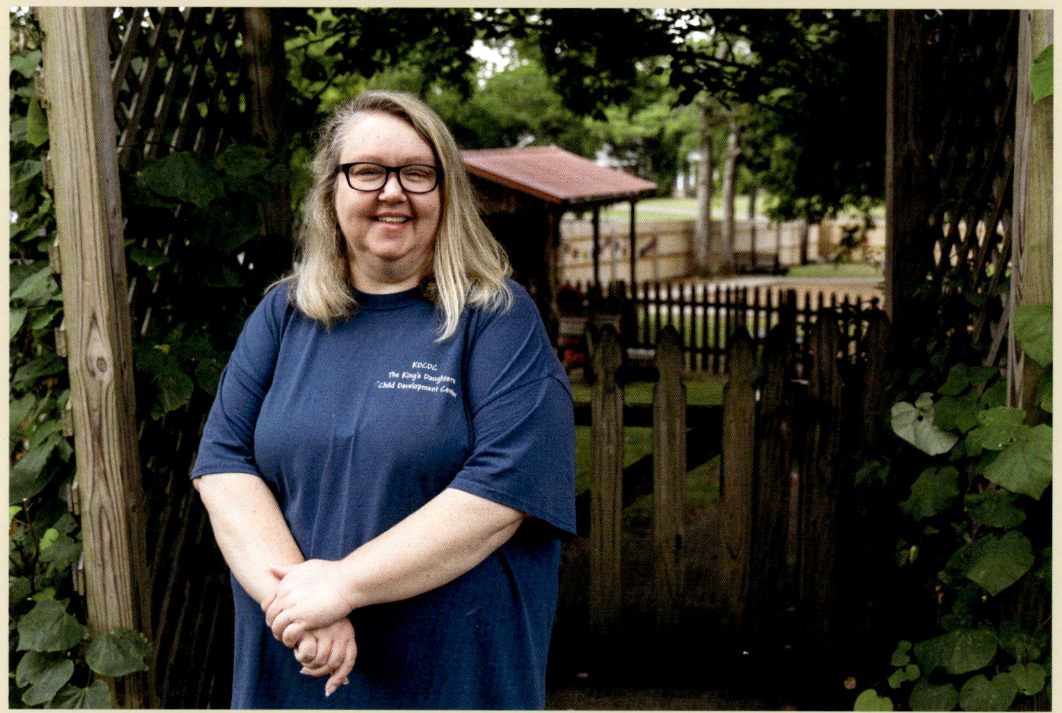

Lee Earls, associate director of King's Daughters Child Development Center, gives a tour of the garden. King's Daughters provides a high-quality, Reggio-inspired, project-based learning experience for children enrolled in their childcare facility.

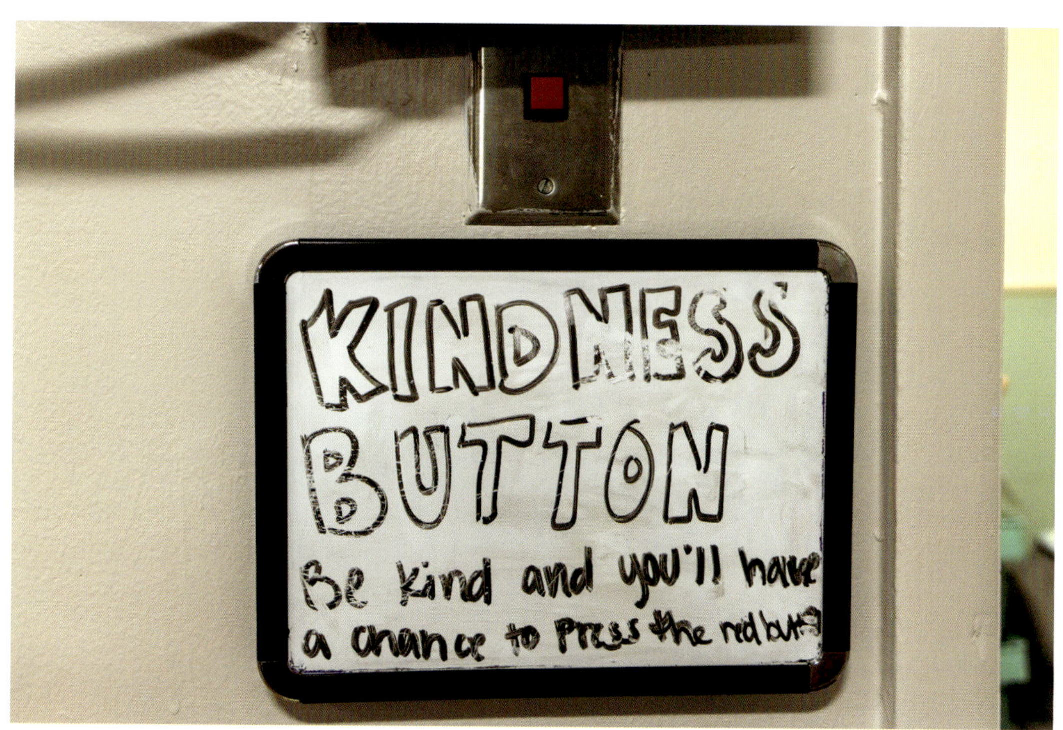
KINDNESS
BUTTON
Be kind and you'll have
a chance to press the red

Bobby Joe Ryman, retired singer, entertainer, and impersonator turned hobbyist woodworker, shows off his custom birdhouses.

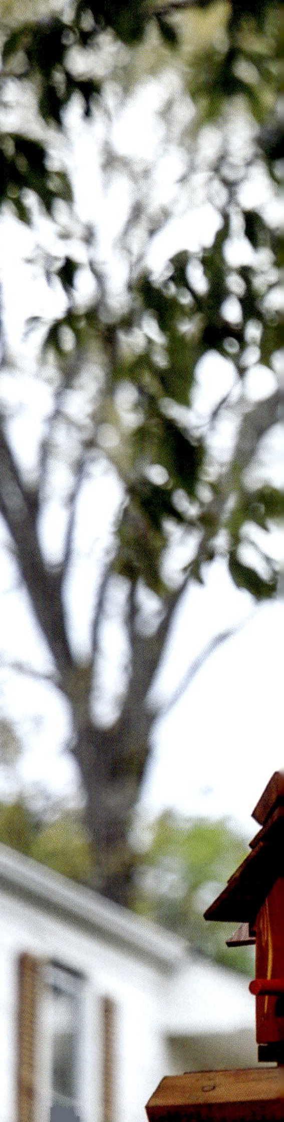

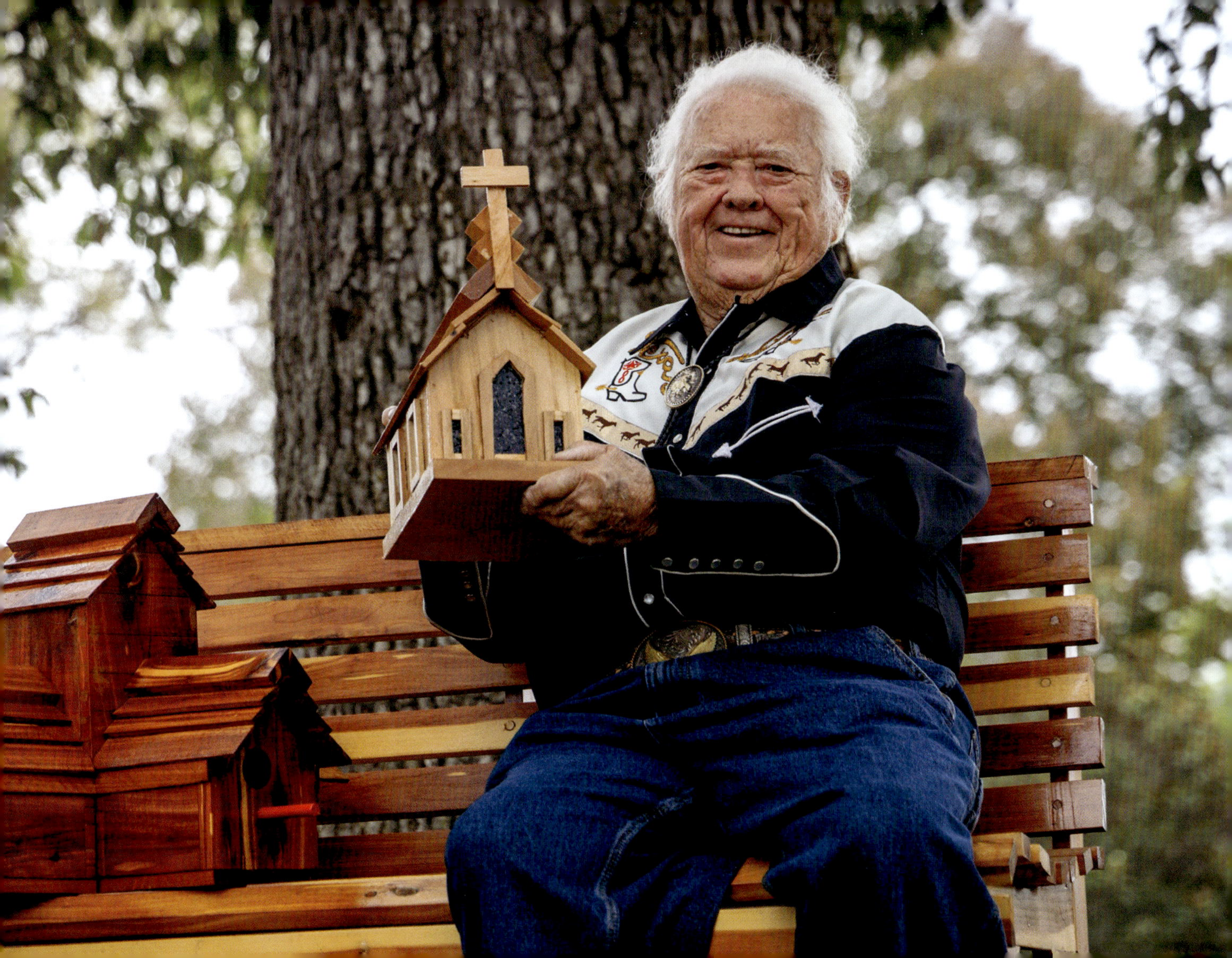

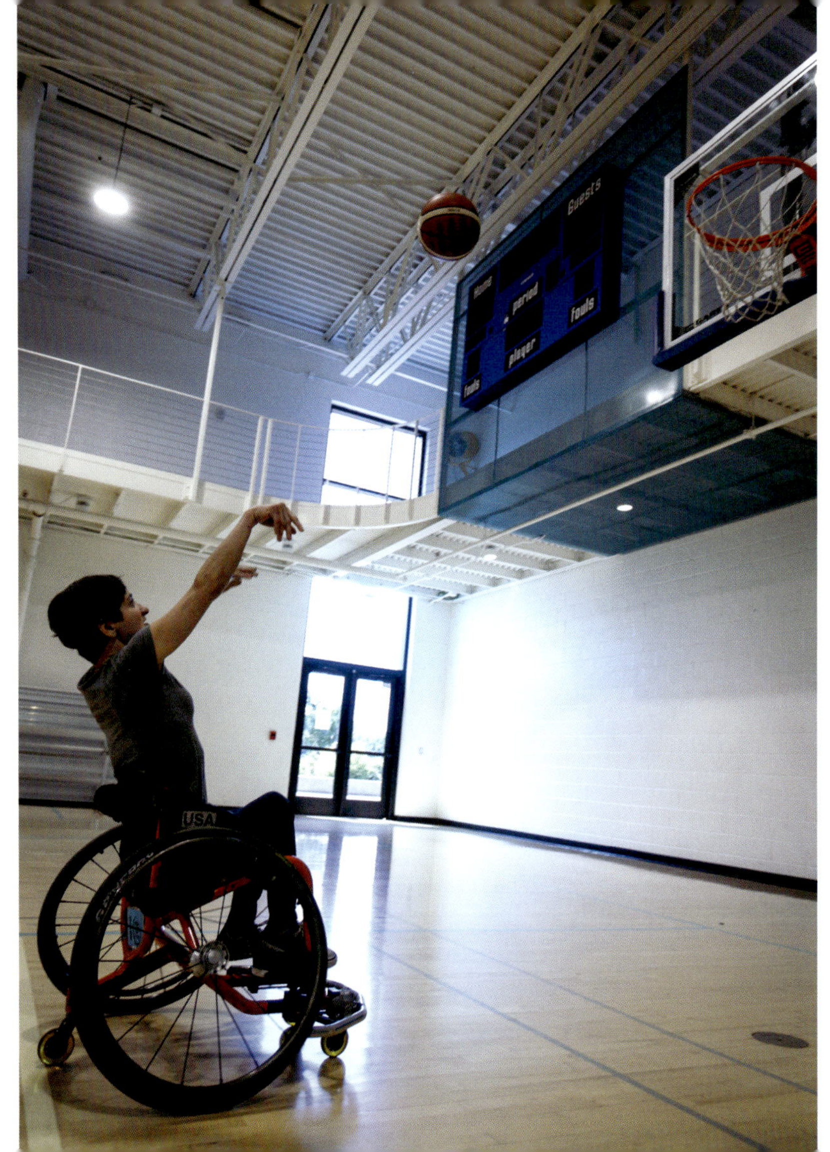
Home
Guests
period
player
fouls
fouls
USA

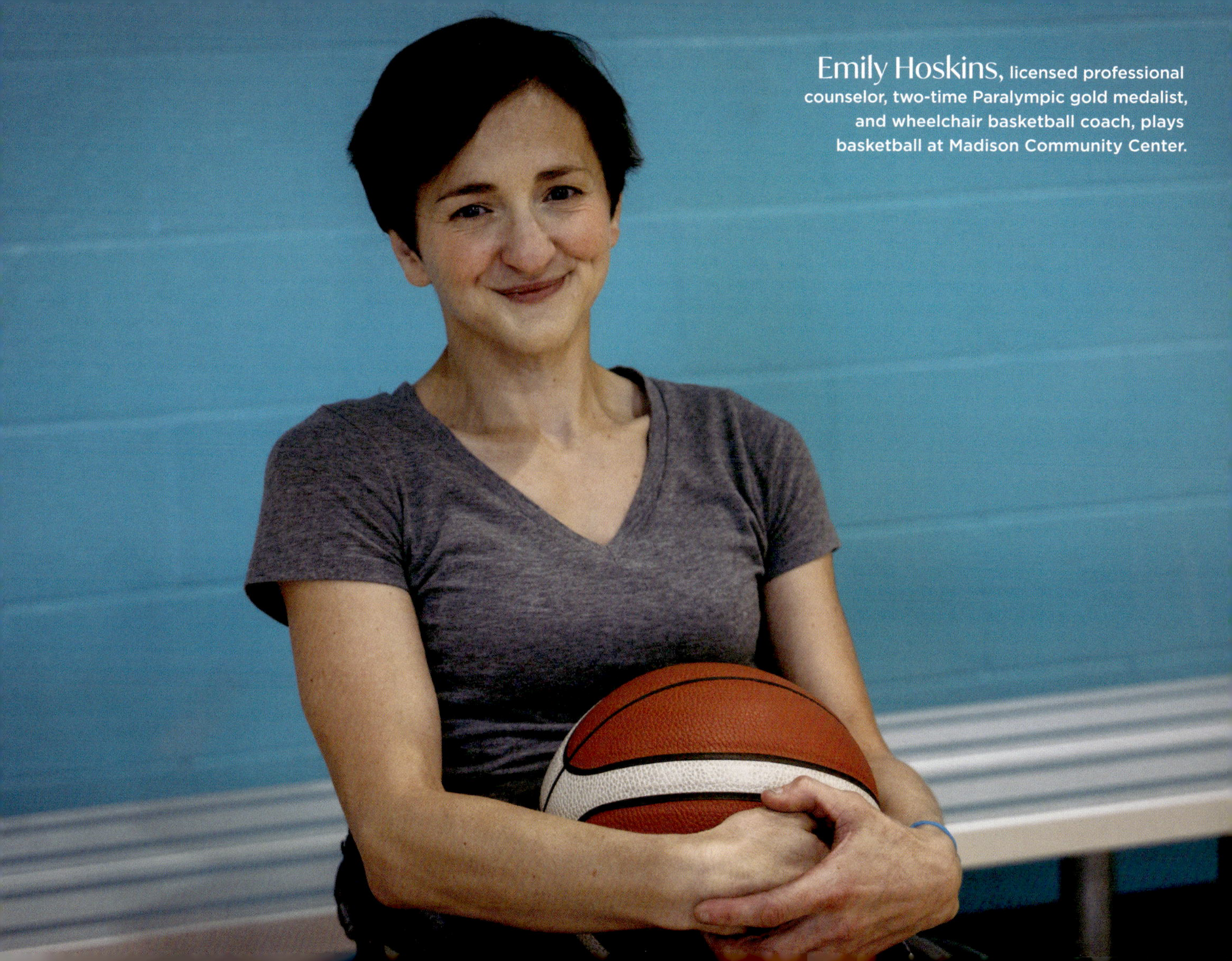

Emily Hoskins, licensed professional counselor, two-time Paralympic gold medalist, and wheelchair basketball coach, plays basketball at Madison Community Center.

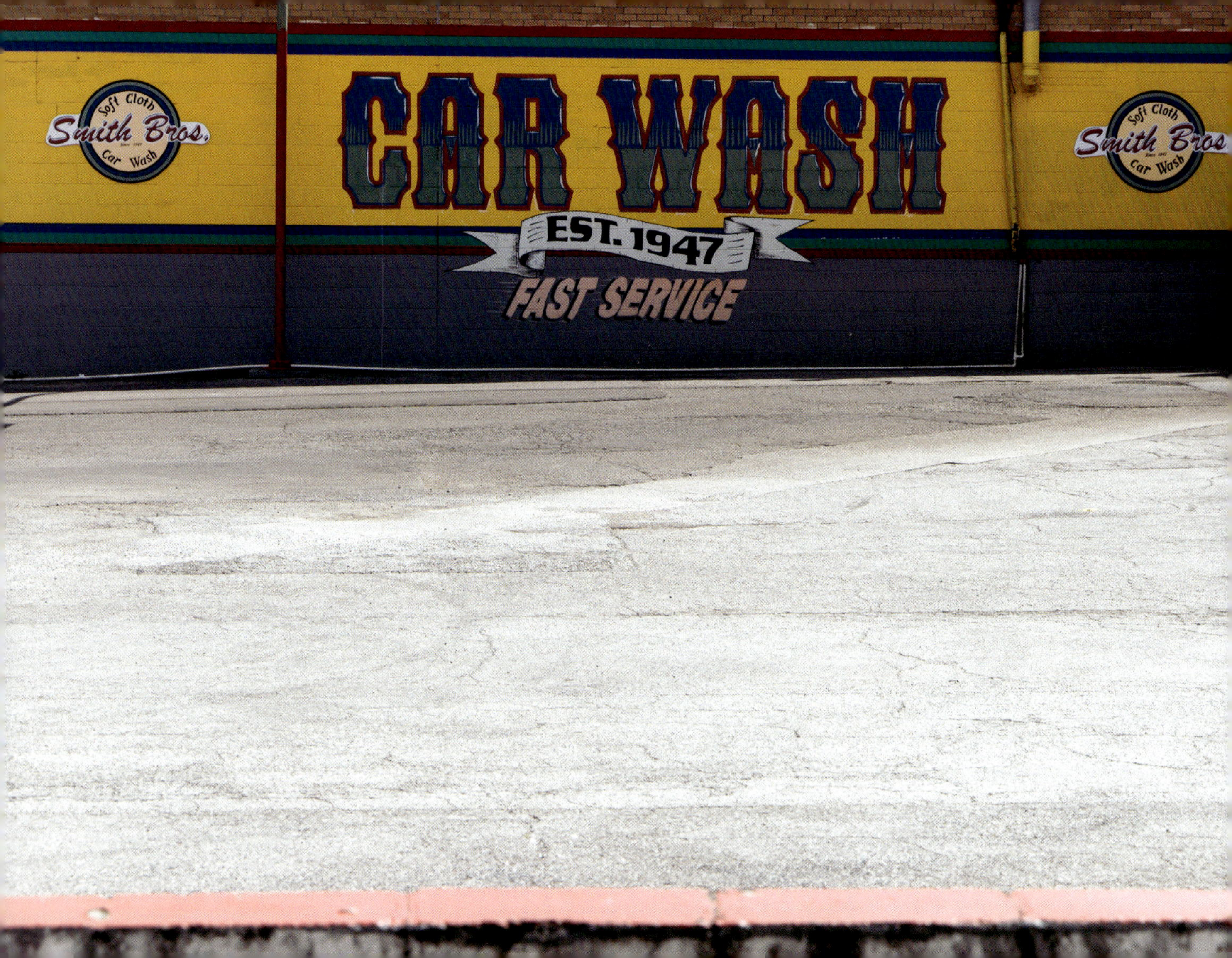

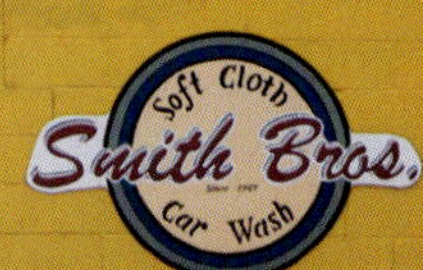
Soft Cloth
Smith Bros.
Car Wash

CAR WASH
EST. 1947
FAST SERVICE

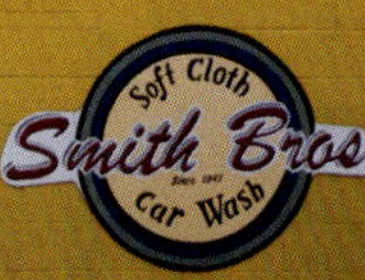
Soft Cloth
Smith Bros
Car Wash

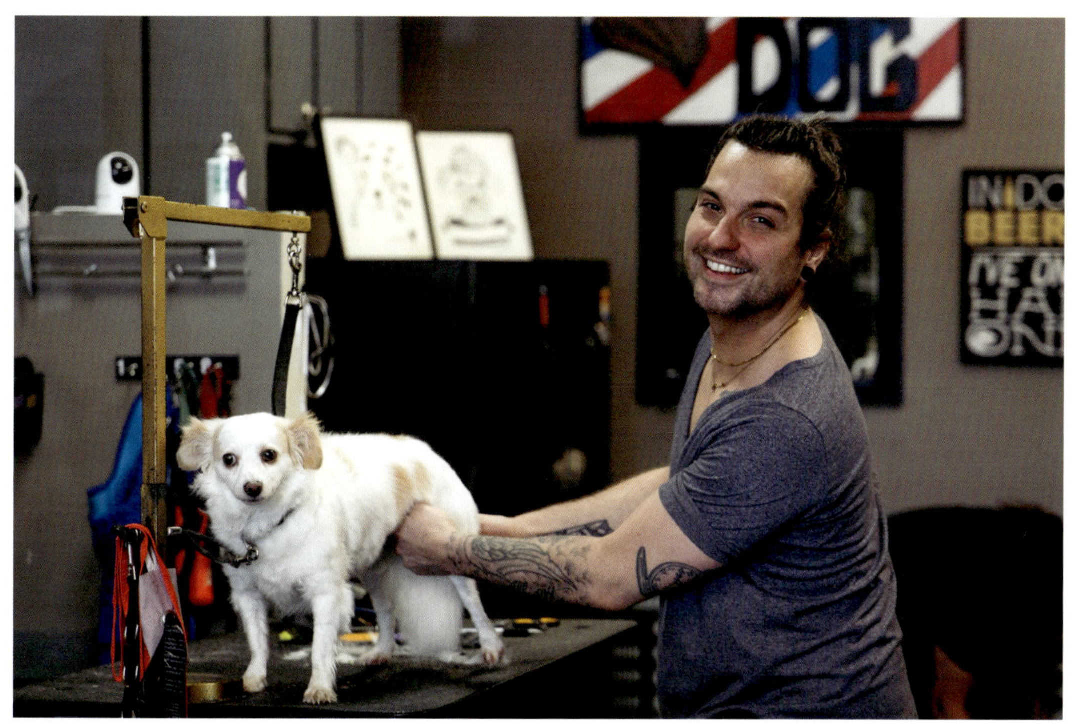

Devin Hathaway, owner of My Puppy Parlor, grooms Sofie, a Papillon mix.

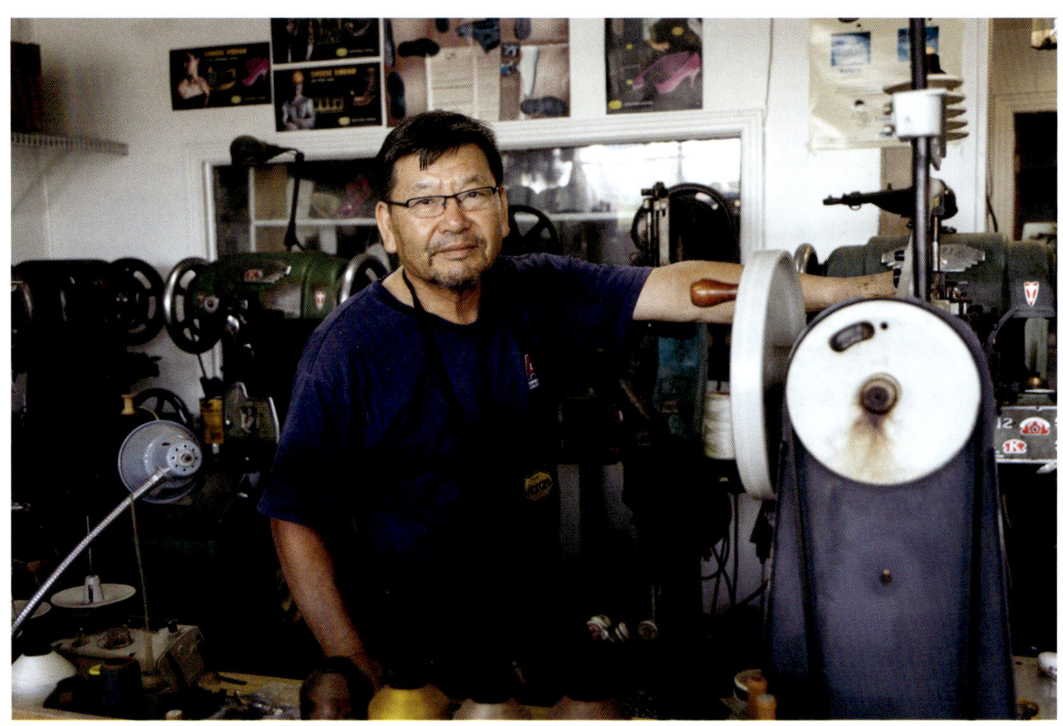

John Lee in front of his equipment at One Stop Shoe Repair, which shares a space with his wife's alterations business next door. The South Korean natives relocated to Nashville by way of NYC for a slower pace of life.

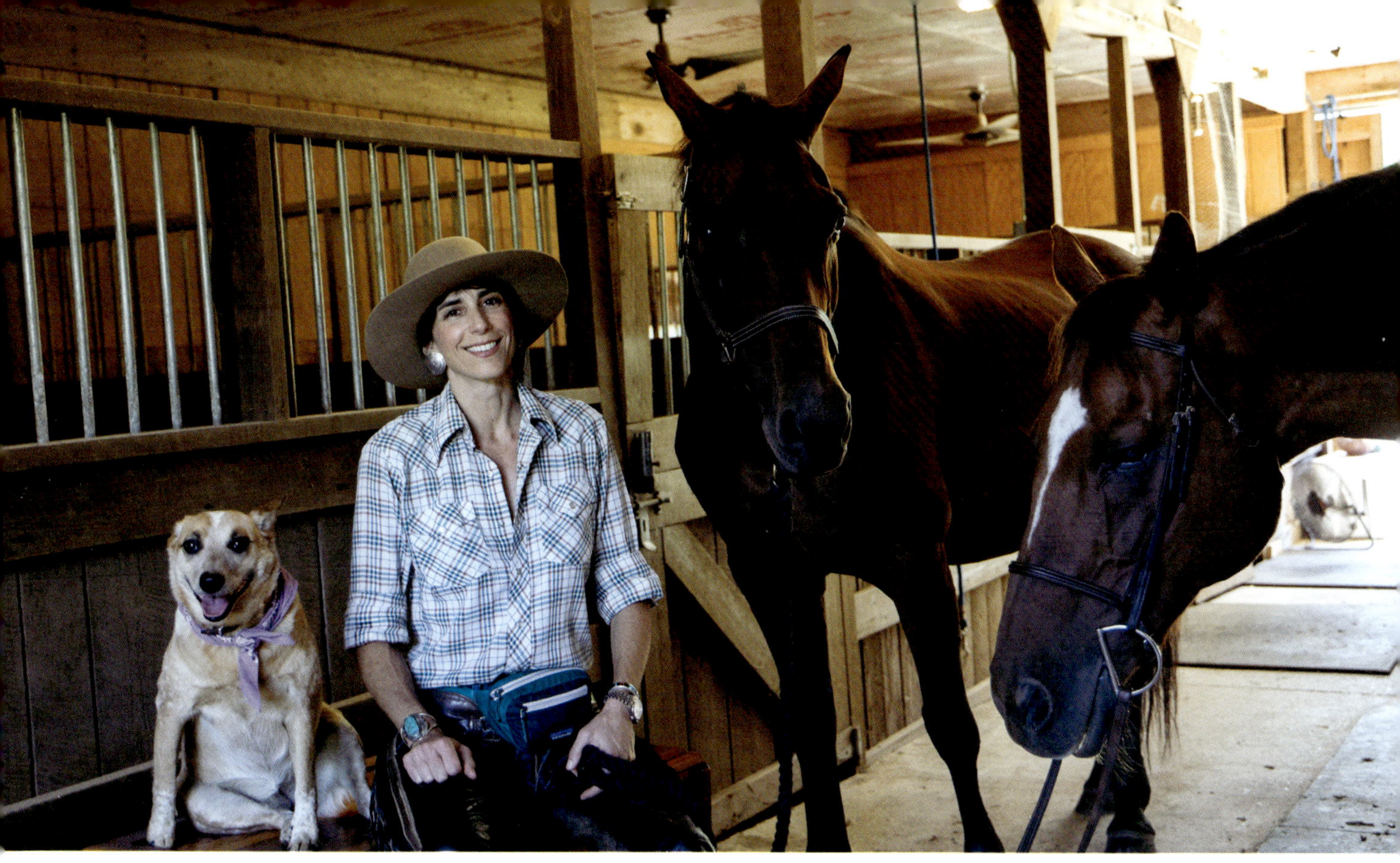

Singer-songwriter Nicki Bluhm in her barn after a ride with her horses, Mo and Omega, and her blue heeler, Birdie.

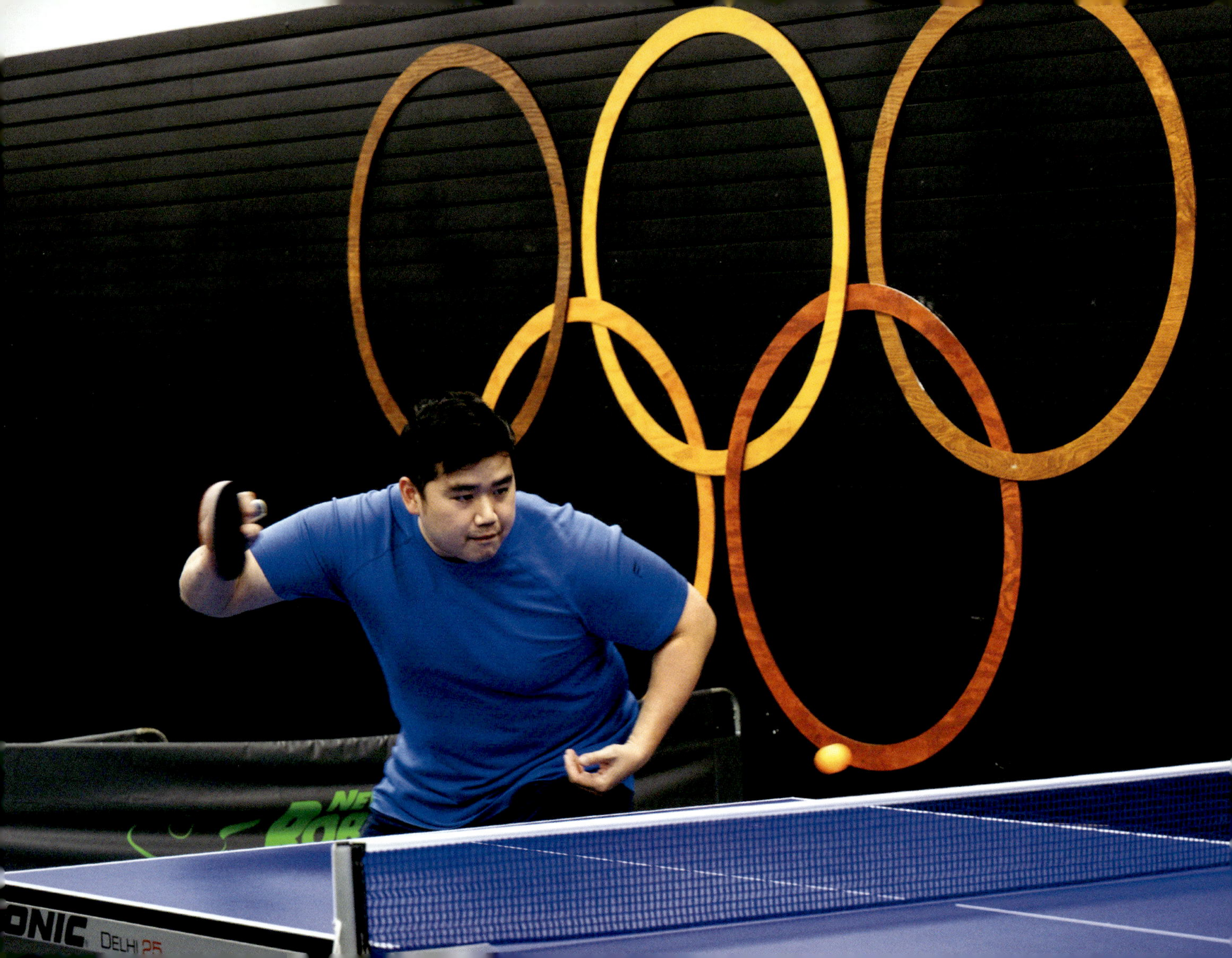
ONIC
DELHI 25

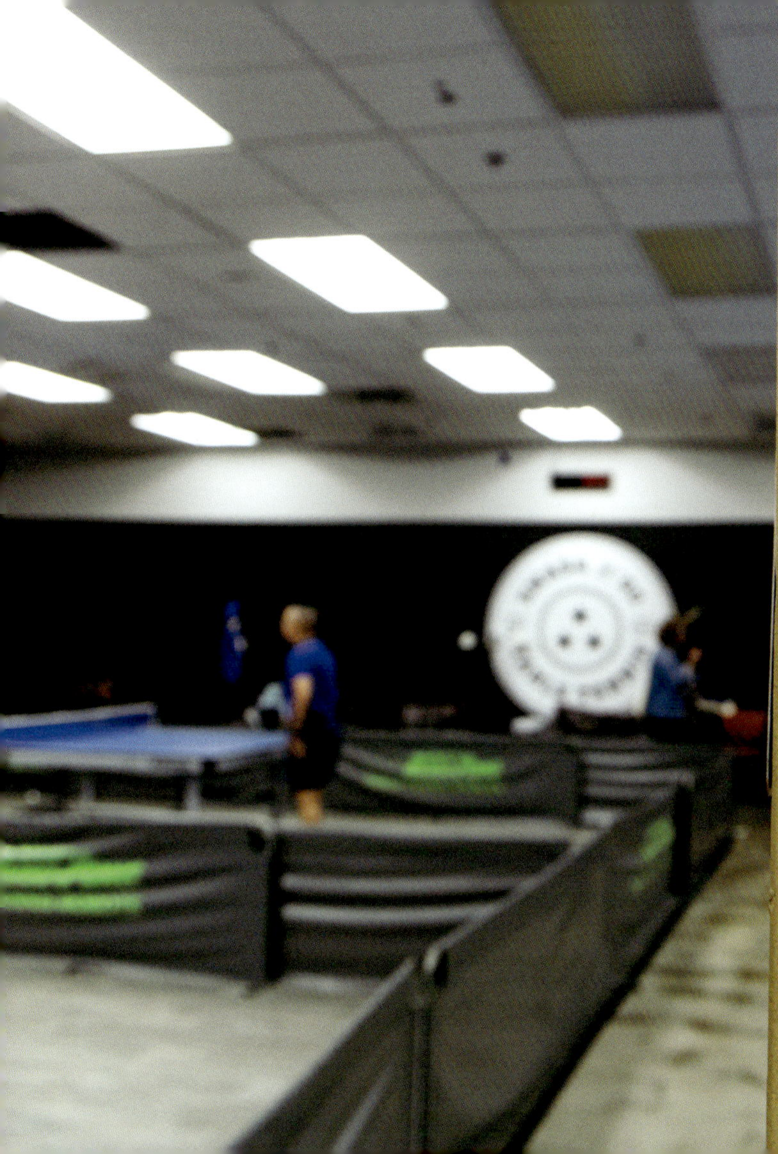

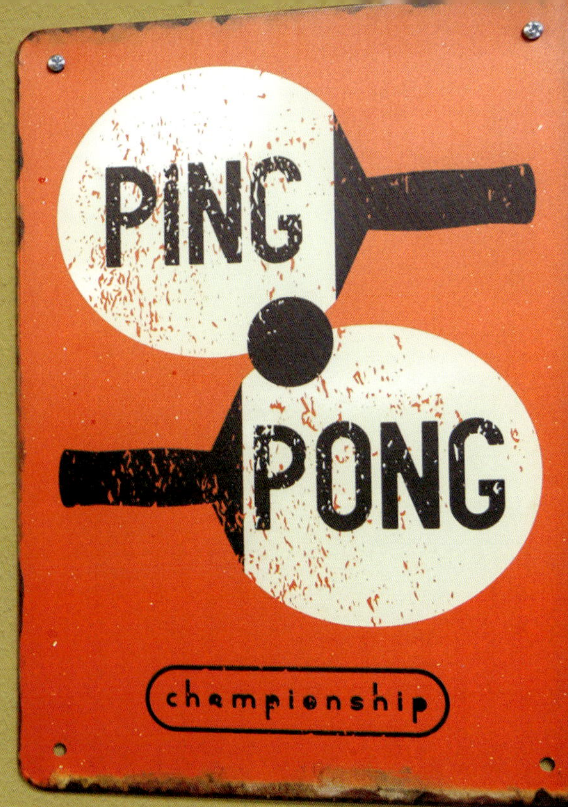

Harrison Ngo, table tennis player, coach, and owner of Smash N'Go Table Tennis. Nashville's first full-time table tennis facility, located inside Rivergate Mall, offers high-level training and league play.

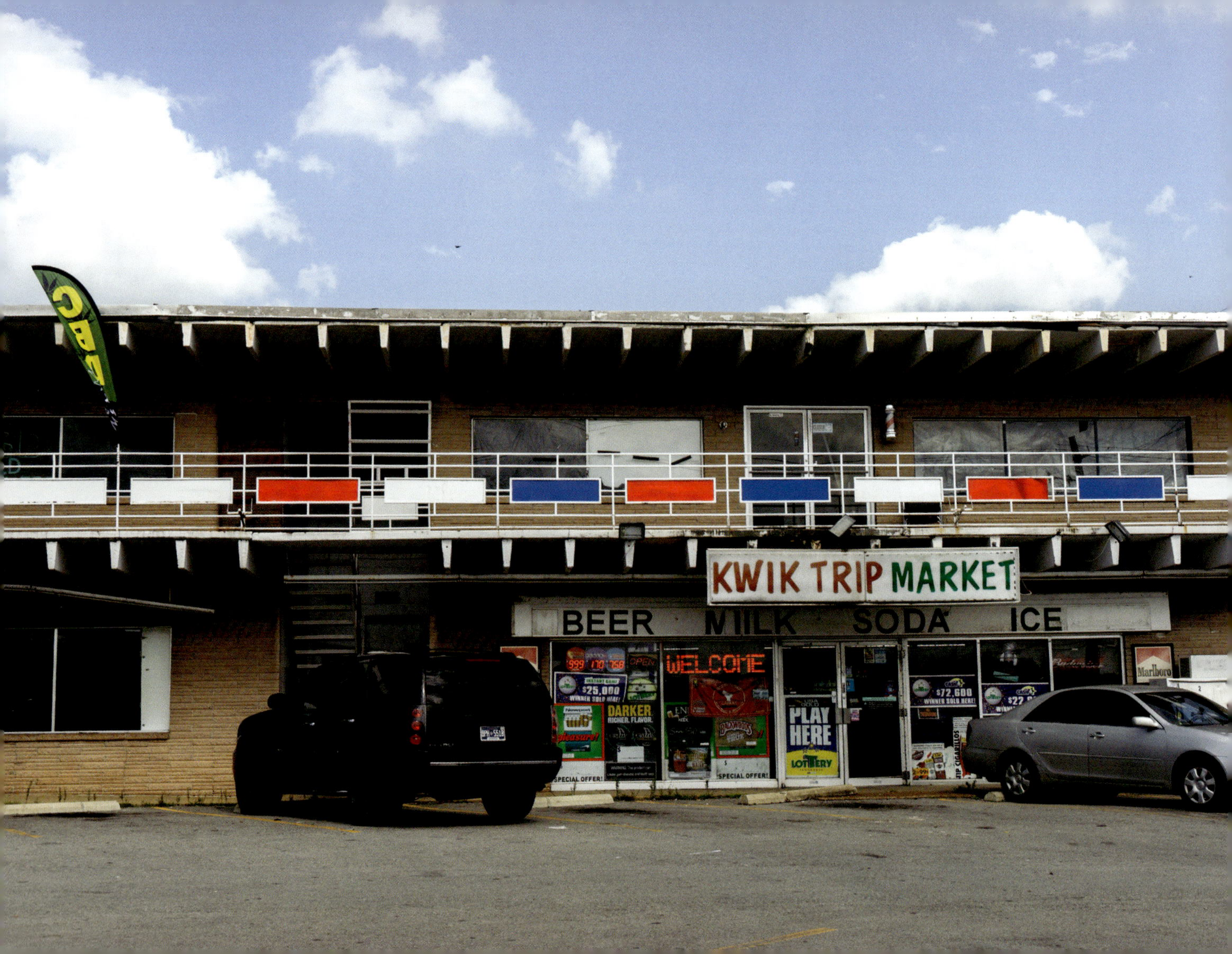
KWIK TRIP MARKET
BEER MILK SODA ICE
WELCOME
PLAY HERE
LOTTERY
DARKER
RICHER. FLAVOR.
SPECIAL OFFER!
SPECIAL OFFER!
$25,000
WINNER SOLD HERE!
$72,600
WINNER SOLD HERE!
Marlboro

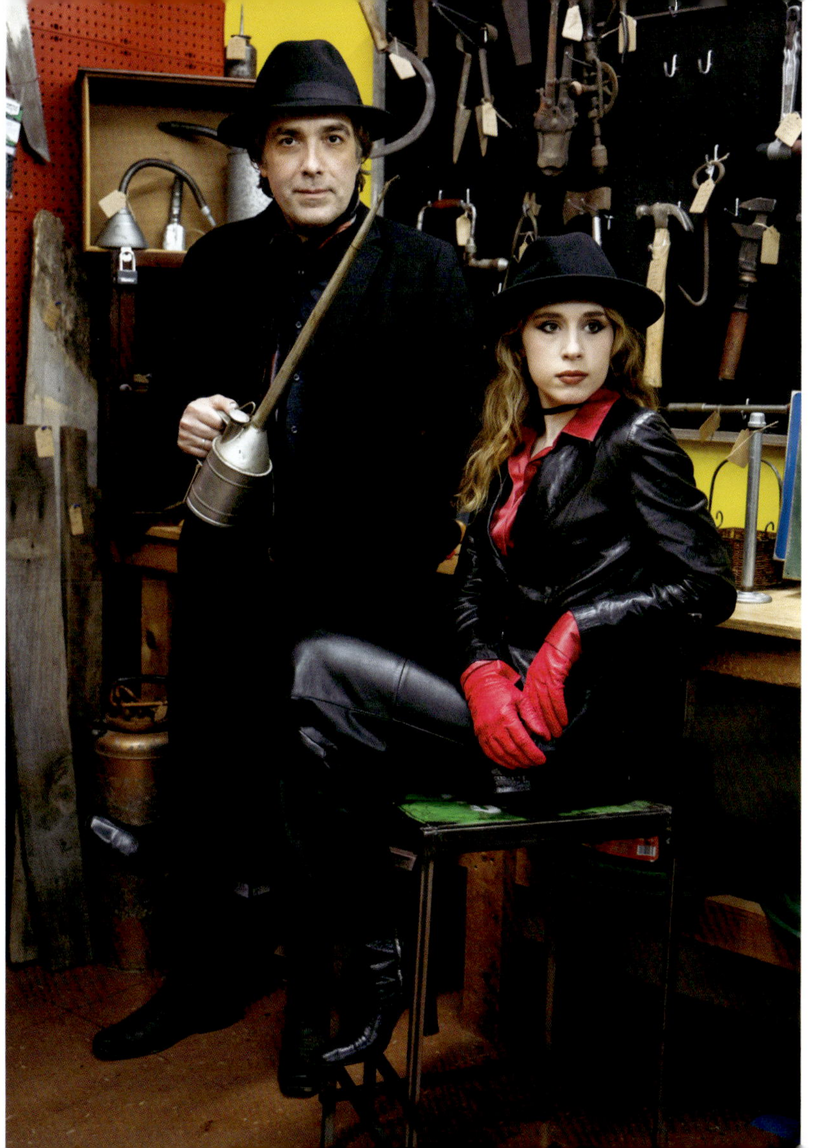

Alt-Americana artists **Irakli Gabriel and Anana Kaye** search for treasures inside Robinson's Flea Market. Natives from the Eastern European nation of Georgia, the multi-faceted artists express themselves through music, visual media, and live performance.

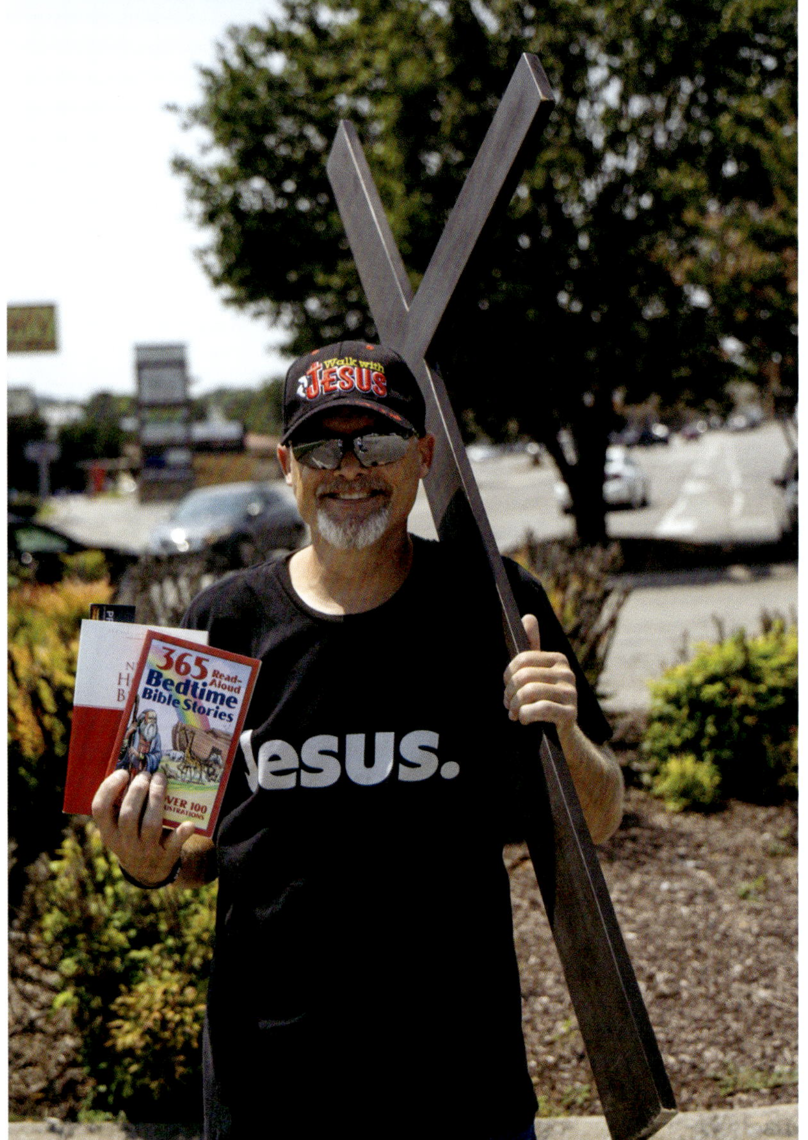

Dale, a passionate roadside evangelical Christian, offers neighbors an opportunity to be baptized along Gallatin Pike.

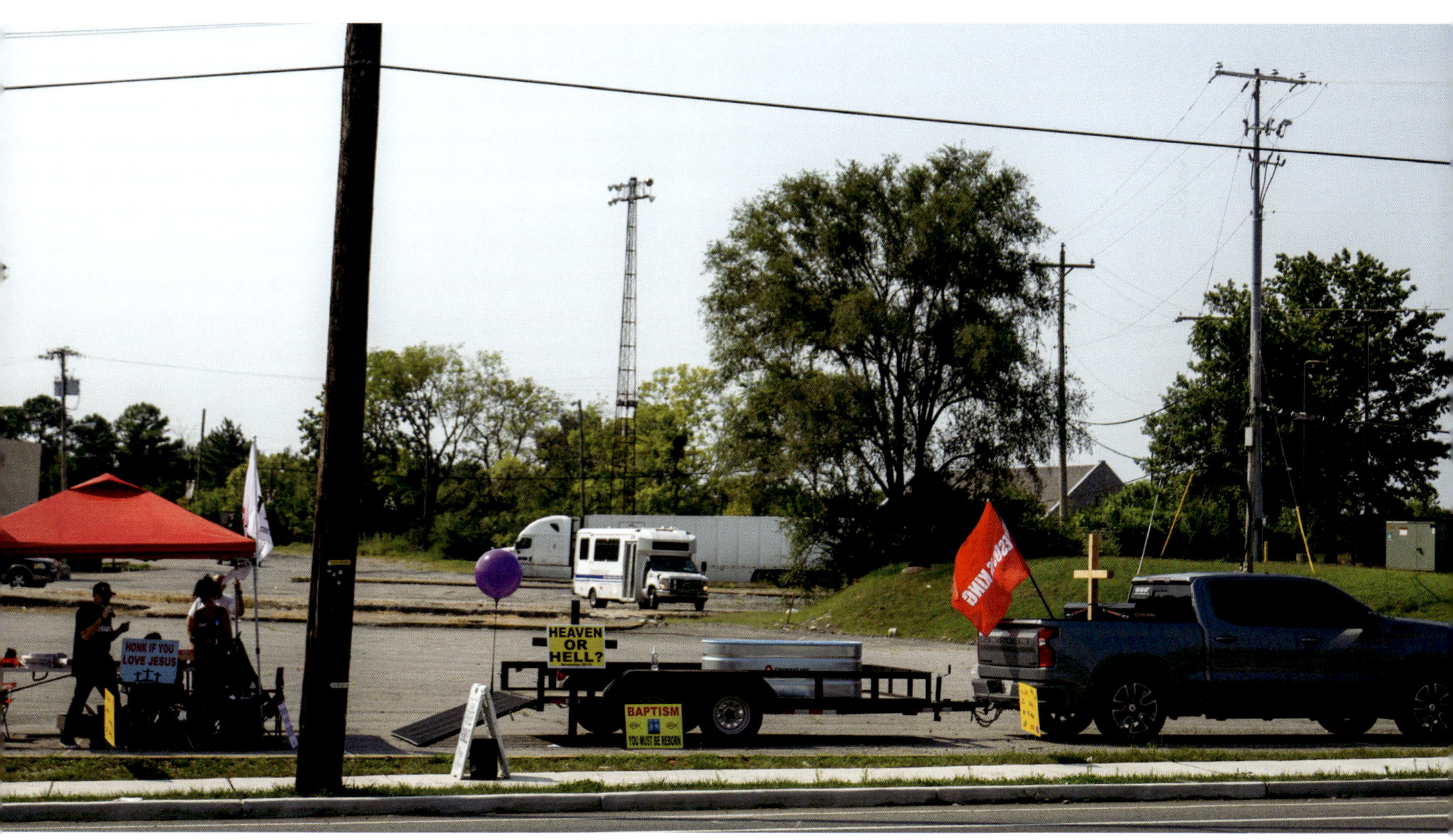
HONK IF YOU
LOVE JESUS
HEAVEN
OR
HELL?
BAPTISM
YOU MUST BE REBORN

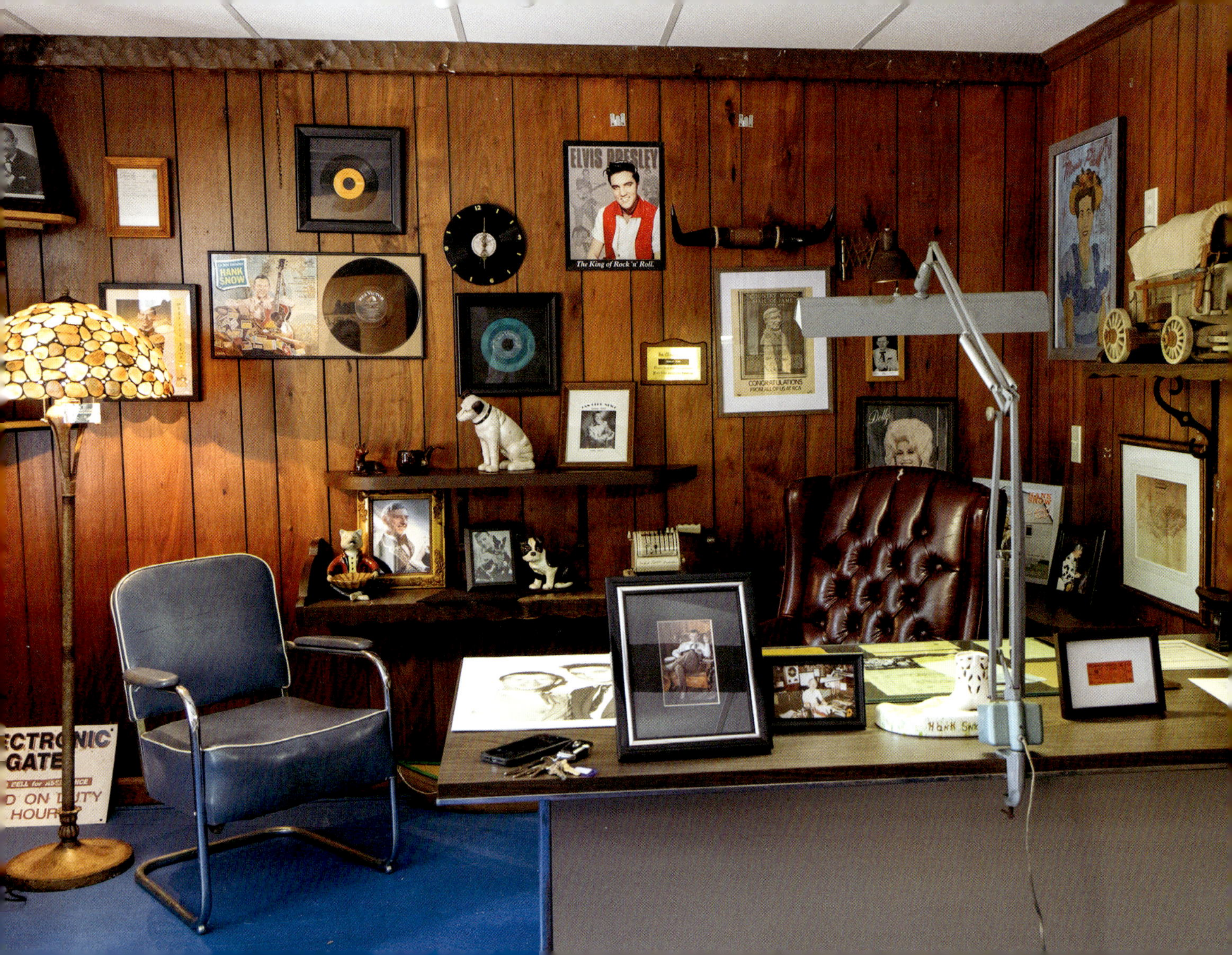
ELVIS PRESLEY
The King of Rock 'n' Roll.
HANK SNOW
CONGRATULATIONS FROM ALL OF US AT RCA
Dolly
GATE
HANK SNOW

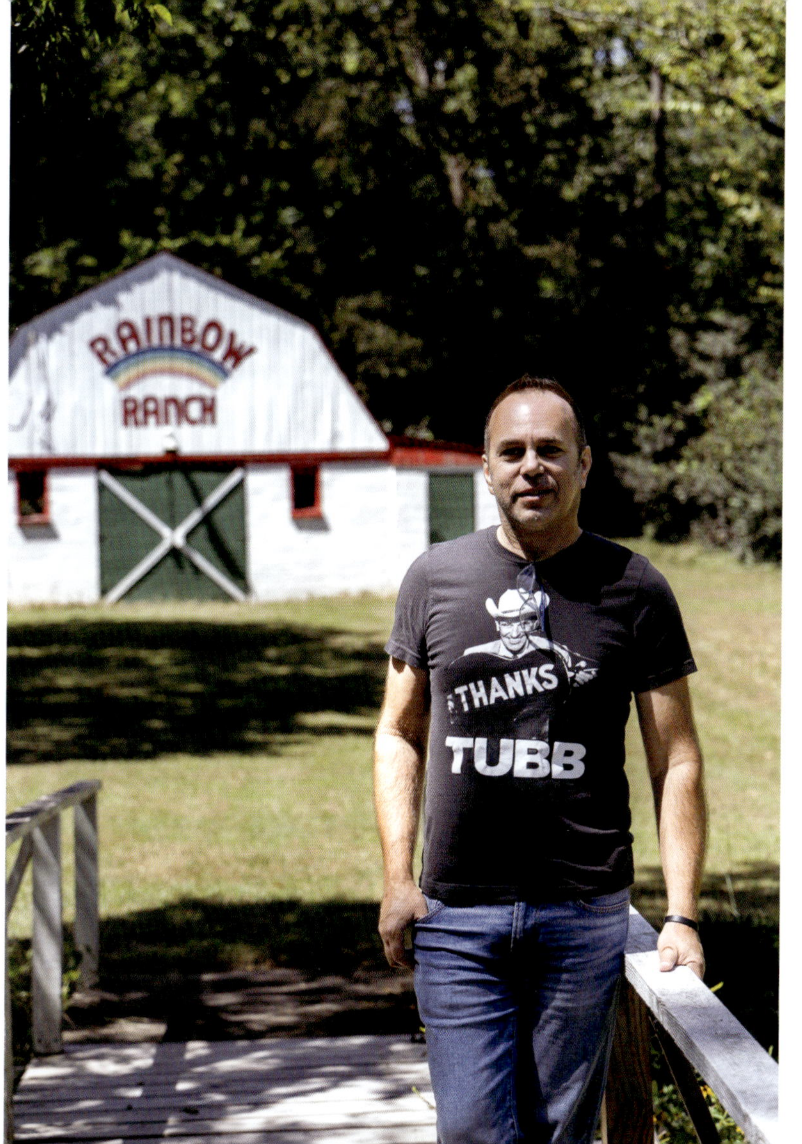

Terry Tyson, the house manager of Hank Snow's Rainbow Ranch, stands outside the home. The property is on the National Register of Historic Places and was designated a historical site by the Metro Historical Commission; it is available as a short-term rental for tourists.

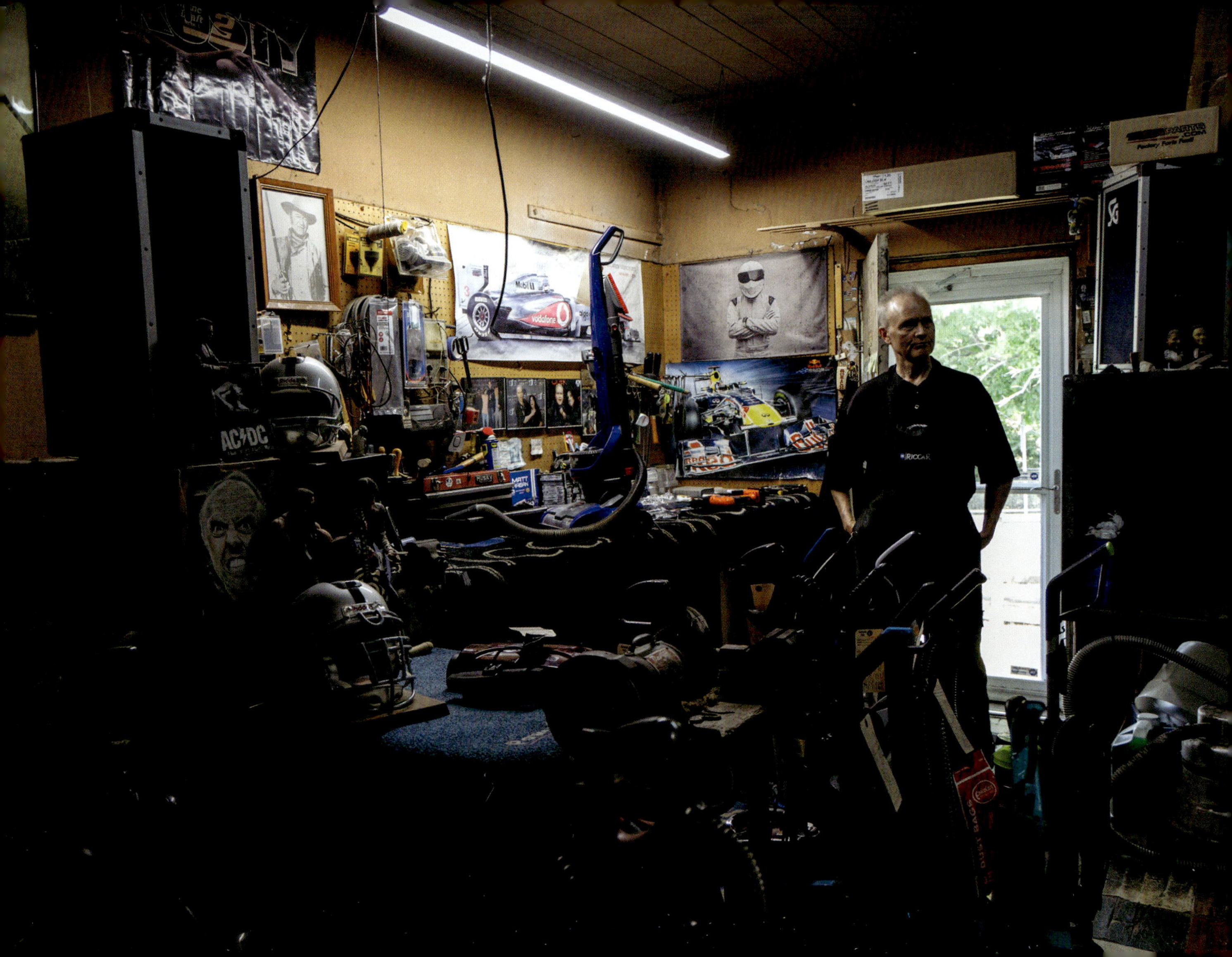
AC/DC
vodafone
RICCAR
DUST BAGS

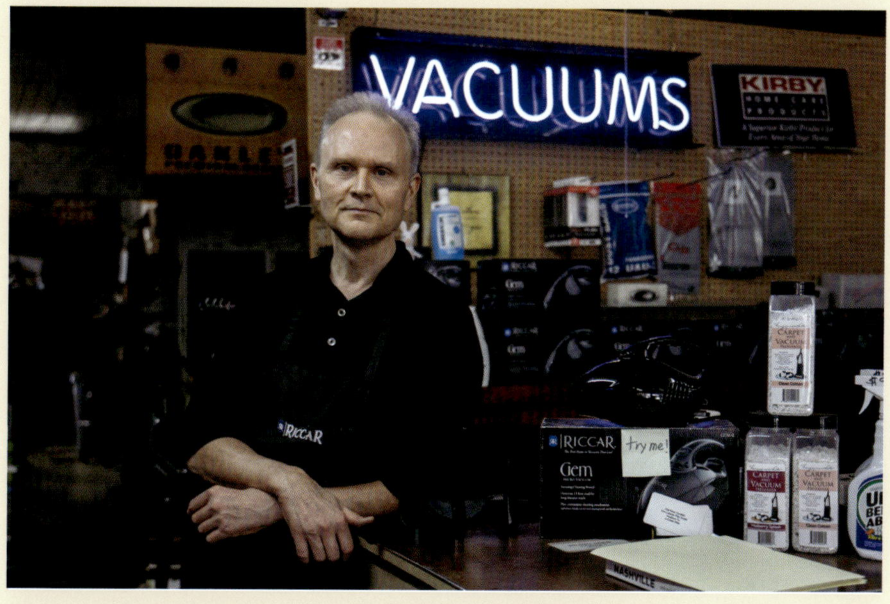

Robert Glover, owner of Mid-State Vacuum. His late father started the vacuum sales and repair company more than thirty-six years ago.

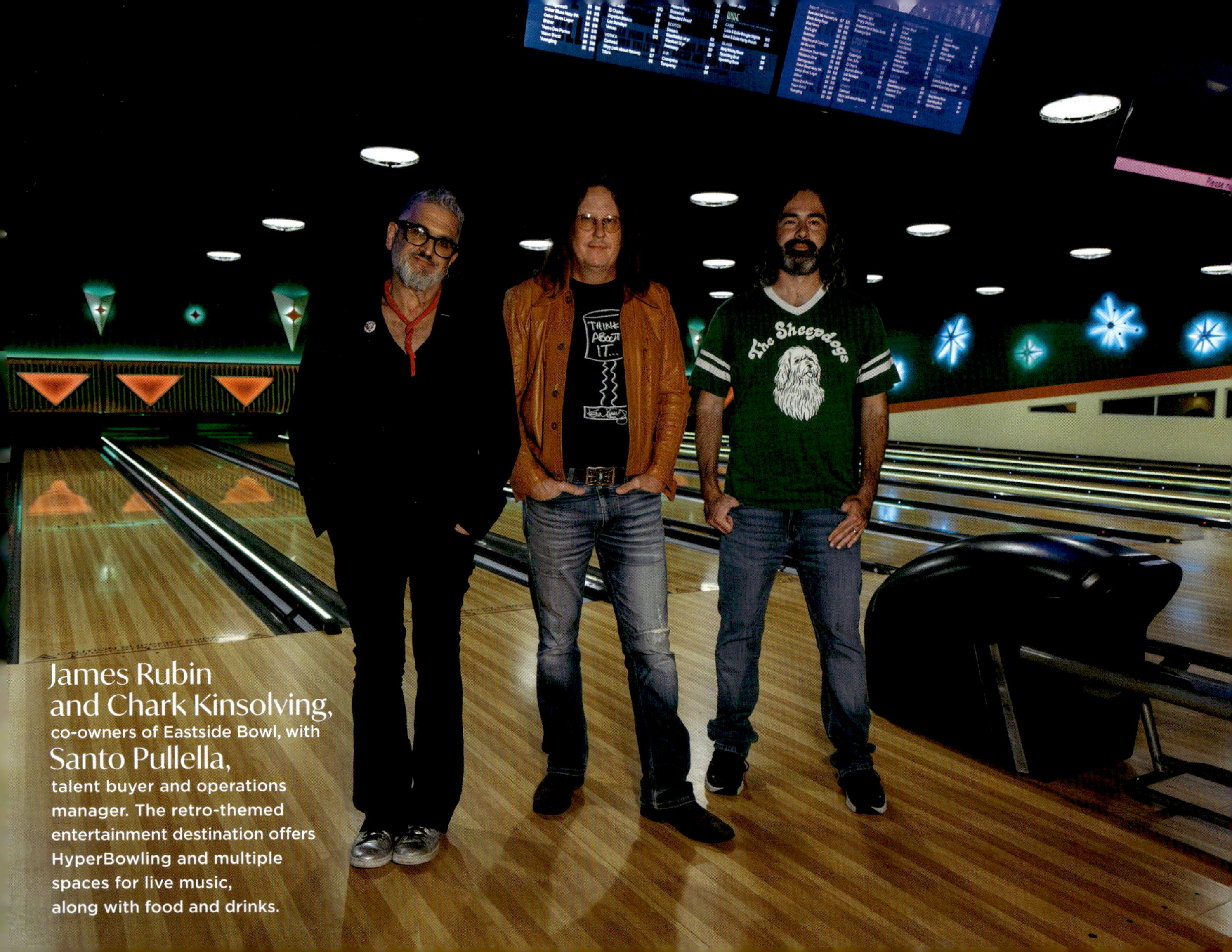

James Rubin and Chark Kinsolving, co-owners of Eastside Bowl, with Santo Pullella, talent buyer and operations manager. The retro-themed entertainment destination offers HyperBowling and multiple spaces for live music, along with food and drinks.

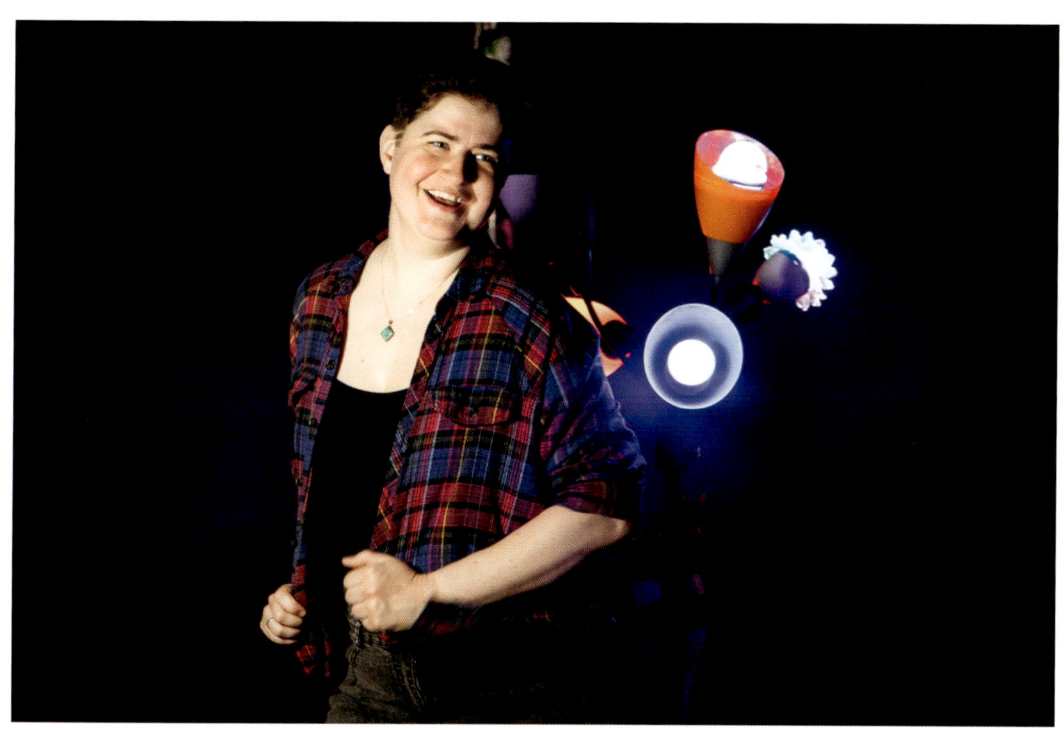

"Betsey Bits," a burlesque dancer and owner of House of Bits, featured in their dance studio and performance space.

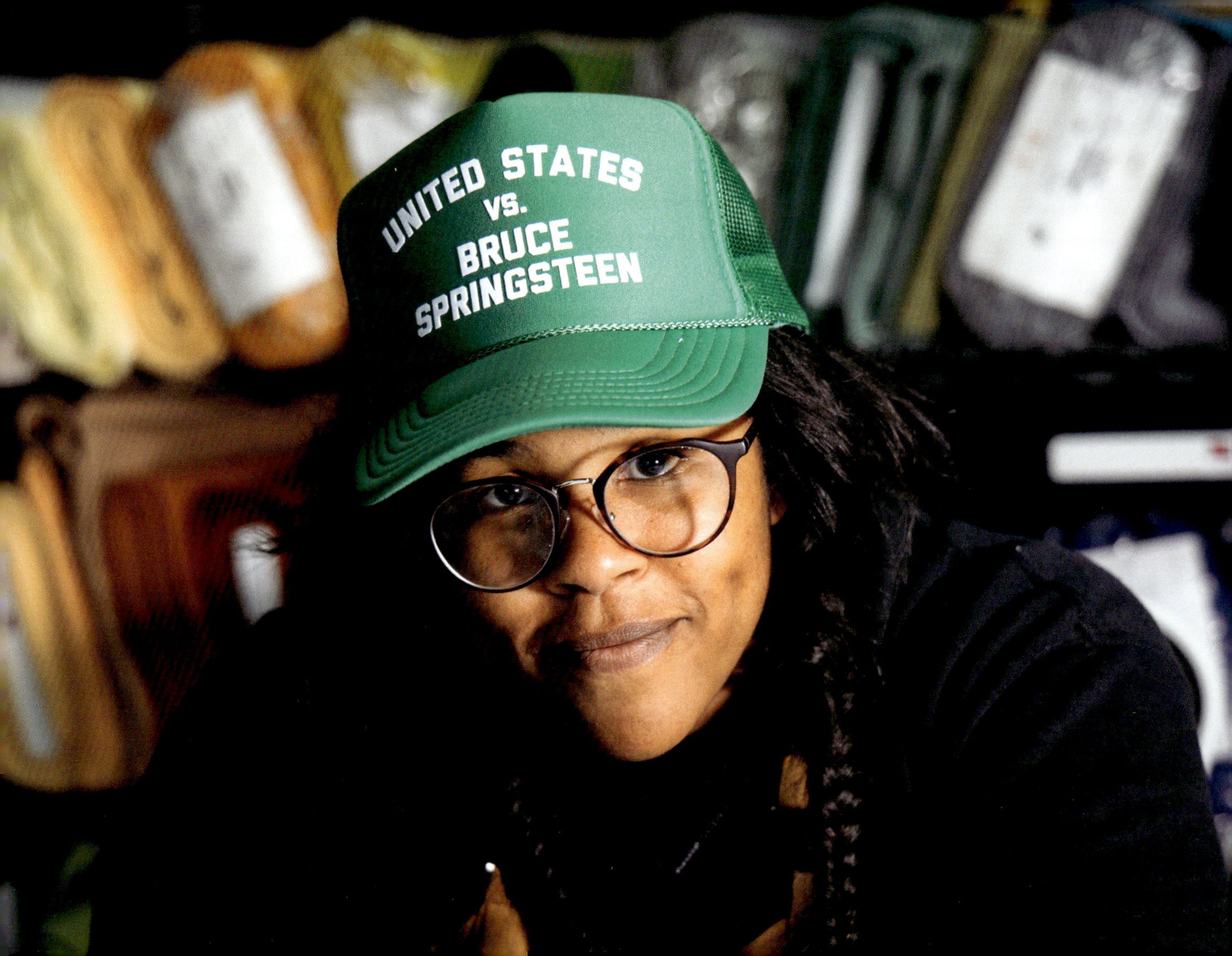
UNITED STATES
VS.
BRUCE
SPRINGSTEEN

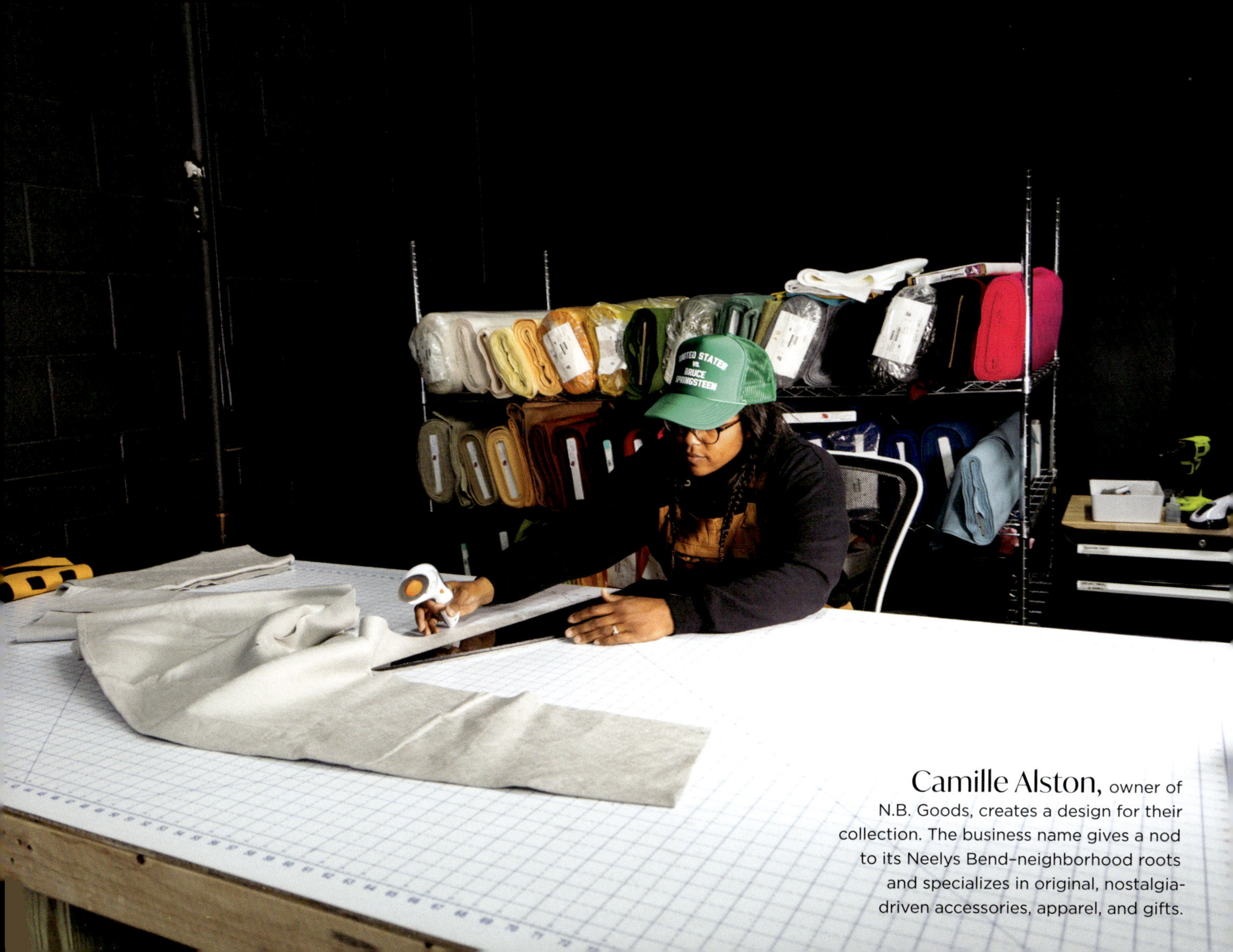

Camille Alston, owner of N.B. Goods, creates a design for their collection. The business name gives a nod to its Neelys Bend–neighborhood roots and specializes in original, nostalgia-driven accessories, apparel, and gifts.

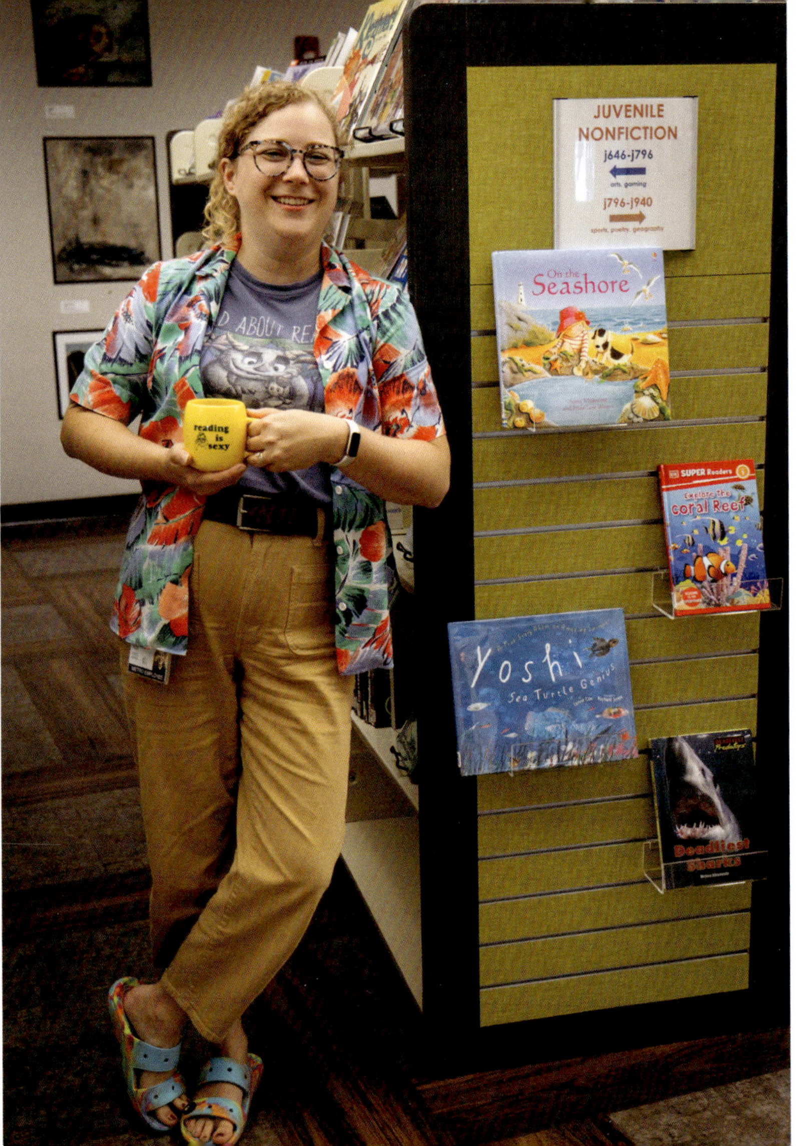

Lisa Bubert, an author and children's librarian at the Madison branch of Nashville Public Library. She contributes to the wider literary community through her writing and editorial services.

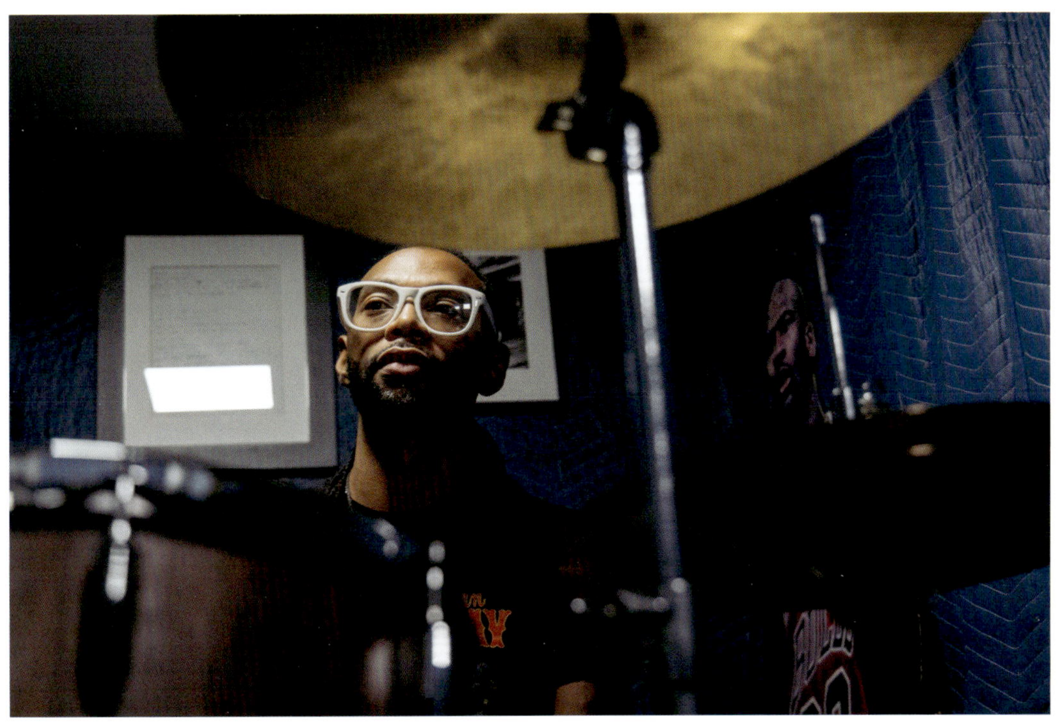

Touring and session drummer and professional DJ **Jerry Pentecost** sits behind his kit in his home studio. His extensive touring credits include Old Crow Medicine Show and Bob Dylan.

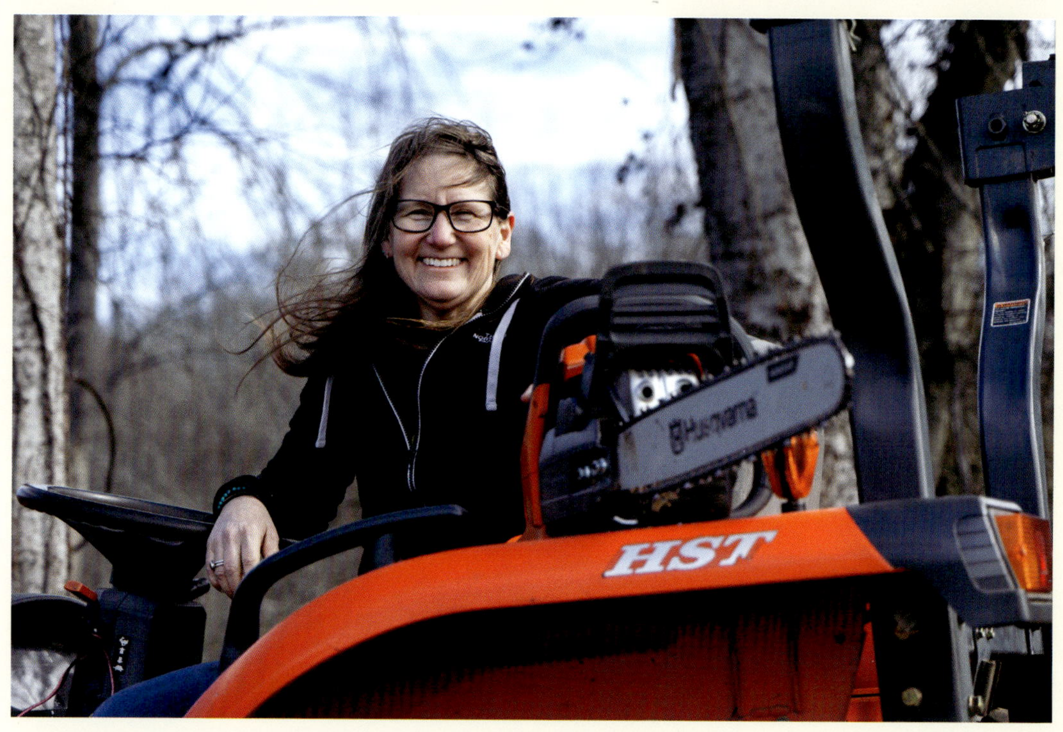

Kelli Boyd, veterinary pathologist and cancer-research scientist, rides a tractor on her Cumberland river property, Ada Mae's Farm.

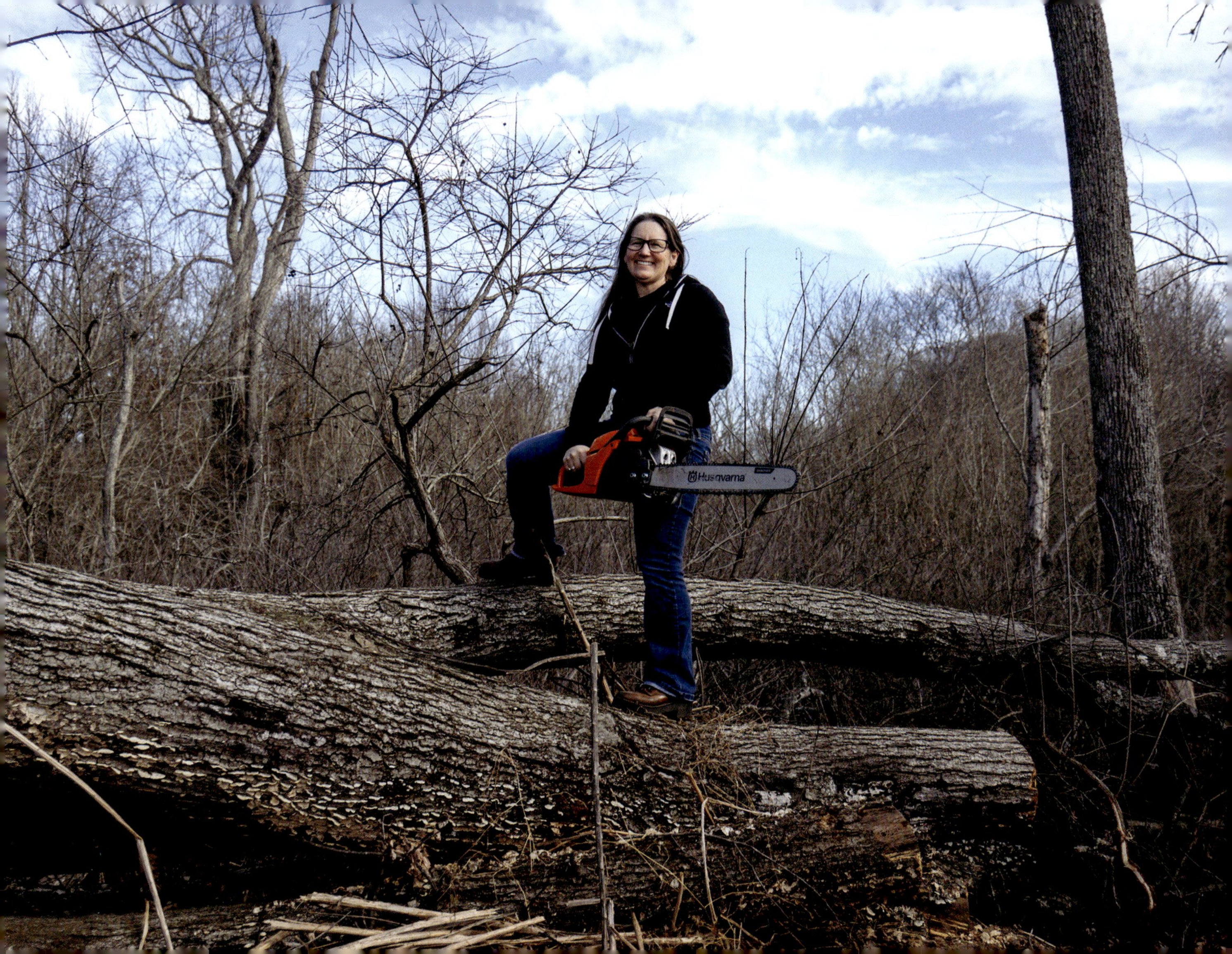
Husqvarna

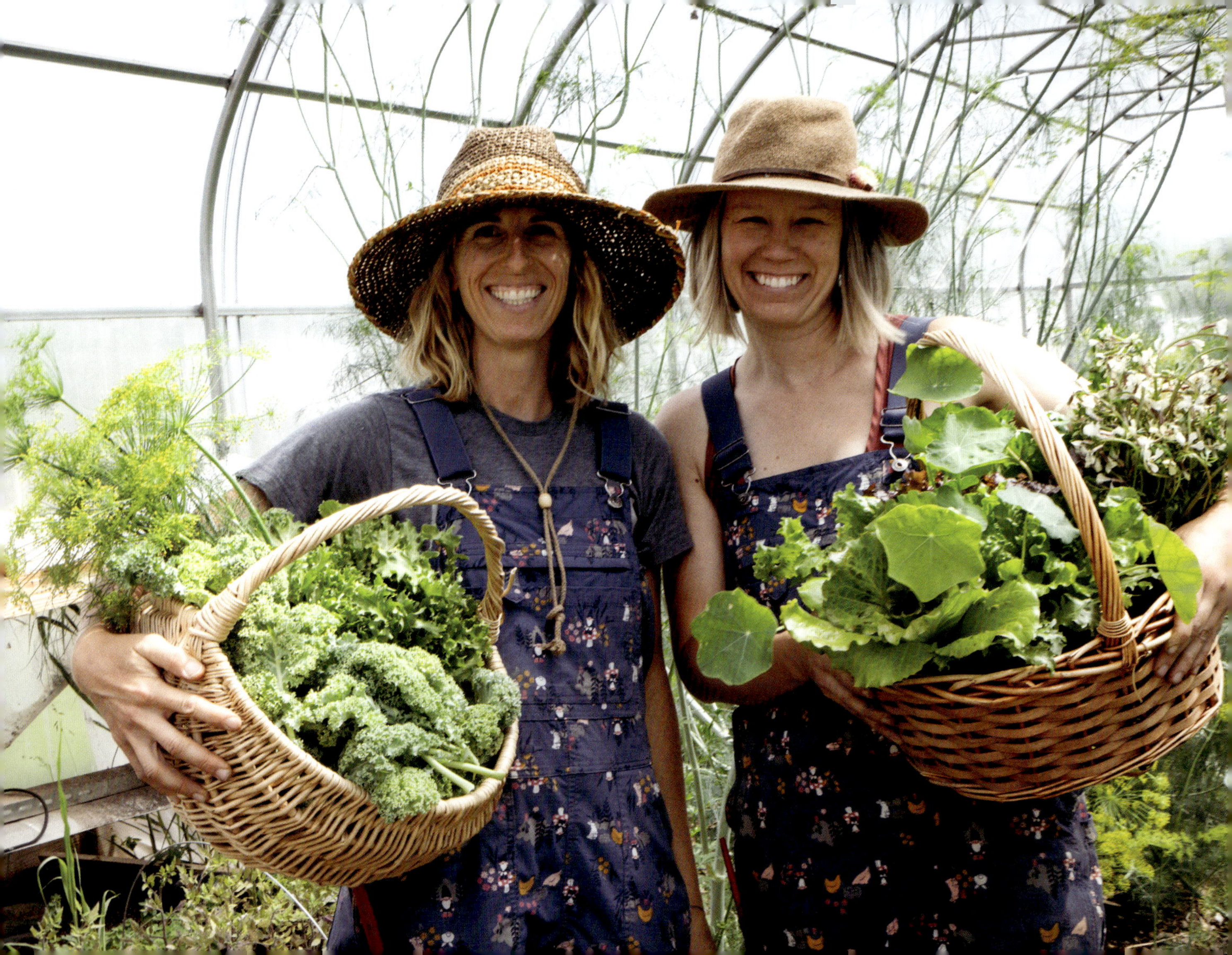

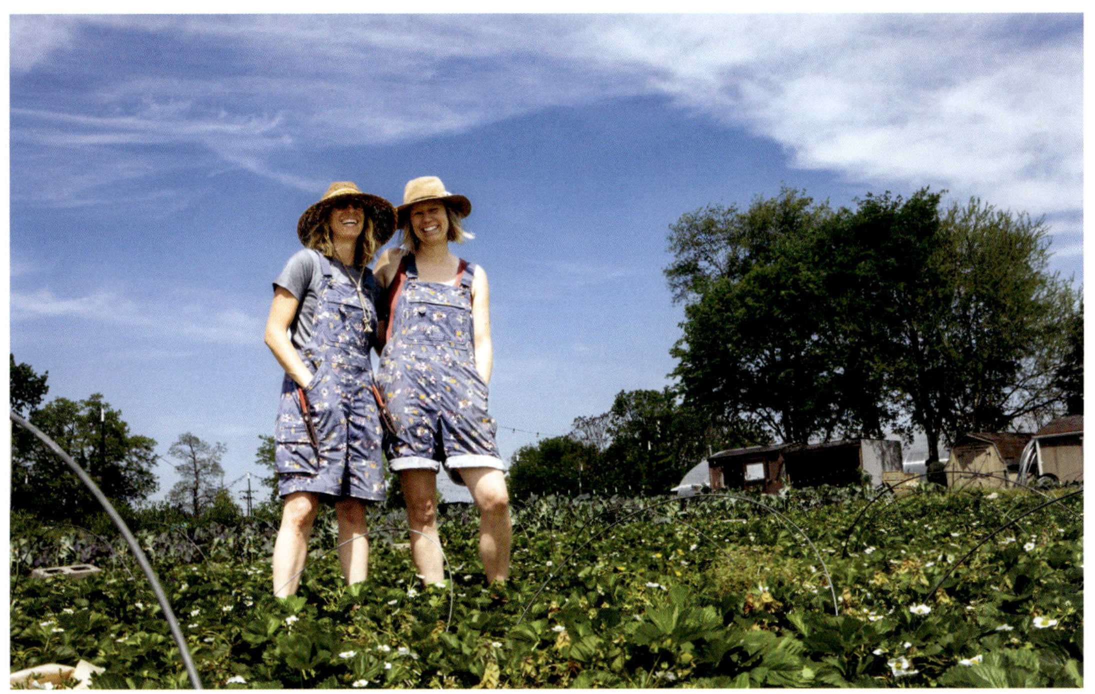

Jenni Adams and Shannon Wilhelm work at The Madison Farm. The farm is committed to organic, bio-intensive, and sustainable farming practices and is an outreach of Madison Campus Church.

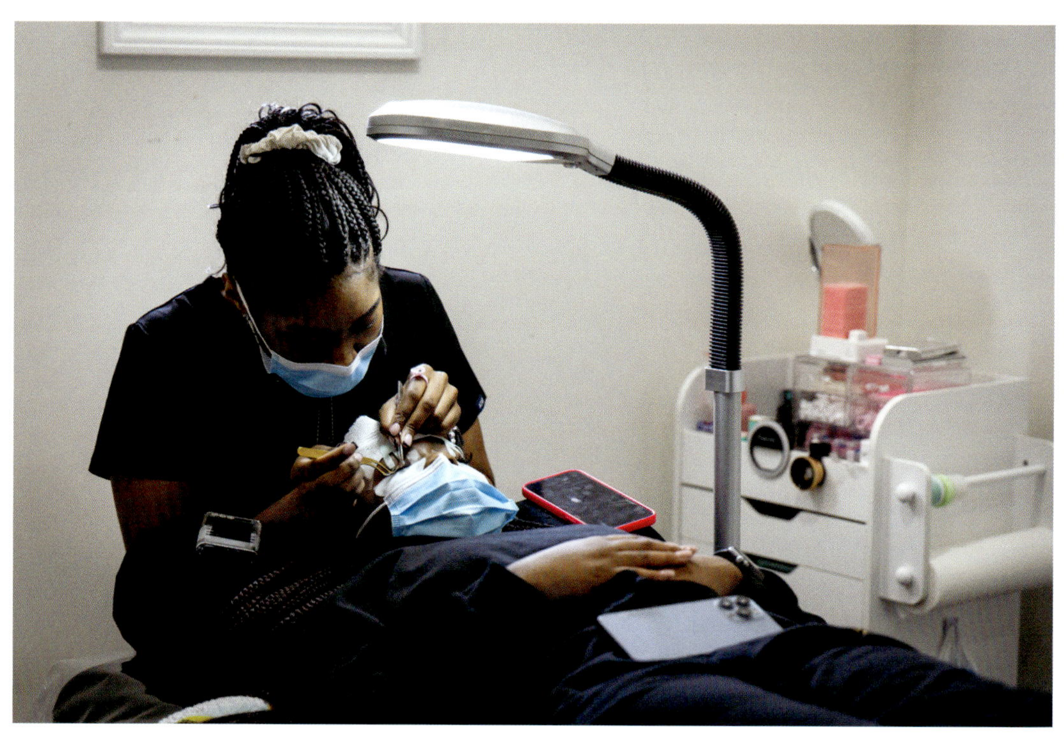

Eyebrow technician Jayla Wiggins works out of her adjacent studio at the Peach Pit Salon.

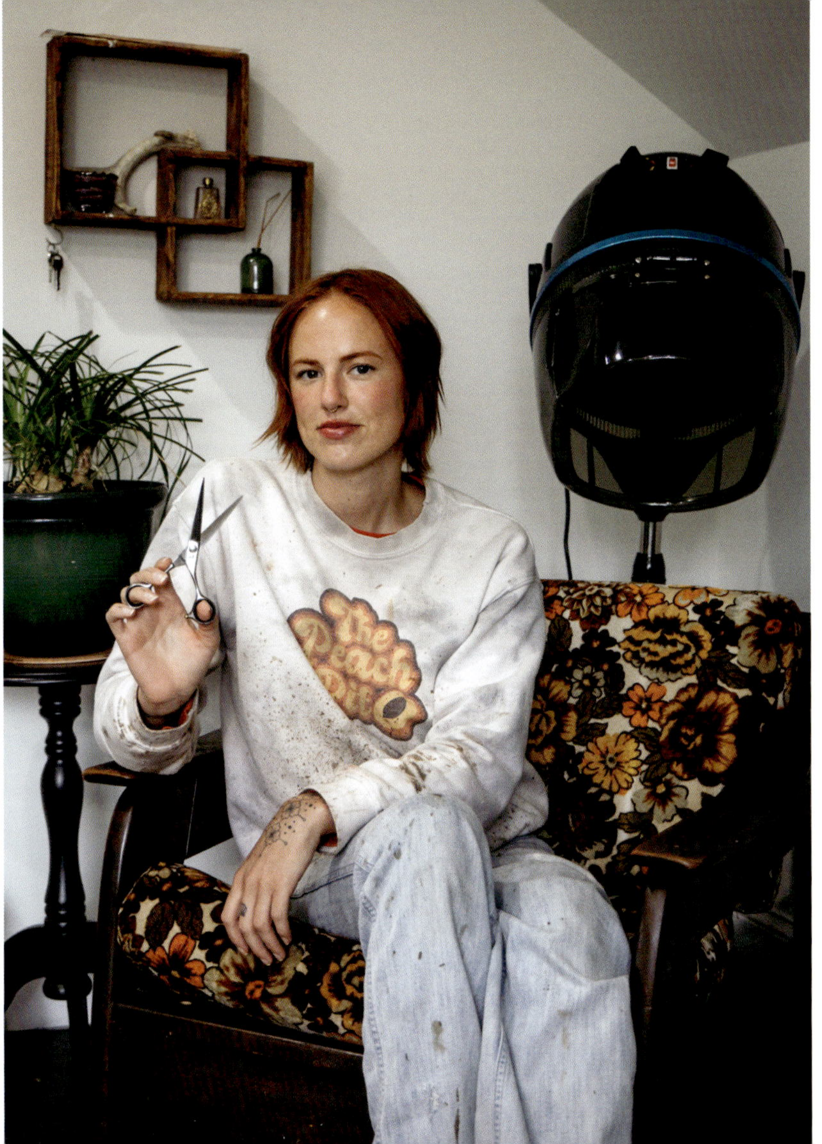

Peach Pit Salon owner **Cassandra Spann** in her shop. She opened the salon with the goal of creating a warm and inclusive space for her clients.

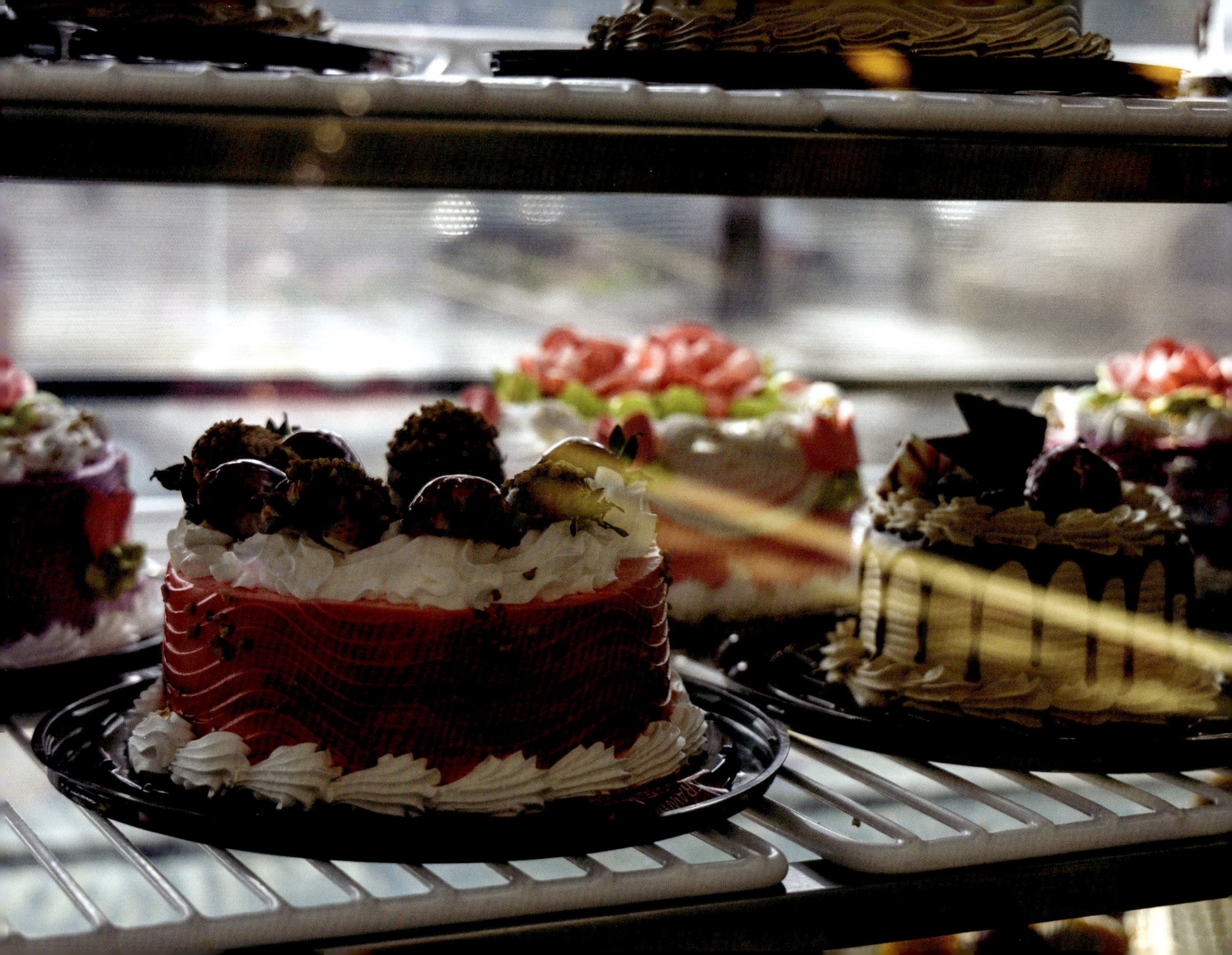

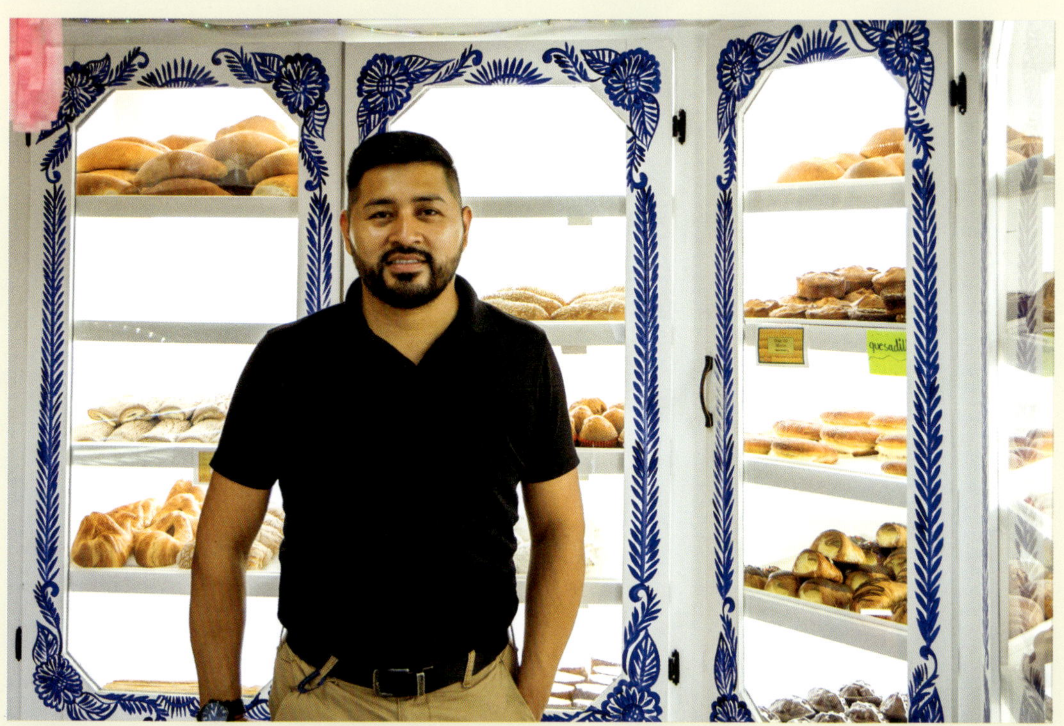

Ariel Valey Lopez, owner of Panaderia y Pasteleria Lopez, stands in front of the bakery's traditional, colorful displays.

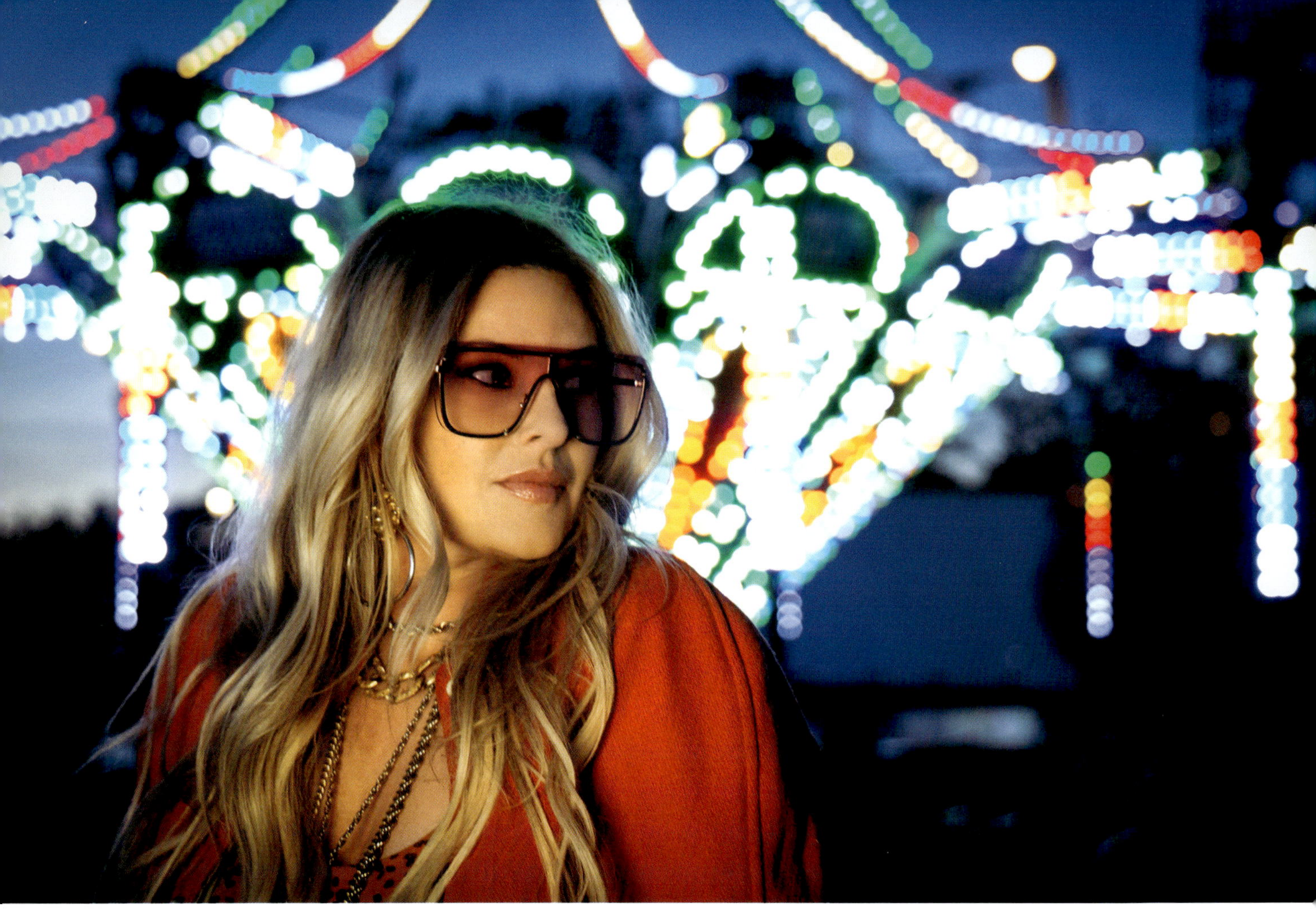

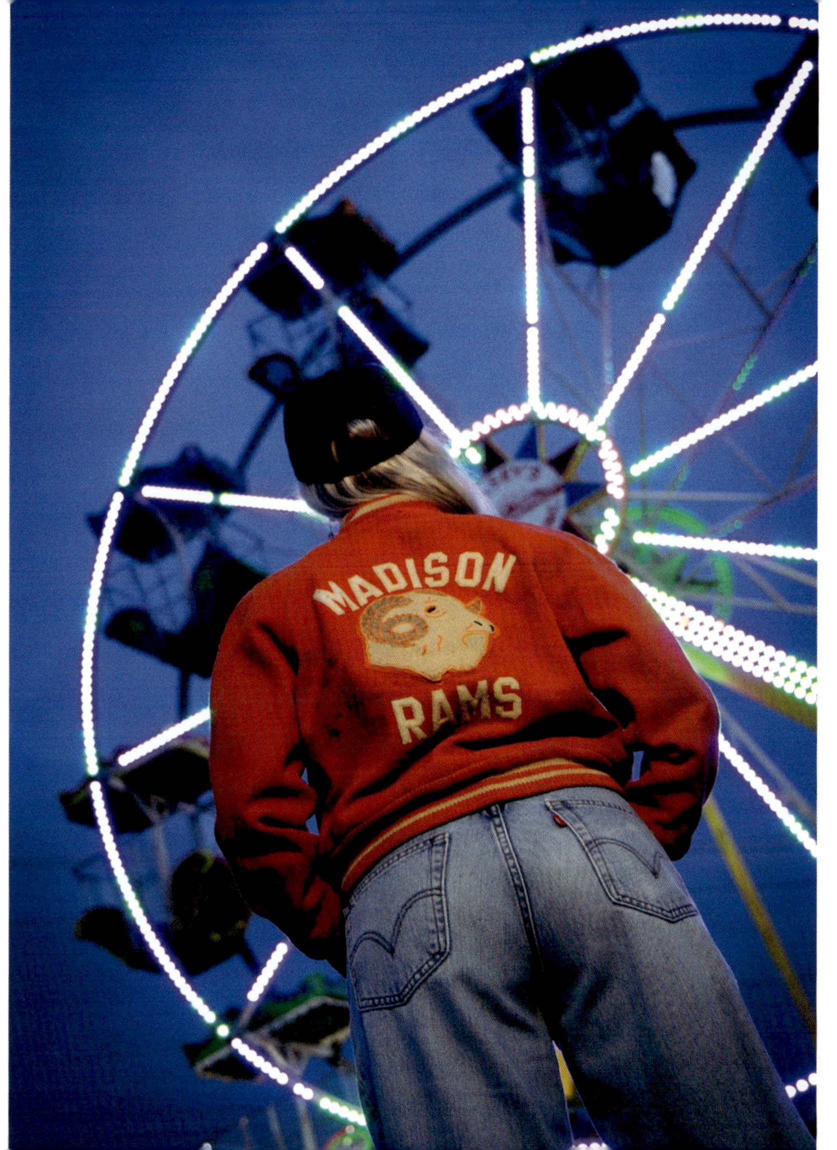

Elizabeth Cook,
singer, songwriter, and Sirius XM radio host, at the Madison Square Carnival sporting her vintage Madison Rams letterman jacket.

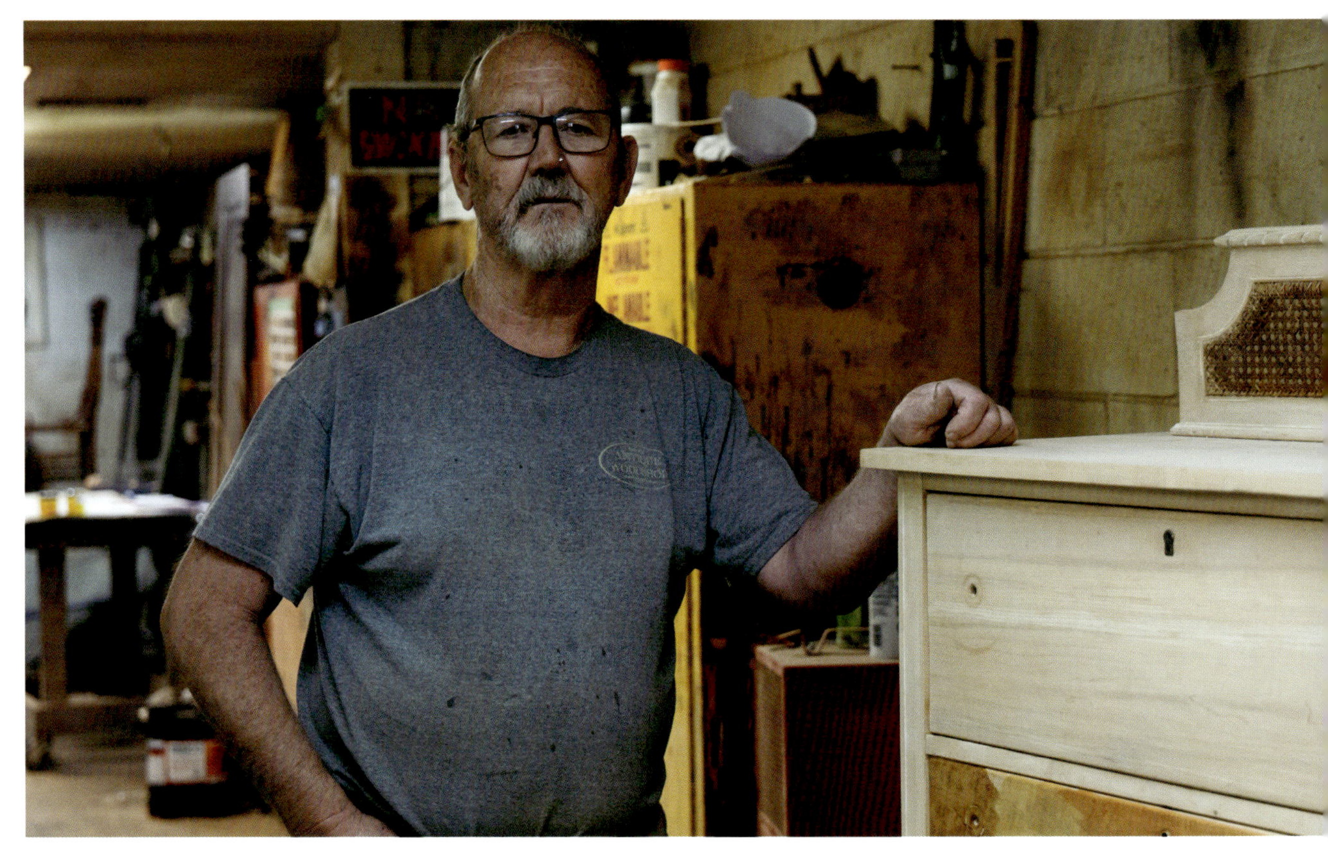

Jeffrey Strain, a skilled woodworker, has offered custom restoration and refinishing at the Antique Woodshop for more than thirty-three years.

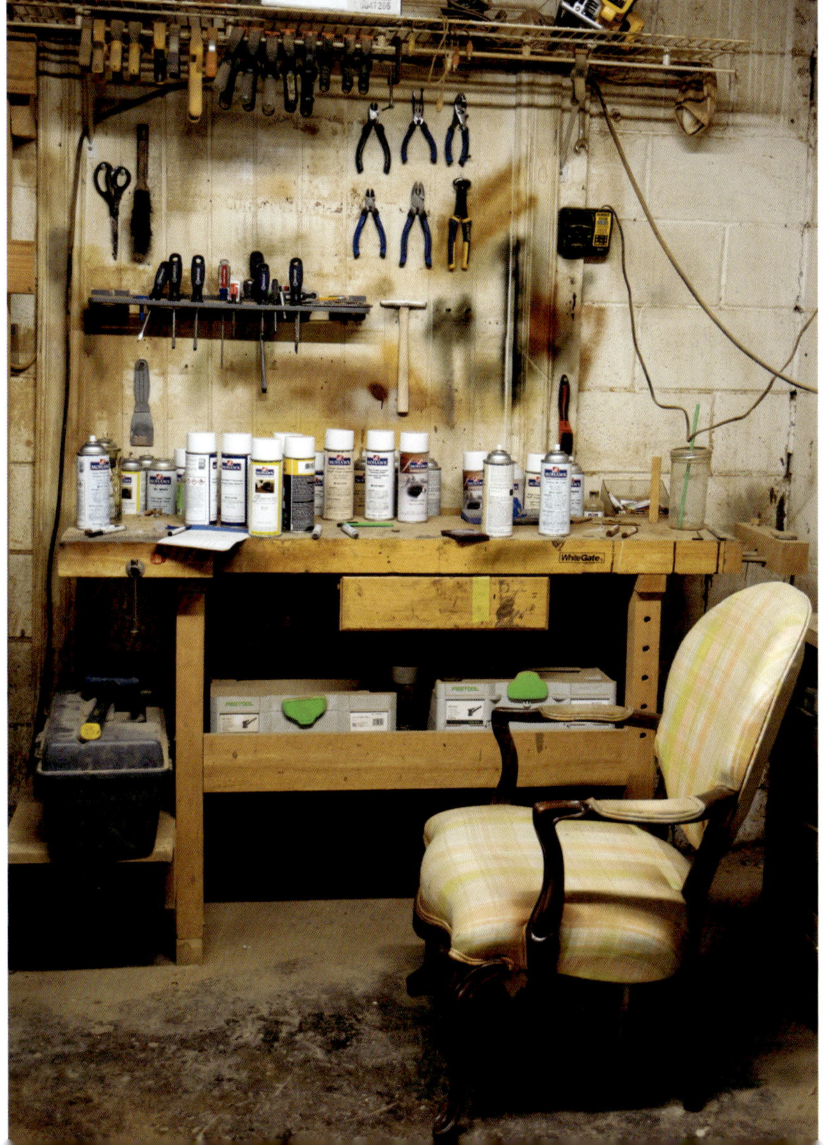
WhiteGate

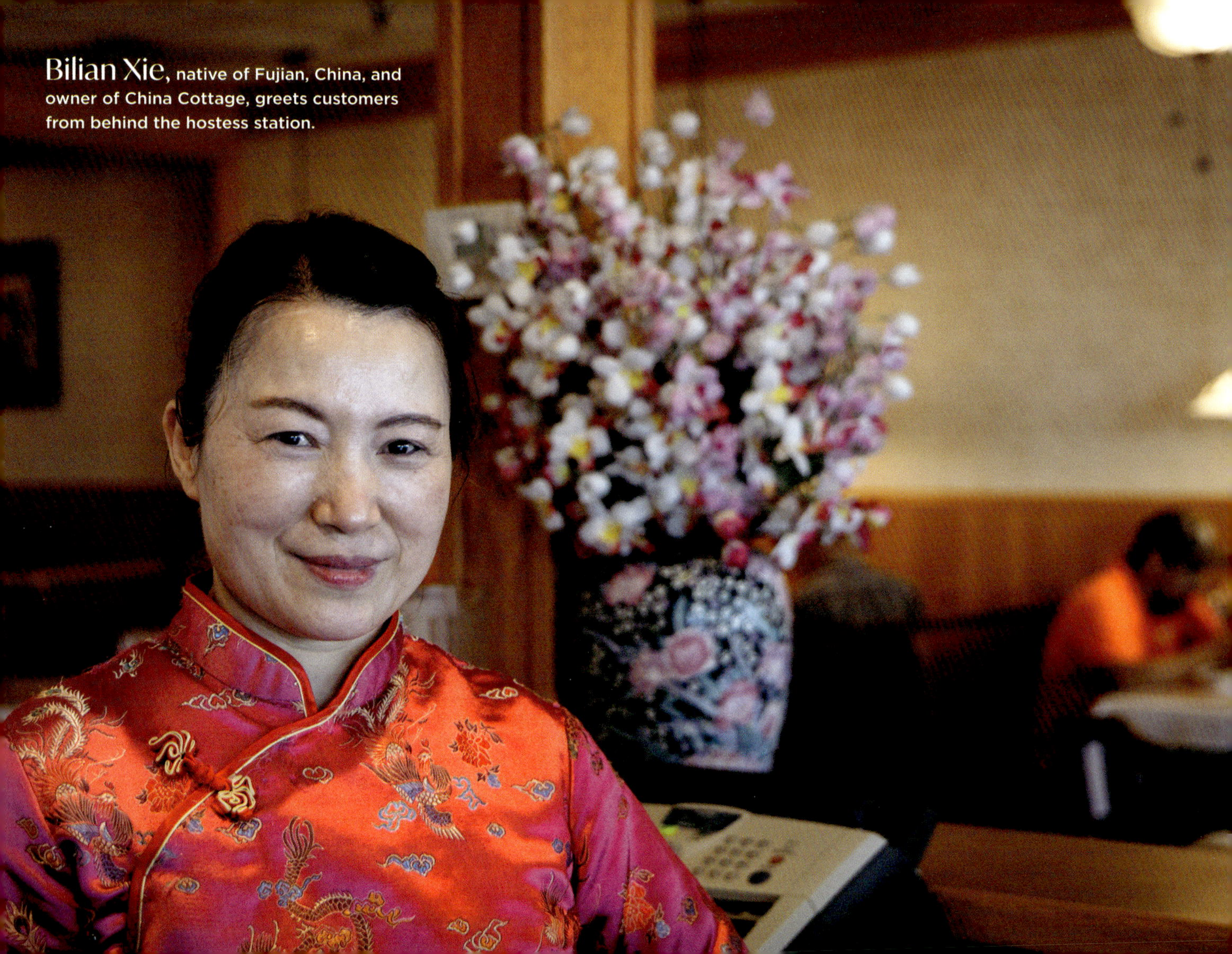

Bilian Xie, native of Fujian, China, and owner of China Cottage, greets customers from behind the hostess station.

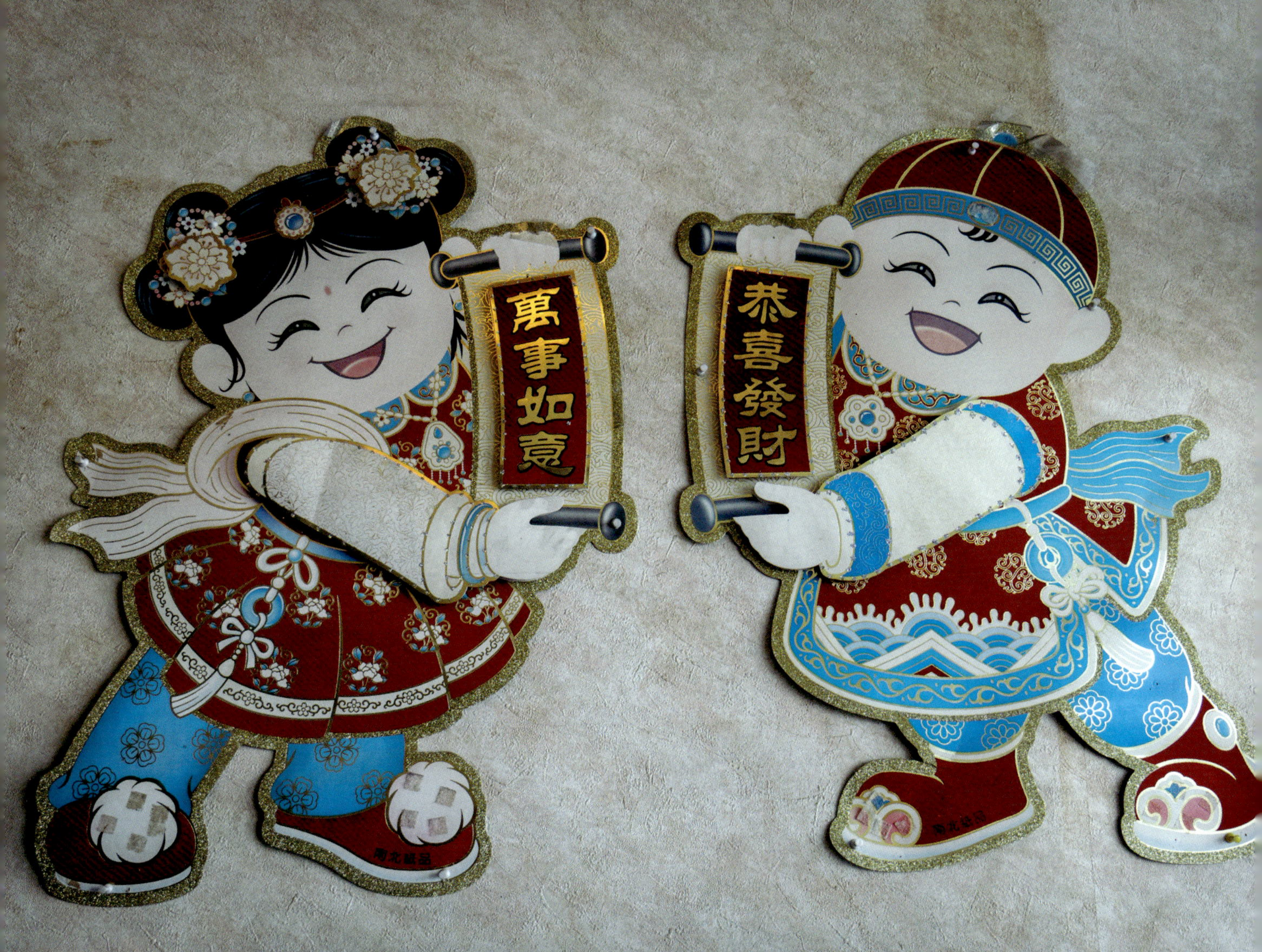
萬事如意
恭喜發財

Rosemary Fossee Stewart, Nashville native, singer, and actress, stands outside her home. An artist since childhood, she's crafted her own unique, genre-blending style for stage and screen.

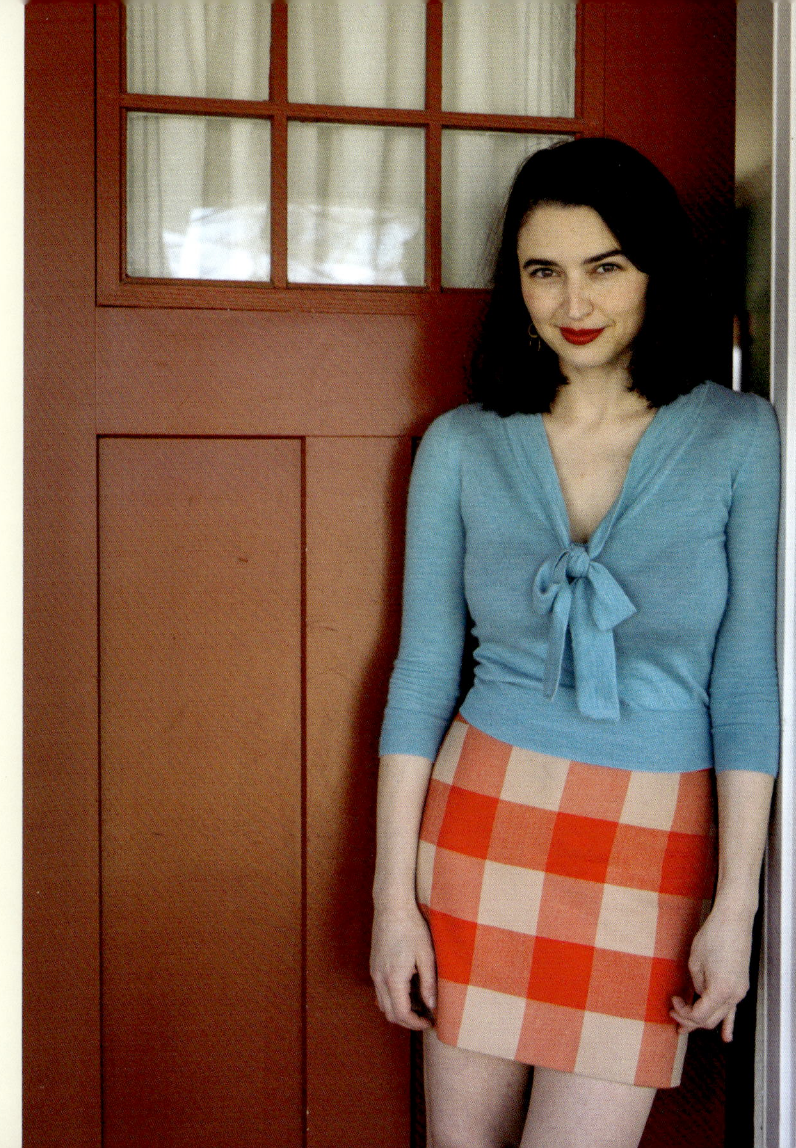

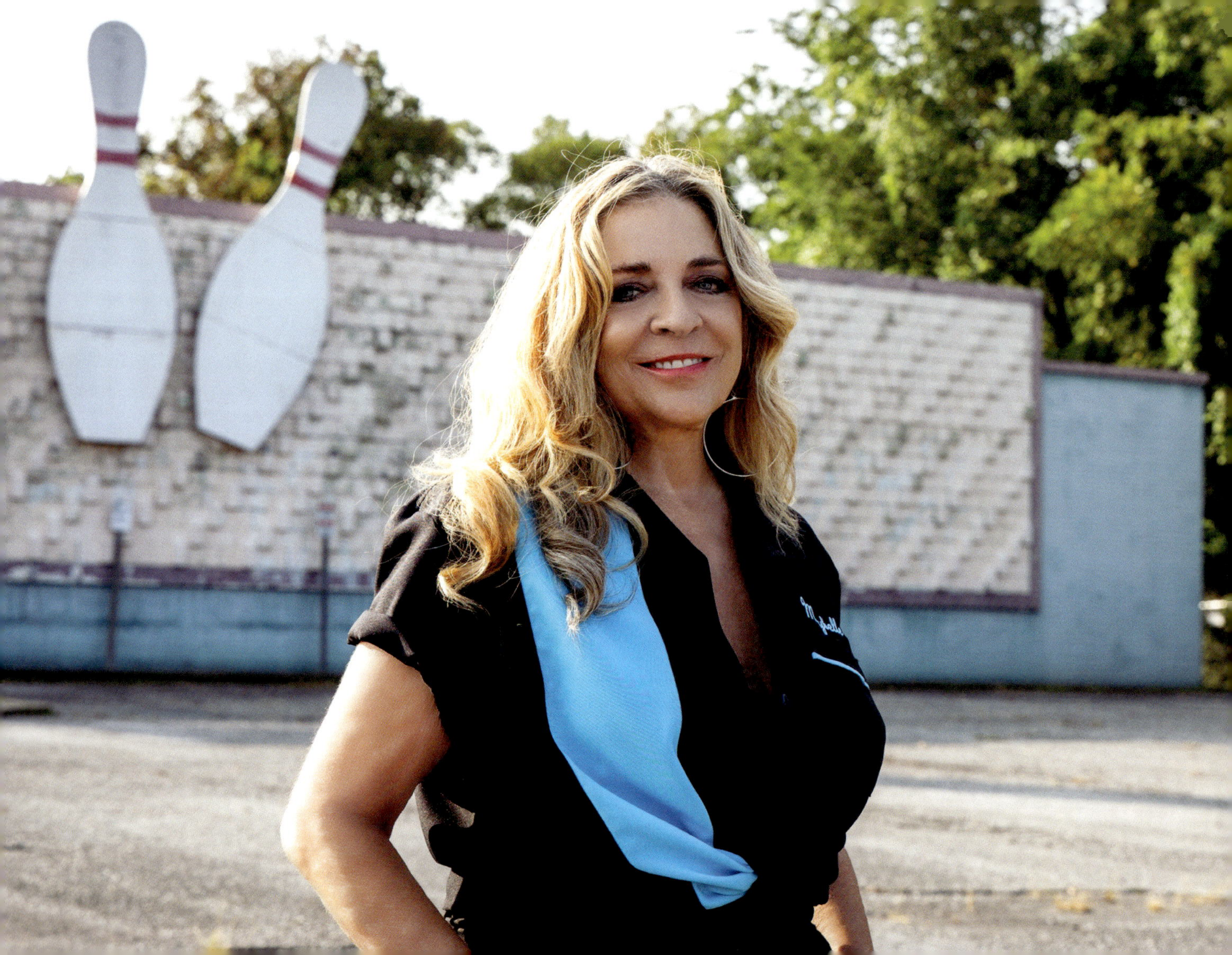

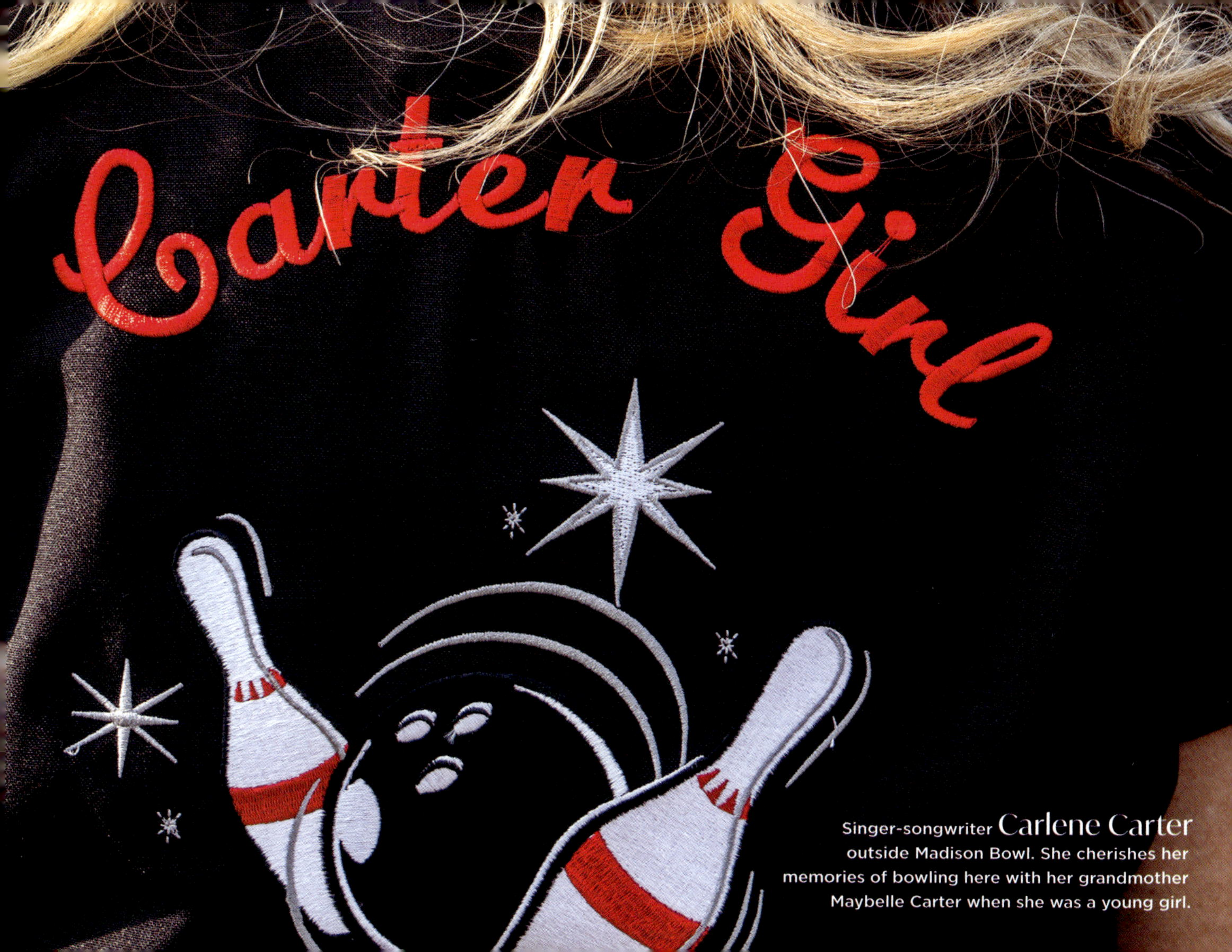

Singer-songwriter Carlene Carter outside Madison Bowl. She cherishes her memories of bowling here with her grandmother Maybelle Carter when she was a young girl.

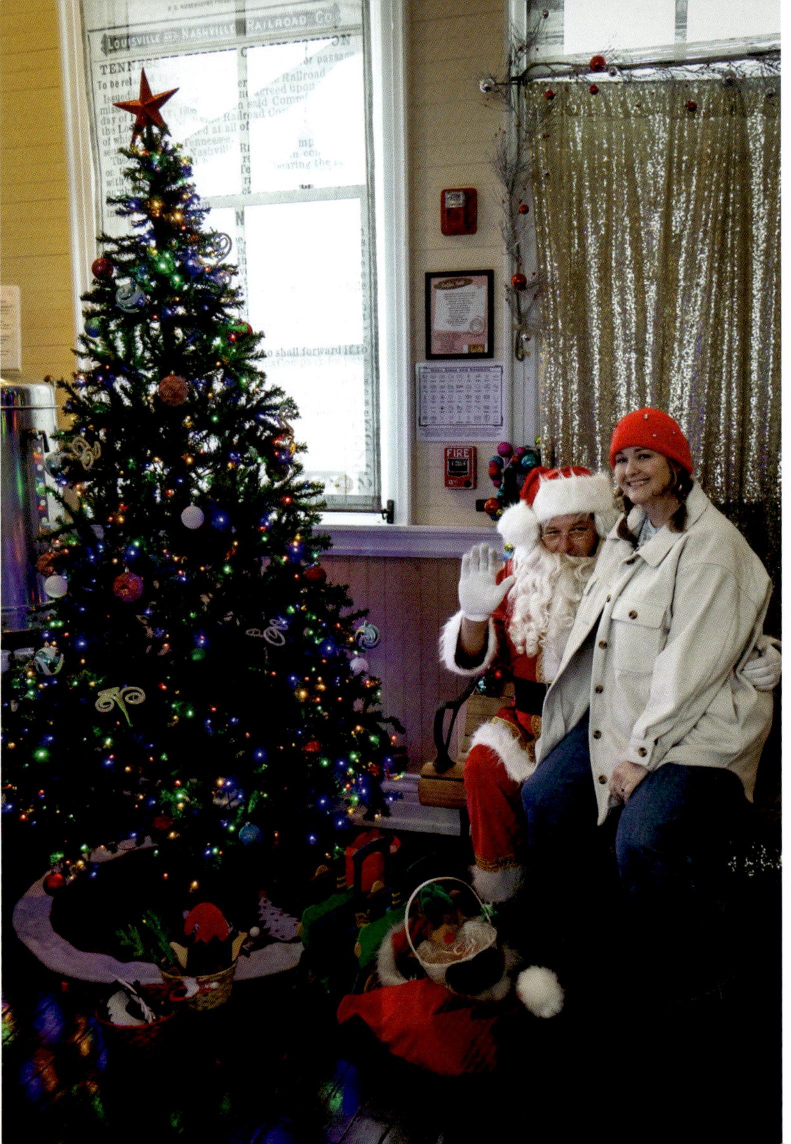

Bel Stuart,
an Amqui Station and Visitors Center board member, at a holiday event with Santa,
Jason Buchanan.

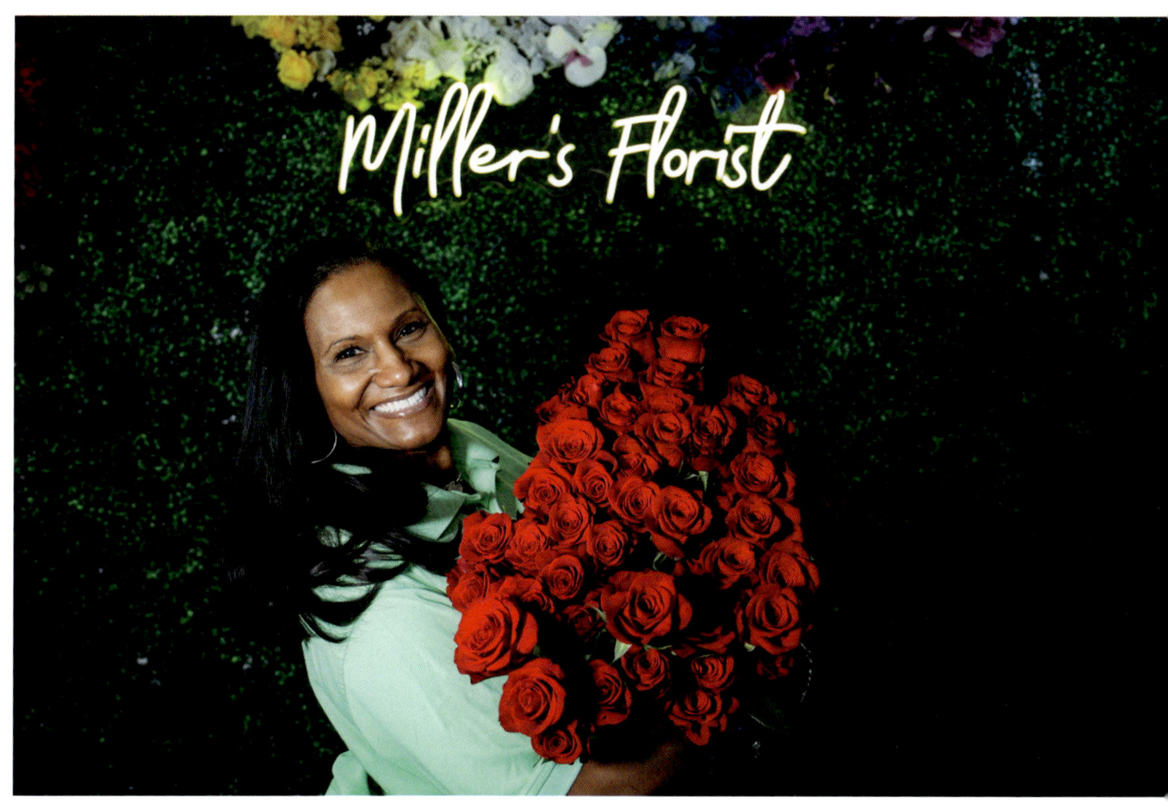

Miller's Florist owner **Konya Williams** playfully displays long-stemmed red roses. A former nurse who loved receiving bouquets from her husband while at work, Konya was inspired to purchase Miller's Florist and begin a new career.

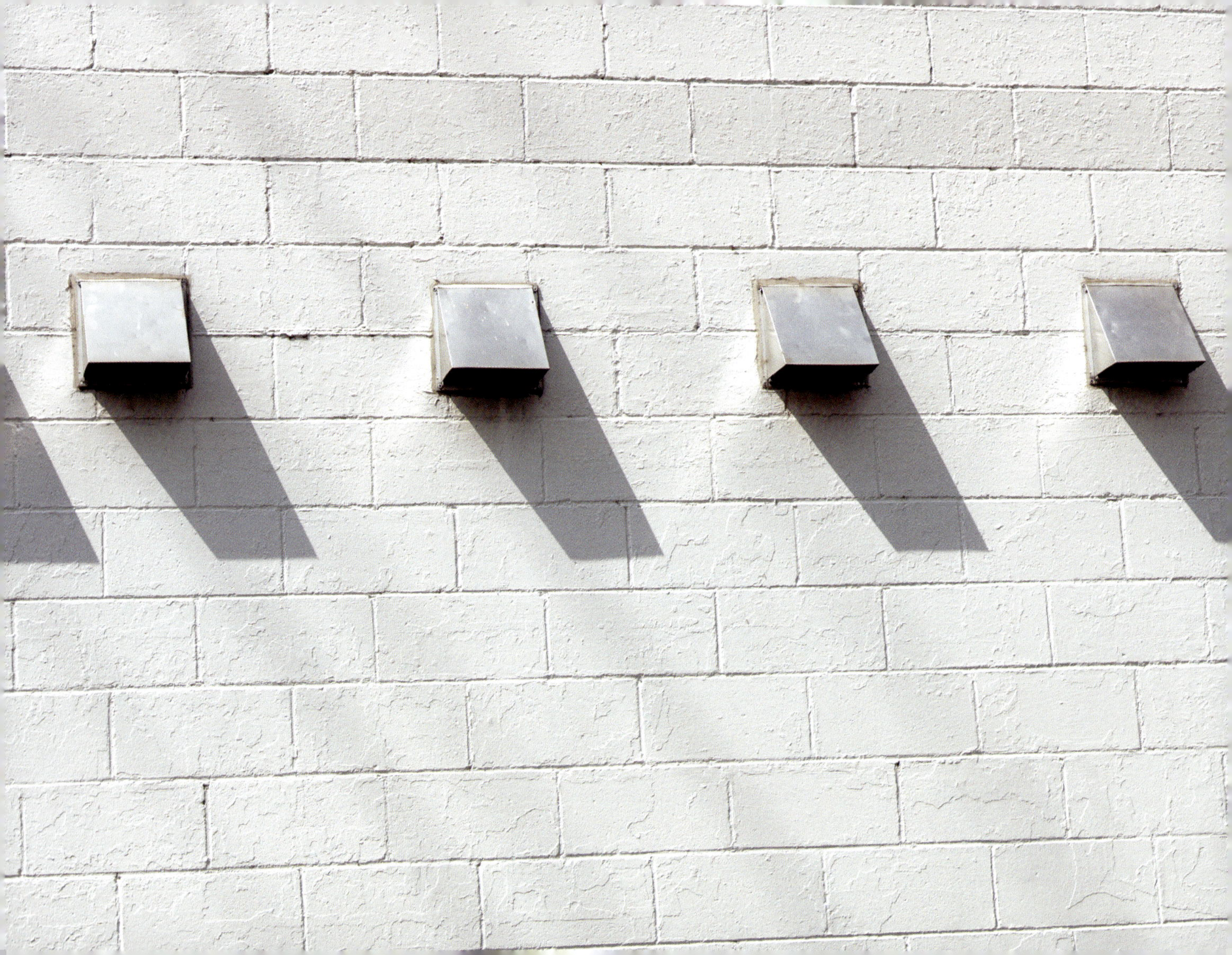

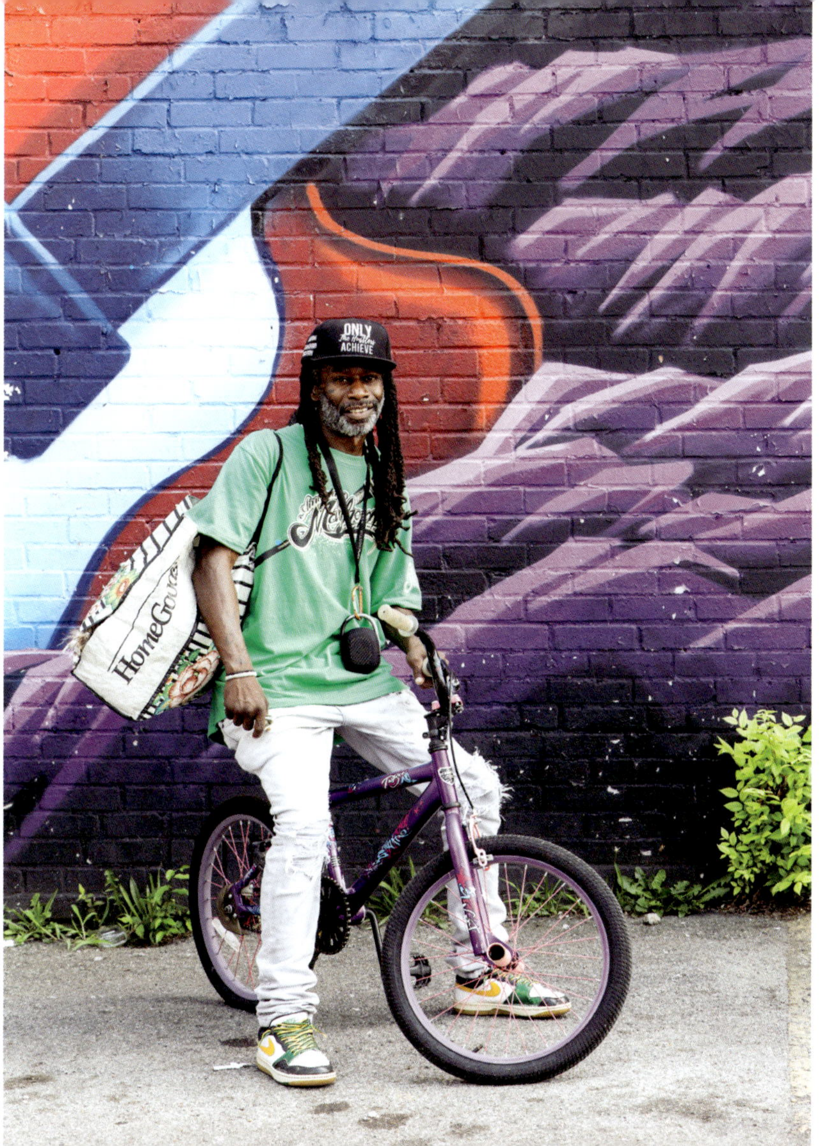

Monty,
a neighborhood staple, stops to pose in front of a mural while riding along Gallatin Pike.

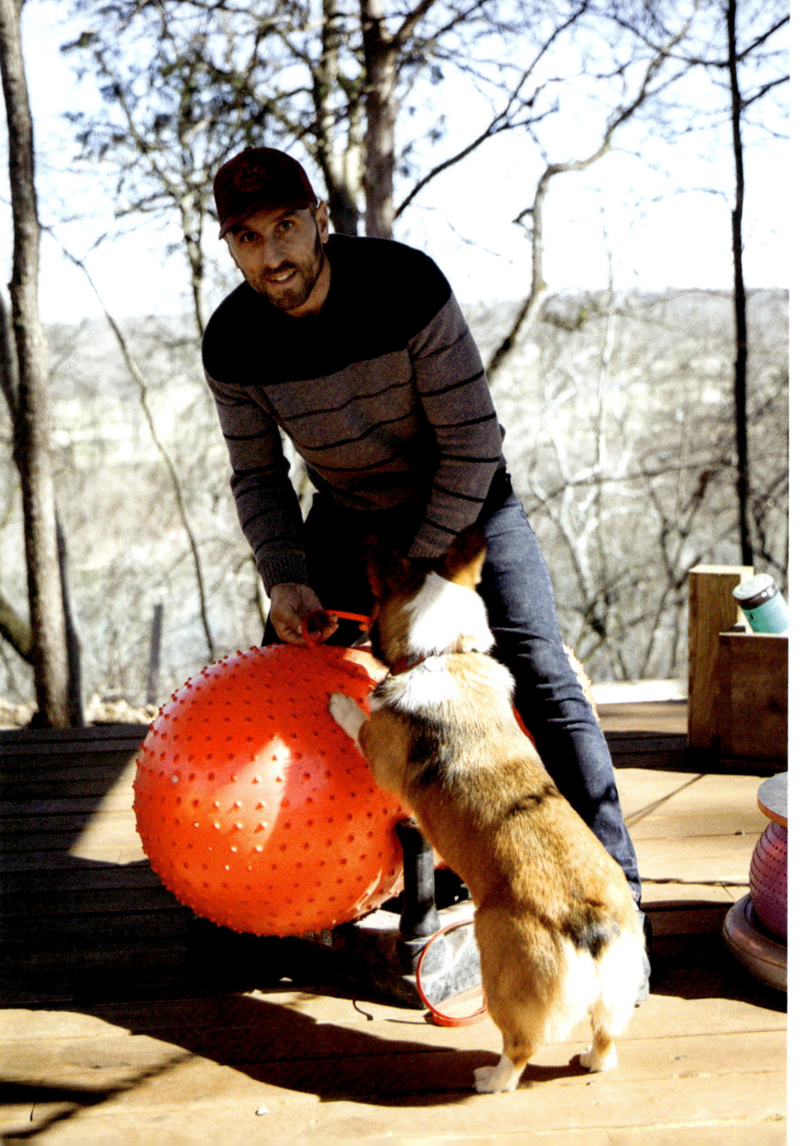

Kevin Kazlauskas,
owner of Full Circle Canine,
works at the training kennel.

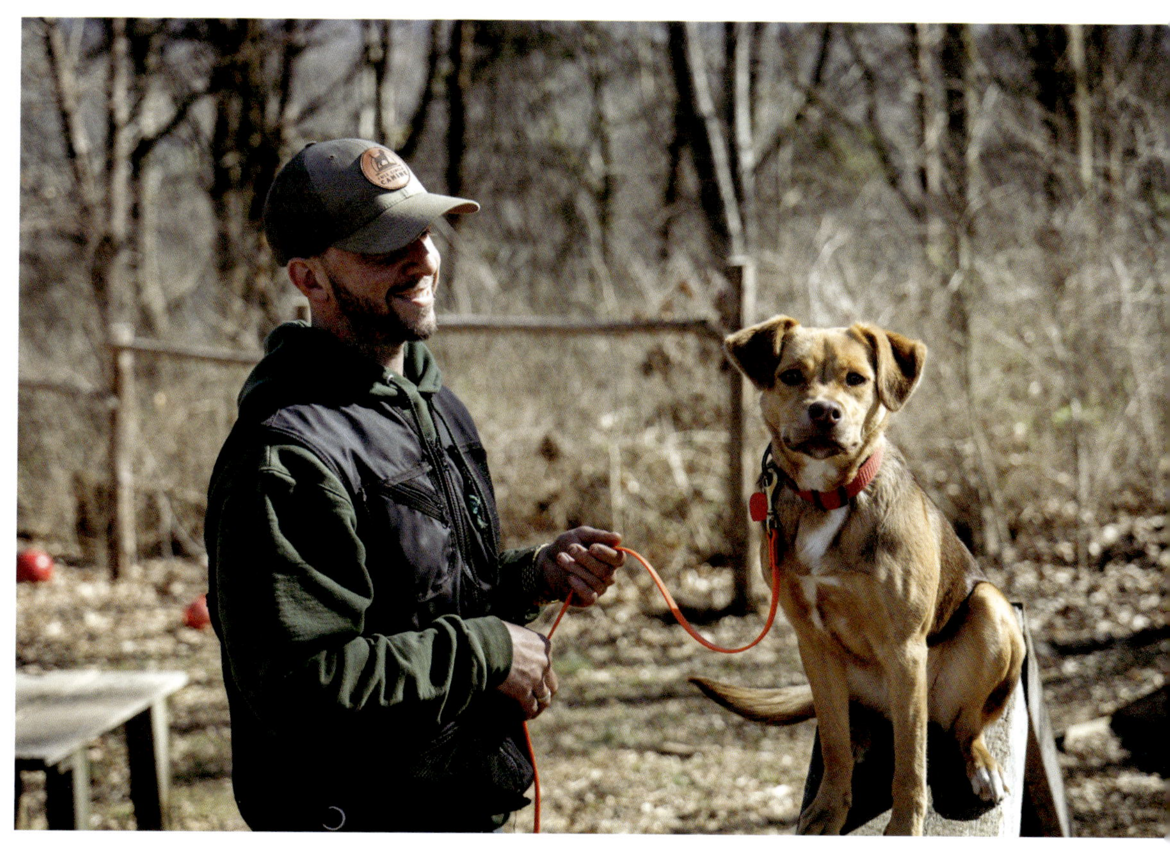

Travis Seidel, dog trainer, working at Full Circle Canine training kennel.

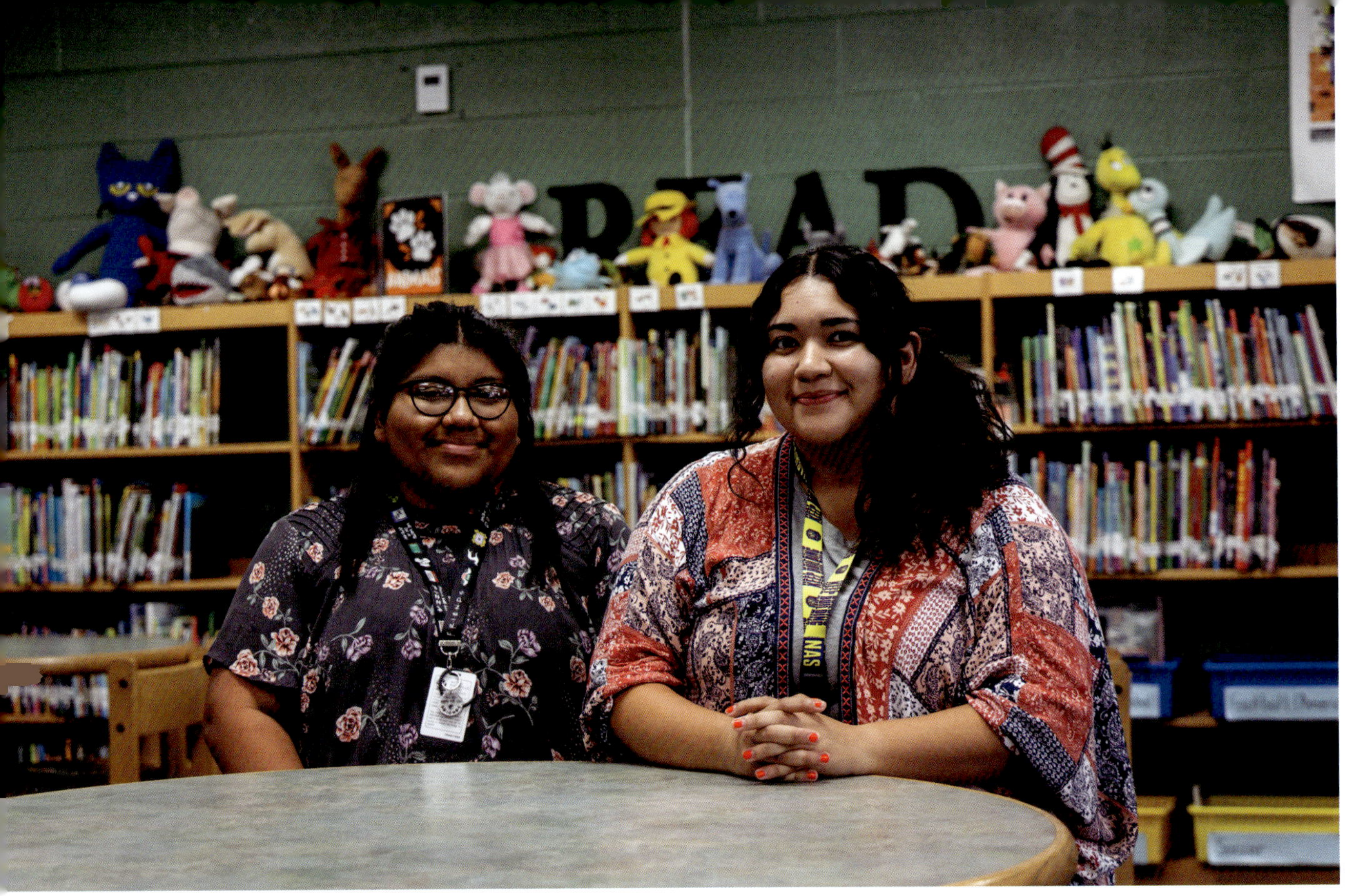

Laura Reyes, general assistant, and **Leslie Valles,** translator, sit inside the library of Amqui Global Communications Magnet School. They serve the Hispanic student and family community at the K-8 Metro Nashville public school.

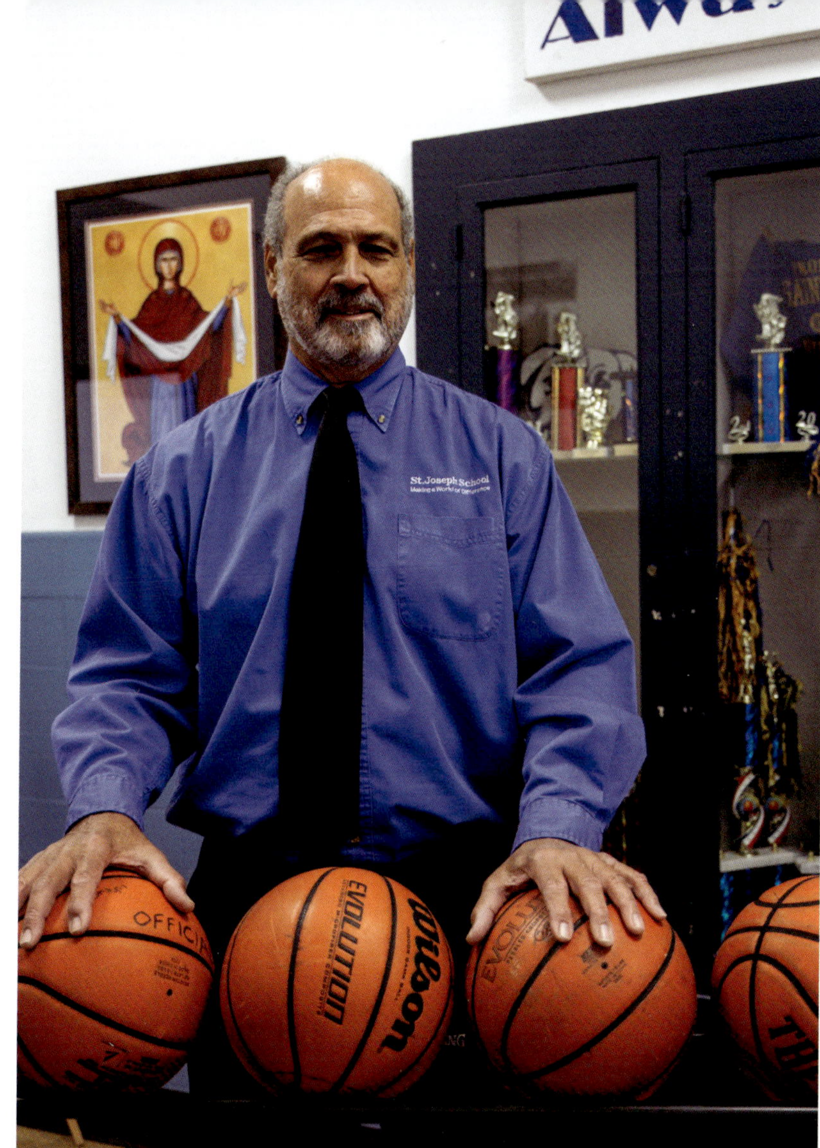

James "Leach" Rucker stands in the hallway of St. Joseph School. Coach Rucker, a beloved employee who retired after forty years of teaching and coaching, still returns to substitute teach.

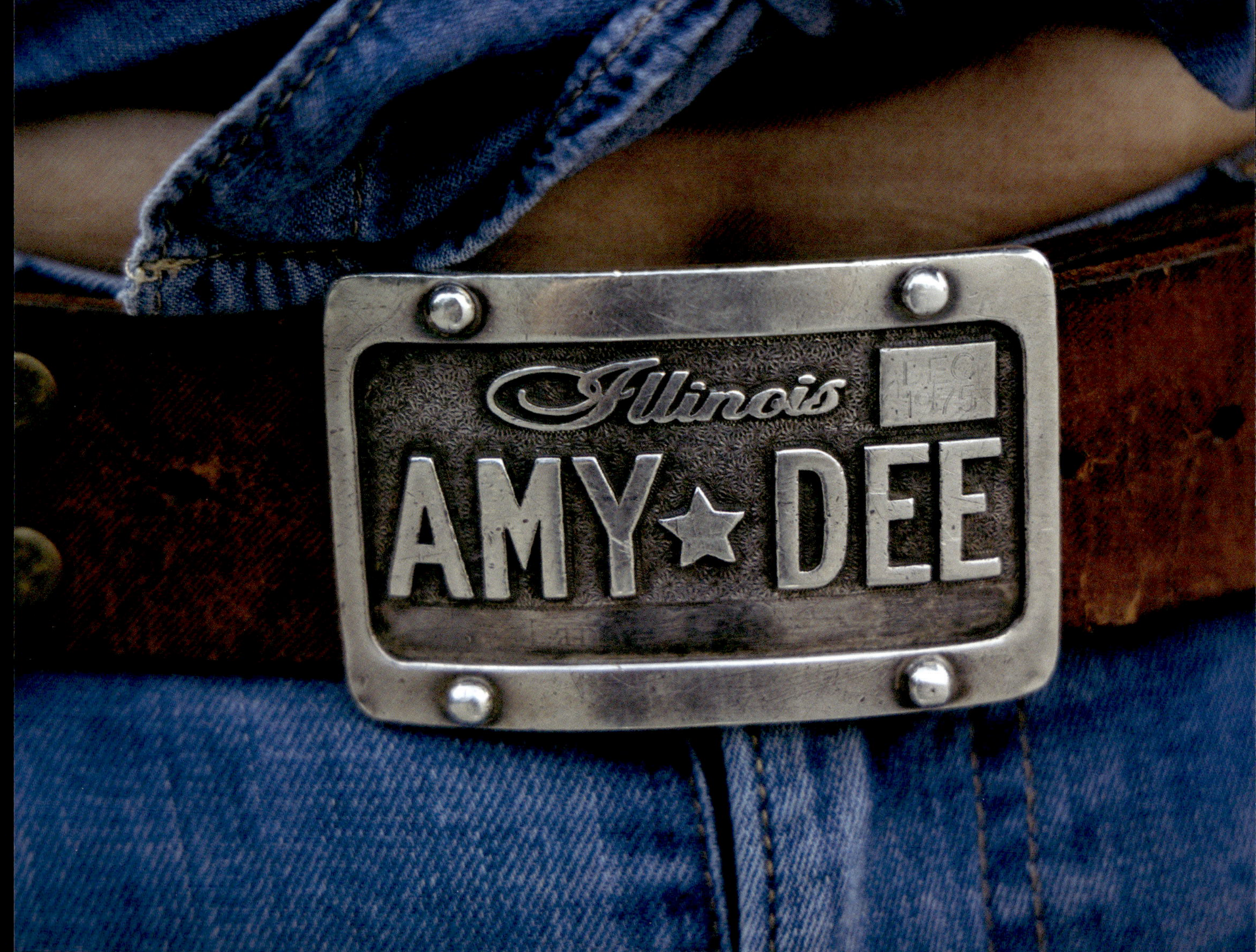
Illinois
AMY ★ DEE

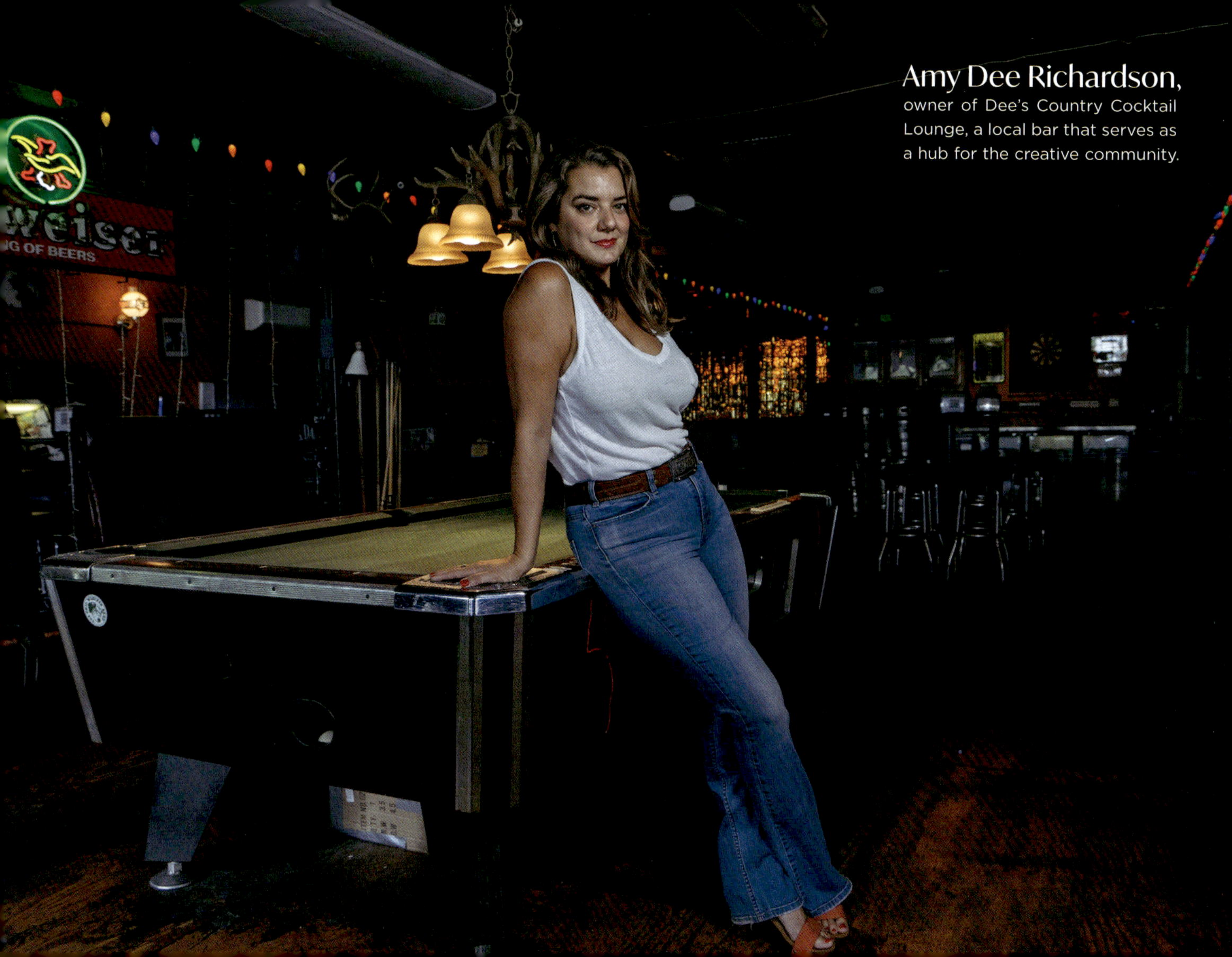

Amy Dee Richardson, owner of Dee's Country Cocktail Lounge, a local bar that serves as a hub for the creative community.

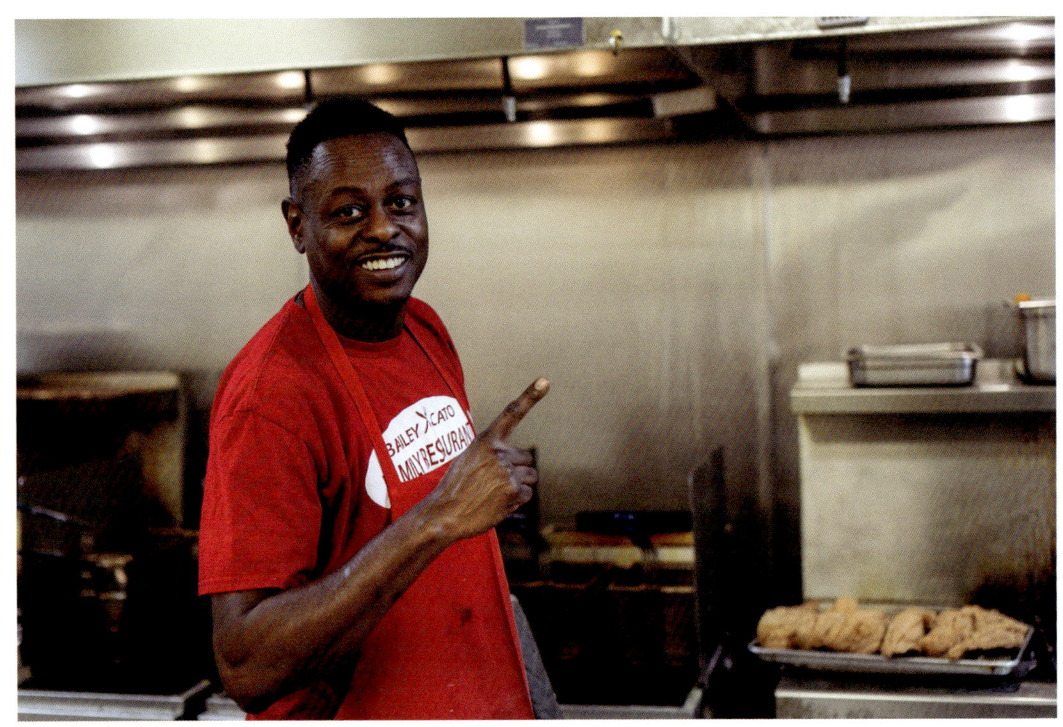

Bailey and Cato owner **Derrick Bailey** works inside the kitchen of his family-owned meat and three-style restaurant.

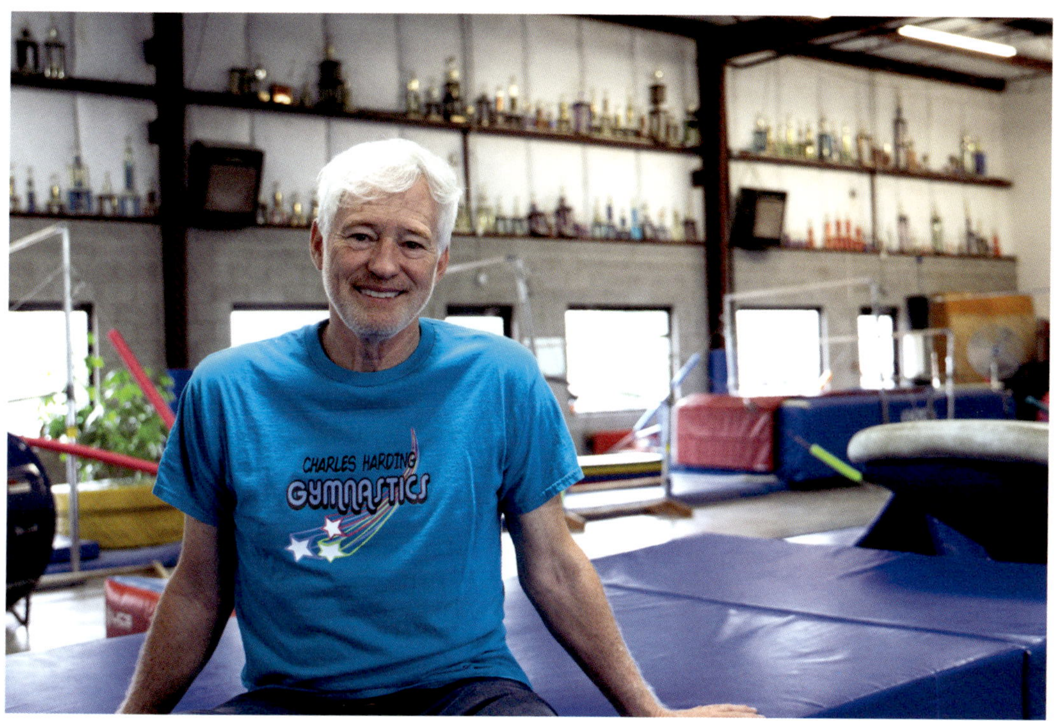

Gymnastics coach and gym owner Charles Harding sits inside the training facility he opened in 1985. Charles Harding Gymnastics studio has a mission of providing high-quality instruction in an inclusive, noncompetitive environment where all people would be welcome.

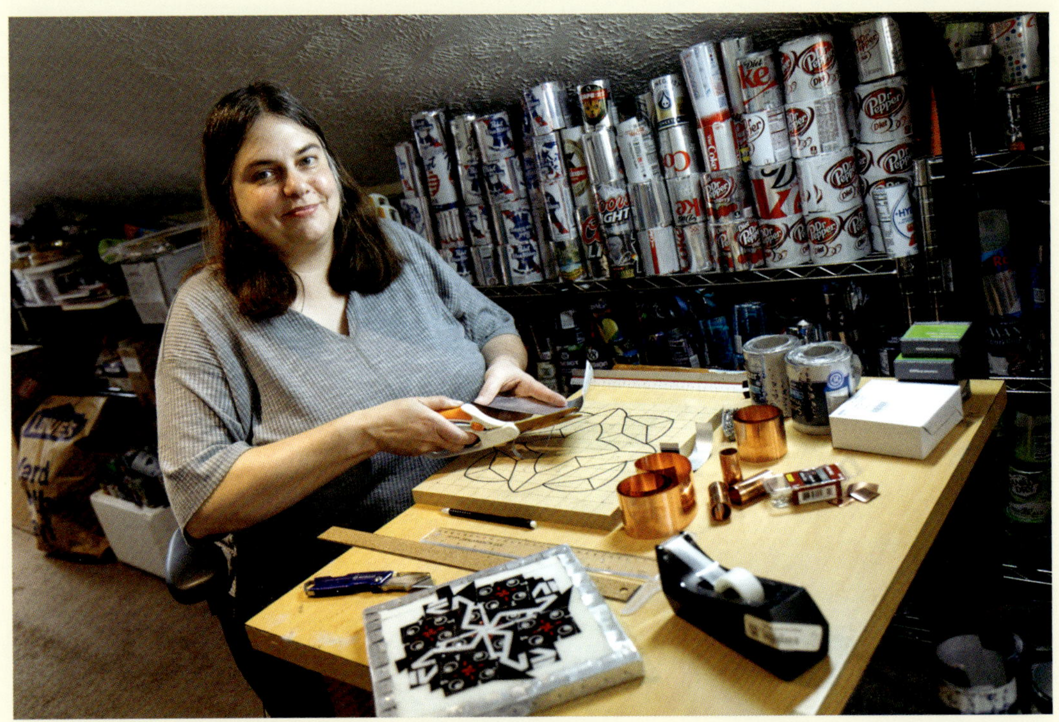

Miranda Herrick, a visual artist who draws and creates structured geometric patterns out of repurposed materials, seen here working with cut aluminum cans in her home's attic studio.

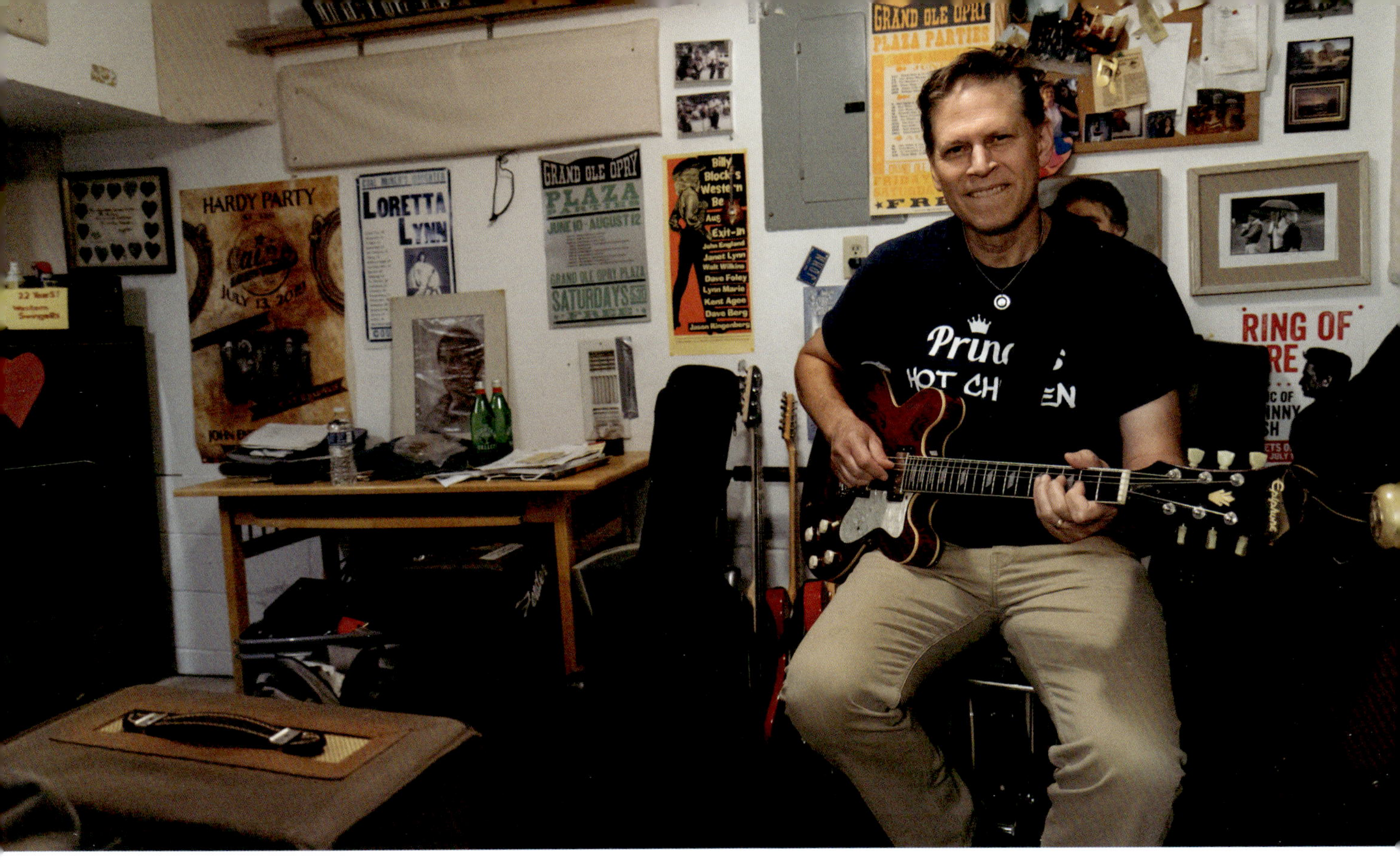

John England, musician and band leader of John England and the Western Swingers, plays guitar inside his home studio.

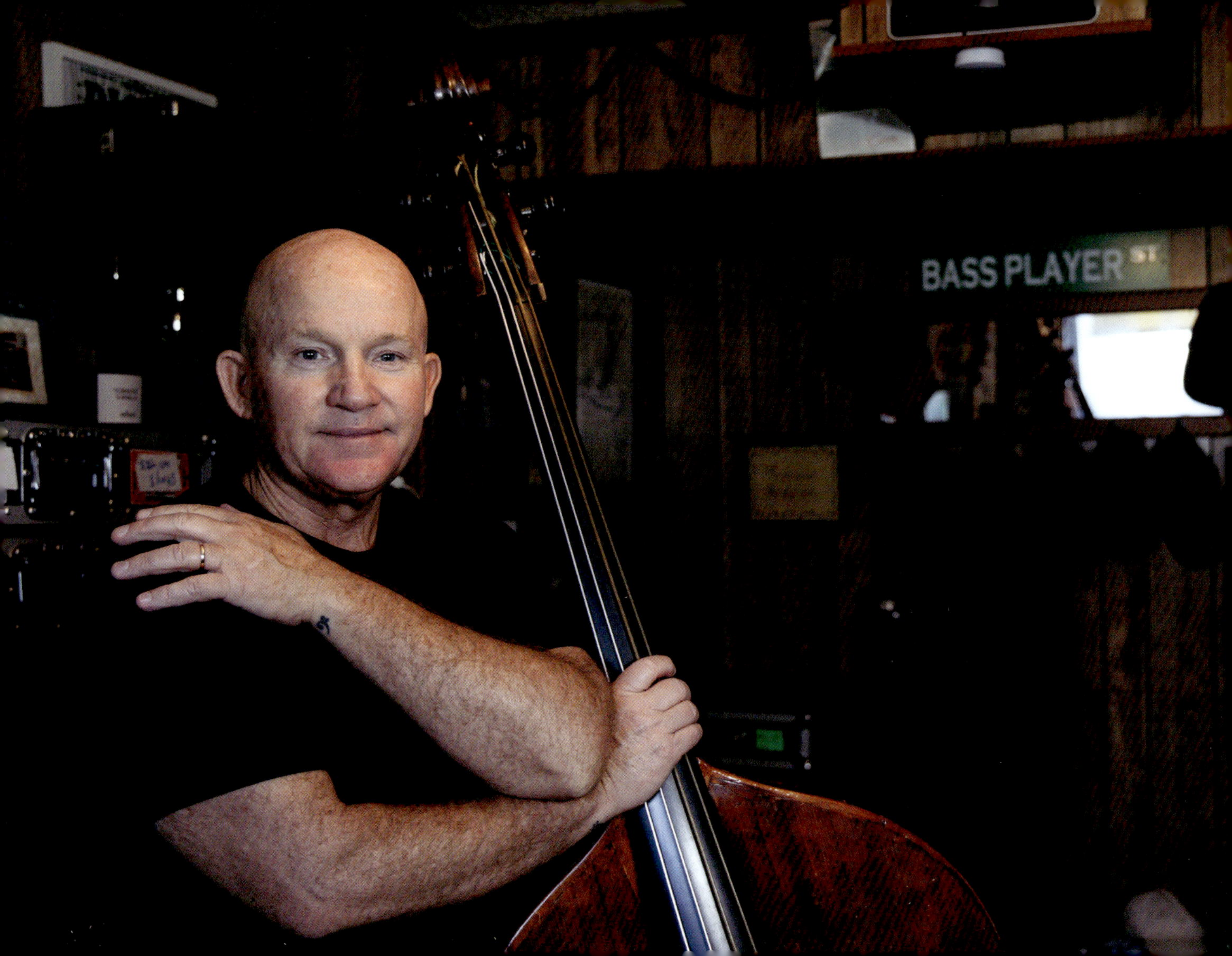
BASS PLAYER ST

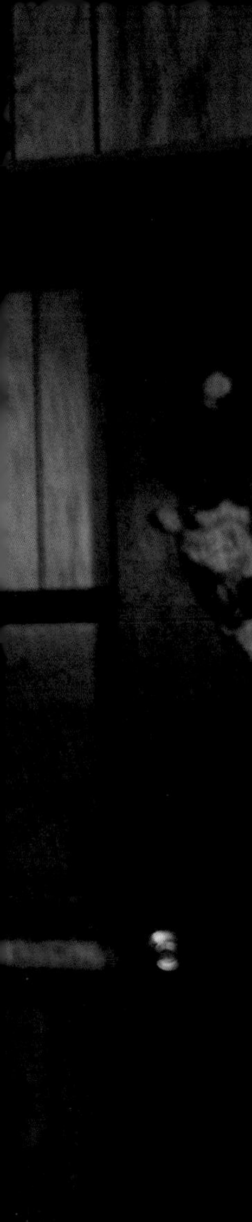

World class double bassist Dennis Crouch plays inside his home studio. He's performed or recorded with artists from Bob Dylan and Elvis Costello to Diana Krall and Alison Krauss.

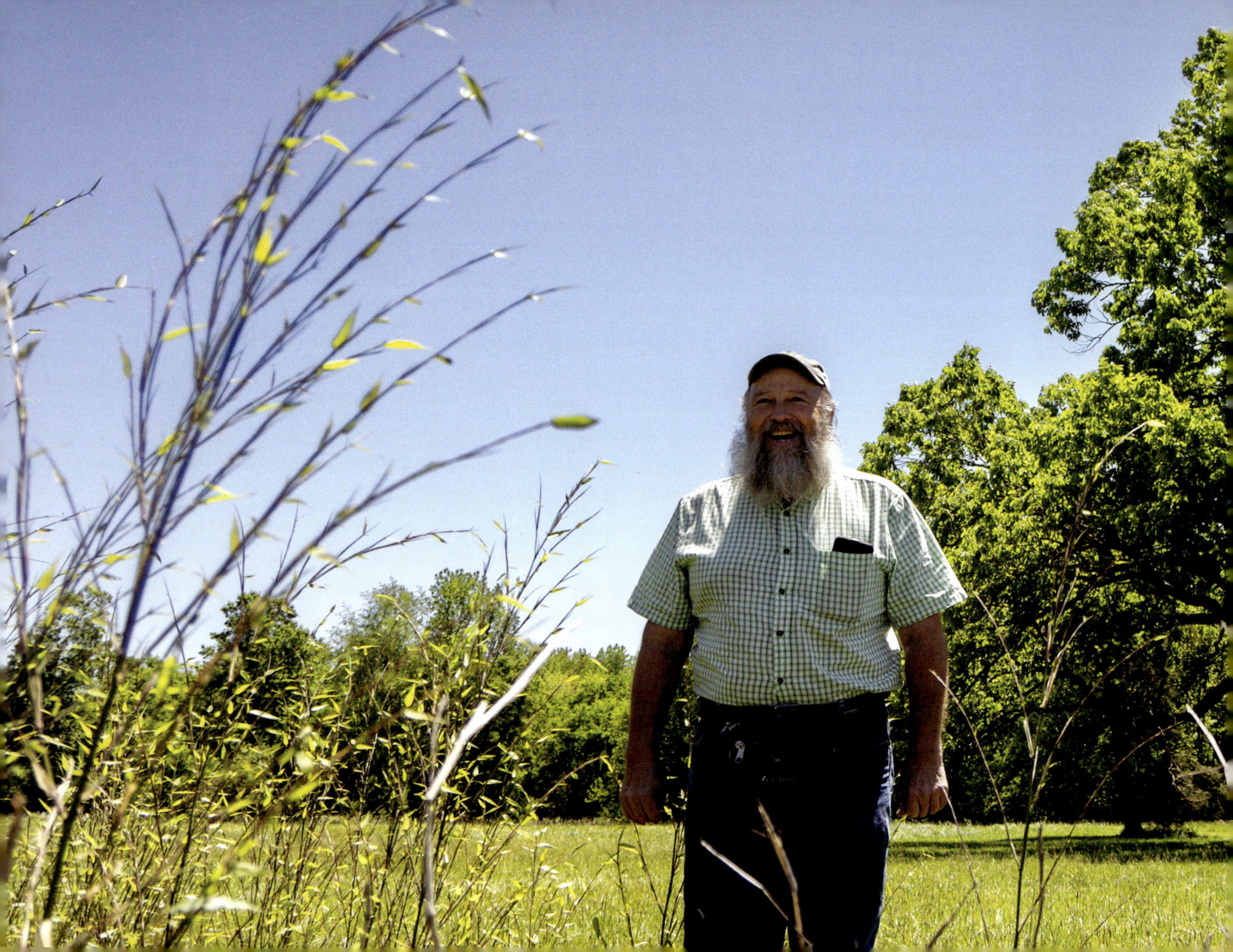

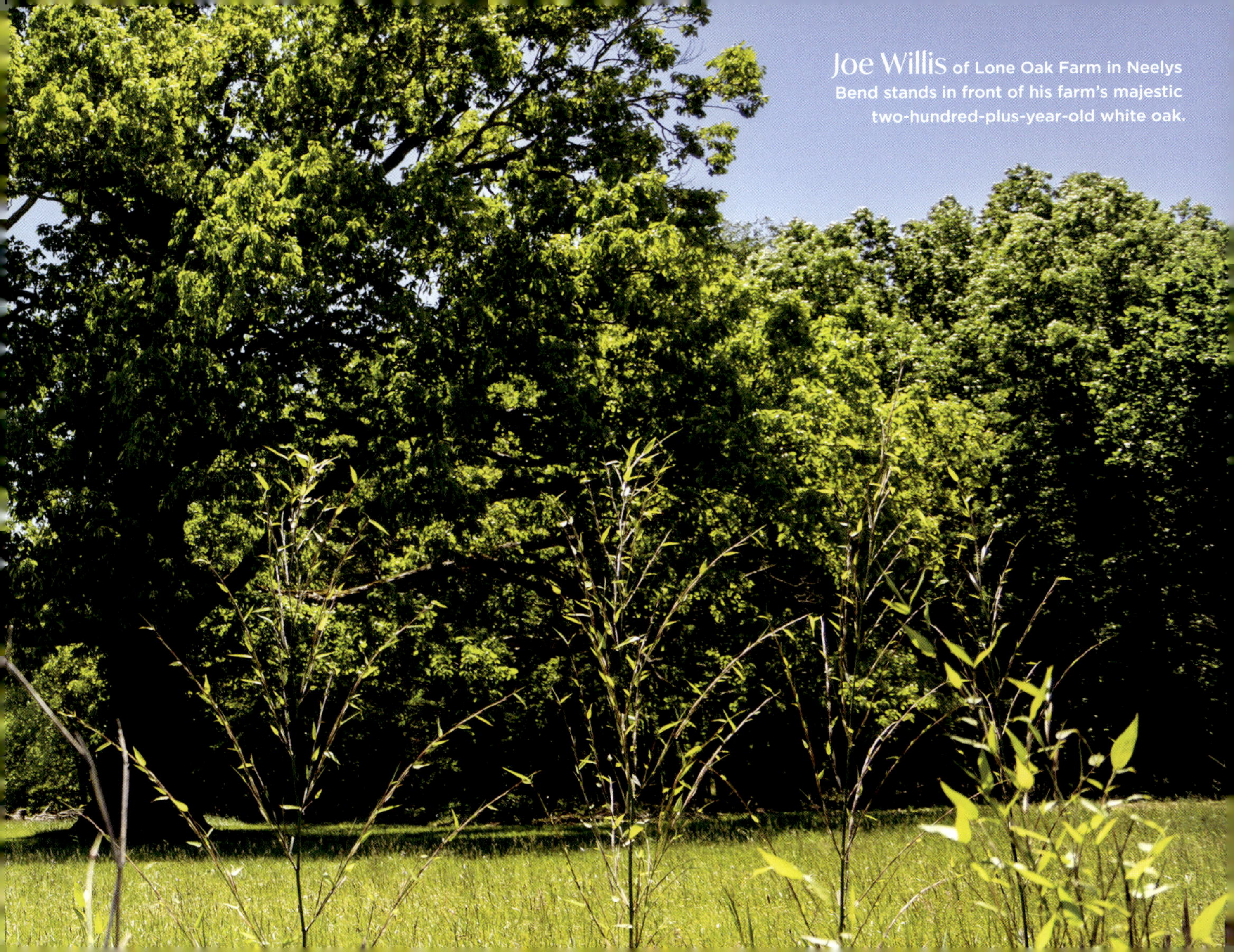

Joe Willis of Lone Oak Farm in Neelys Bend stands in front of his farm's majestic two-hundred-plus-year-old white oak.

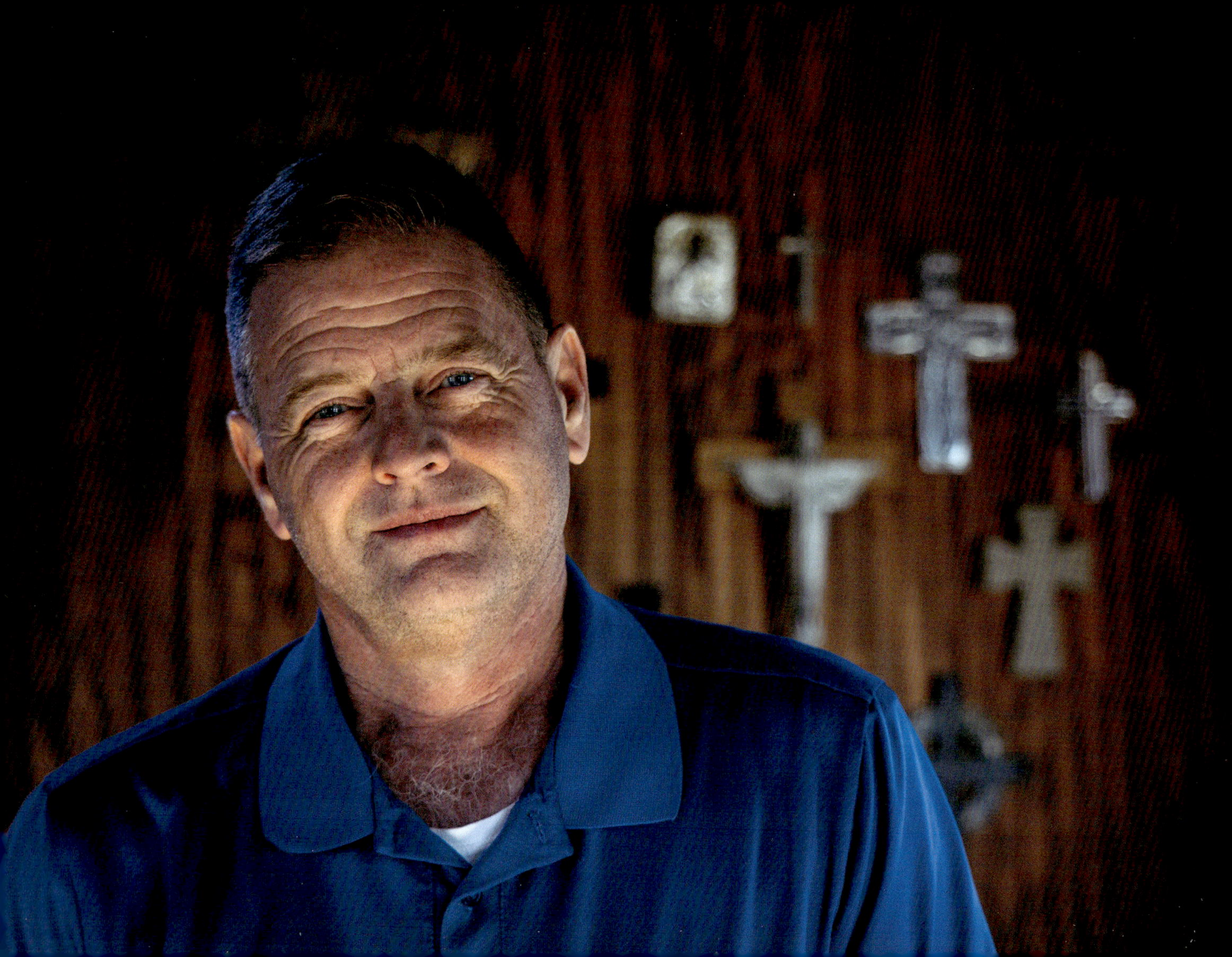

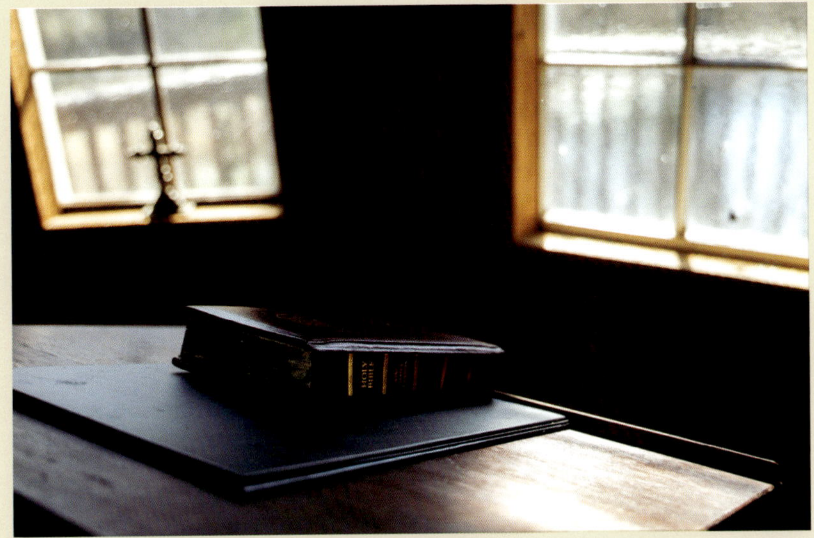

Greg Bullard, pastor of Covenant of the Cross, inside The Chapel at Stewards' Grove, a treehouse chapel on his family's farm. The chapel provides a warm, affirming, faith-based space for all people, especially those who are LGBTQ+, to gather in the sanctuary.

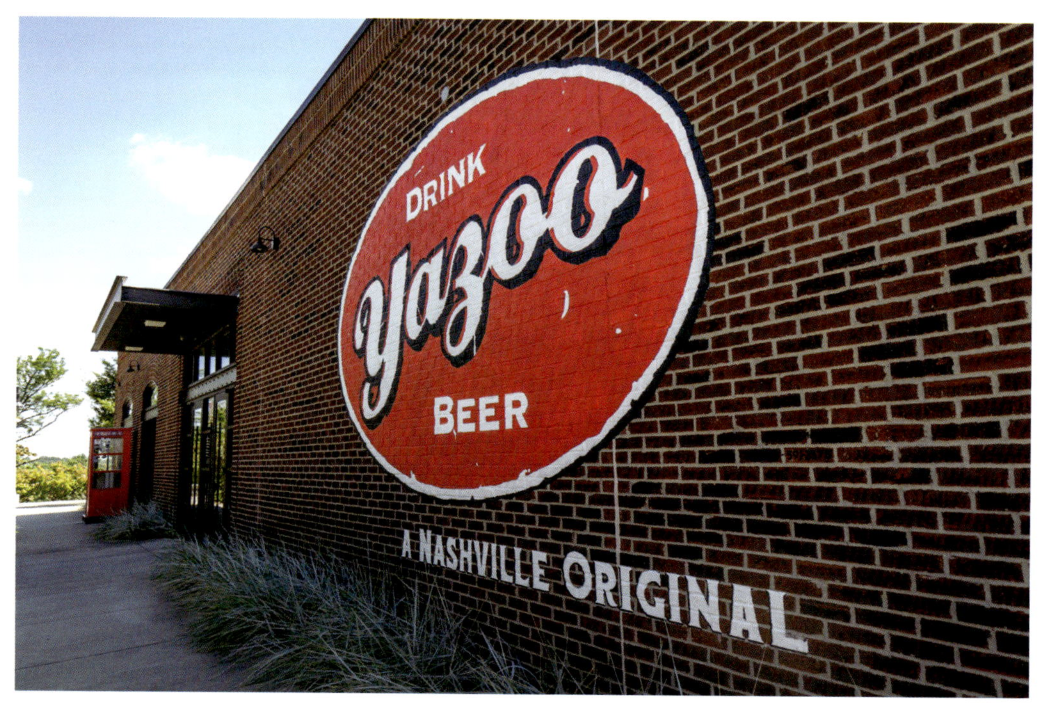
DRINK
Yazoo
BEER
A NASHVILLE ORIGINAL

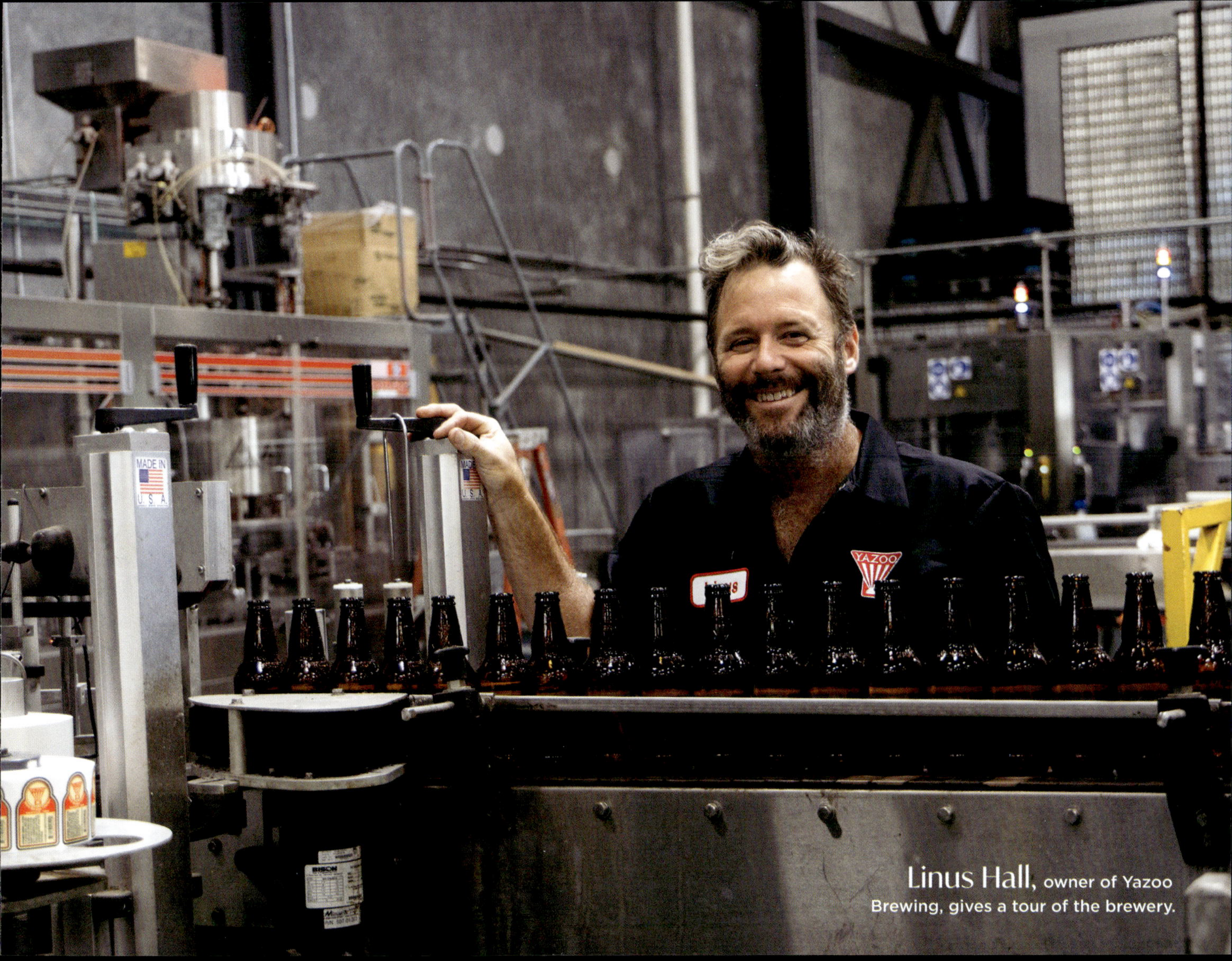

Linus Hall, owner of Yazoo Brewing, gives a tour of the brewery.

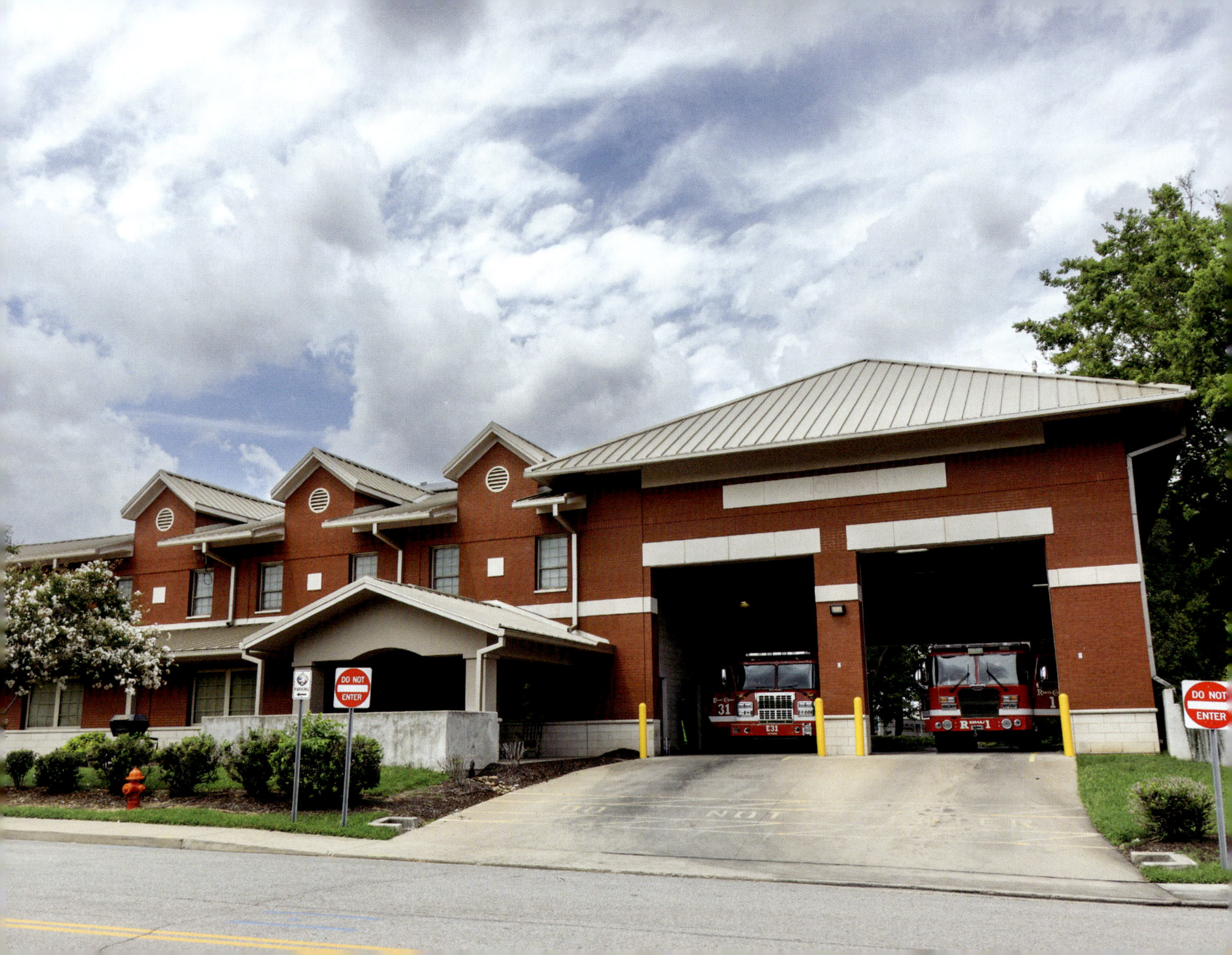
DO NOT
ENTER
DO NOT
ENTER

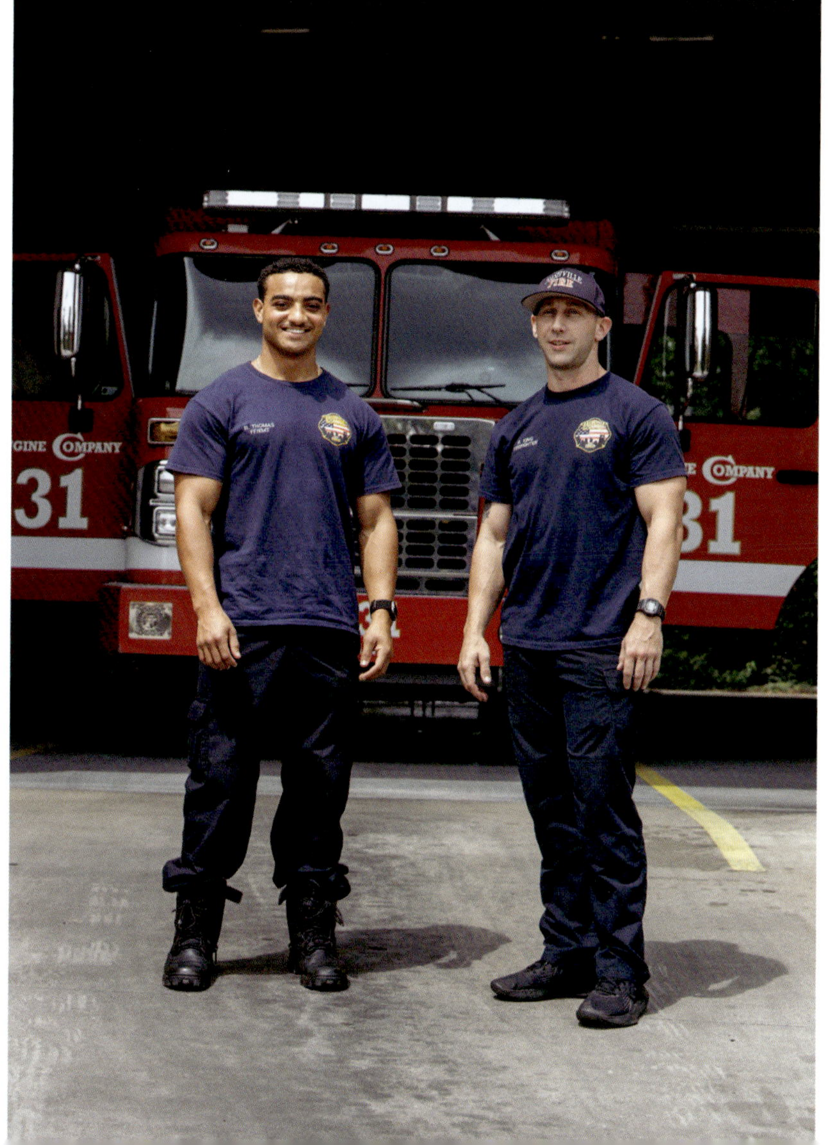

Blaise Thomas and Ryan King,

firefighters at Nashville Fire Department Station 31, stand in the driveway.

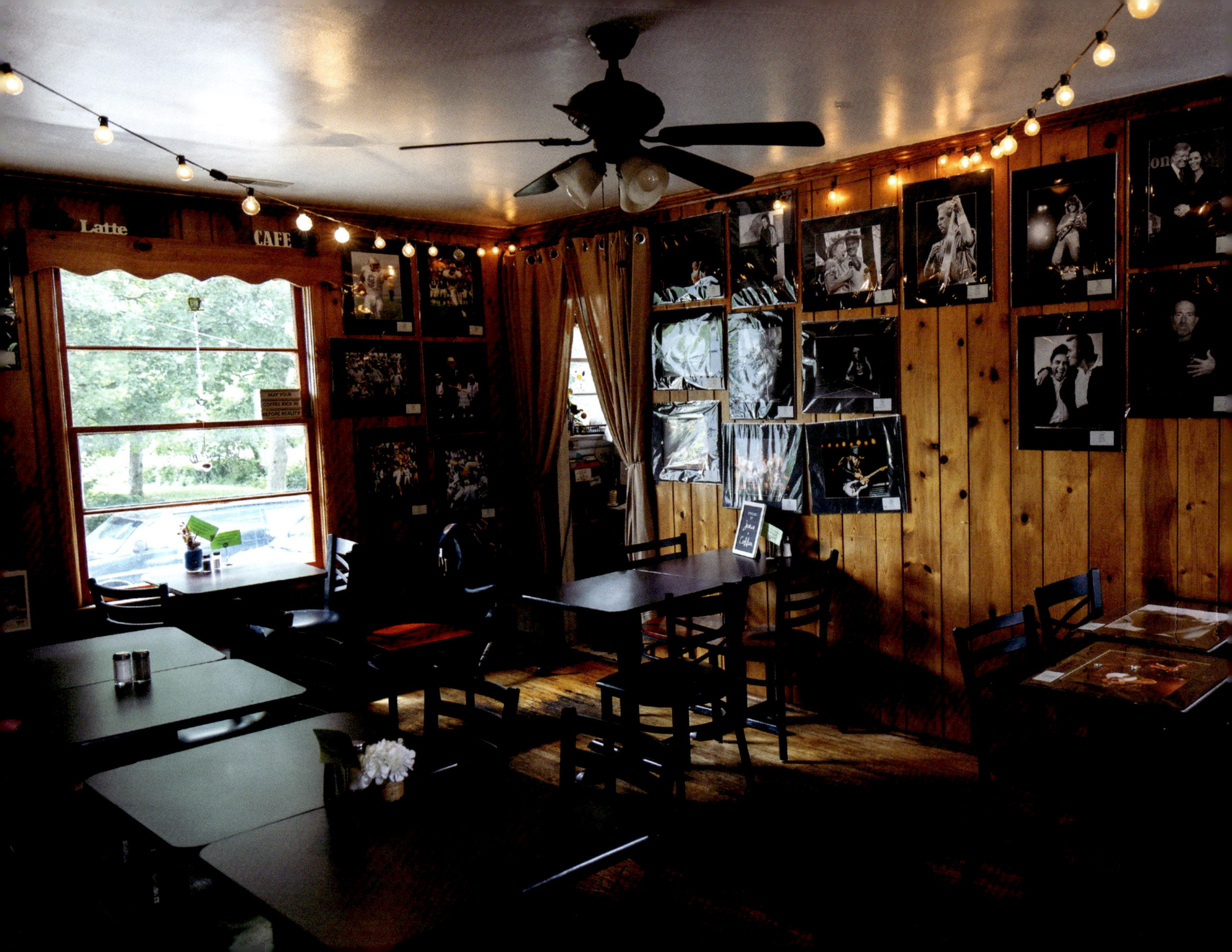
Latte
CAFE

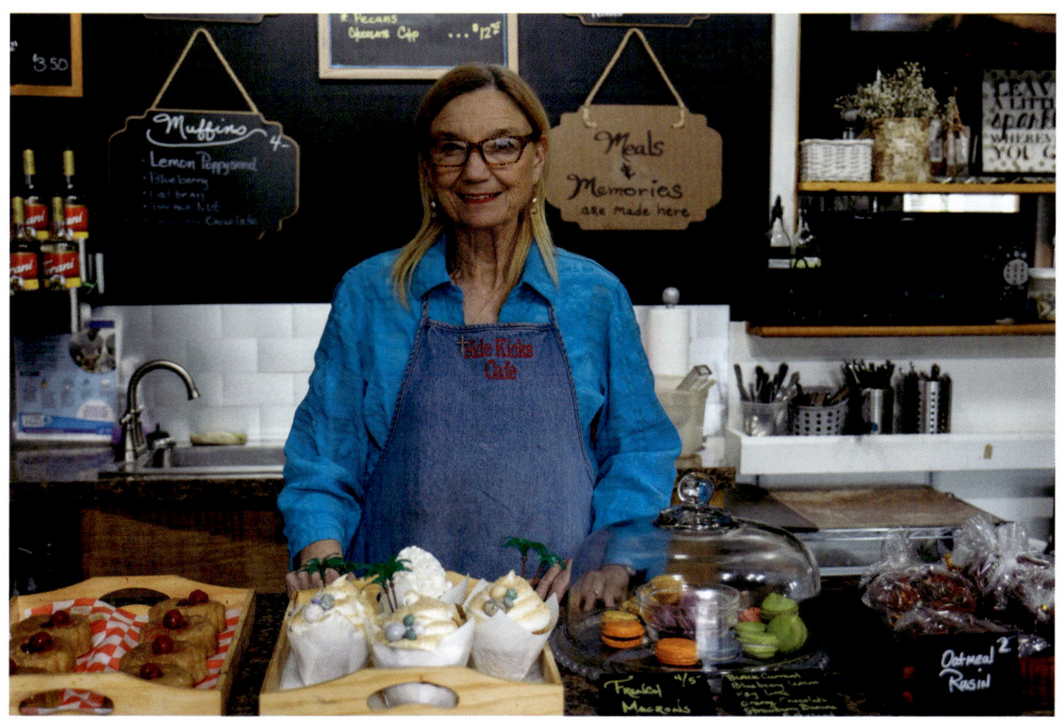

Cathy Hoormann, owner of Sidekicks Cafe, stands behind the counter. She opened the cafe to be a community gathering spot similar to one she remembered from her childhood.

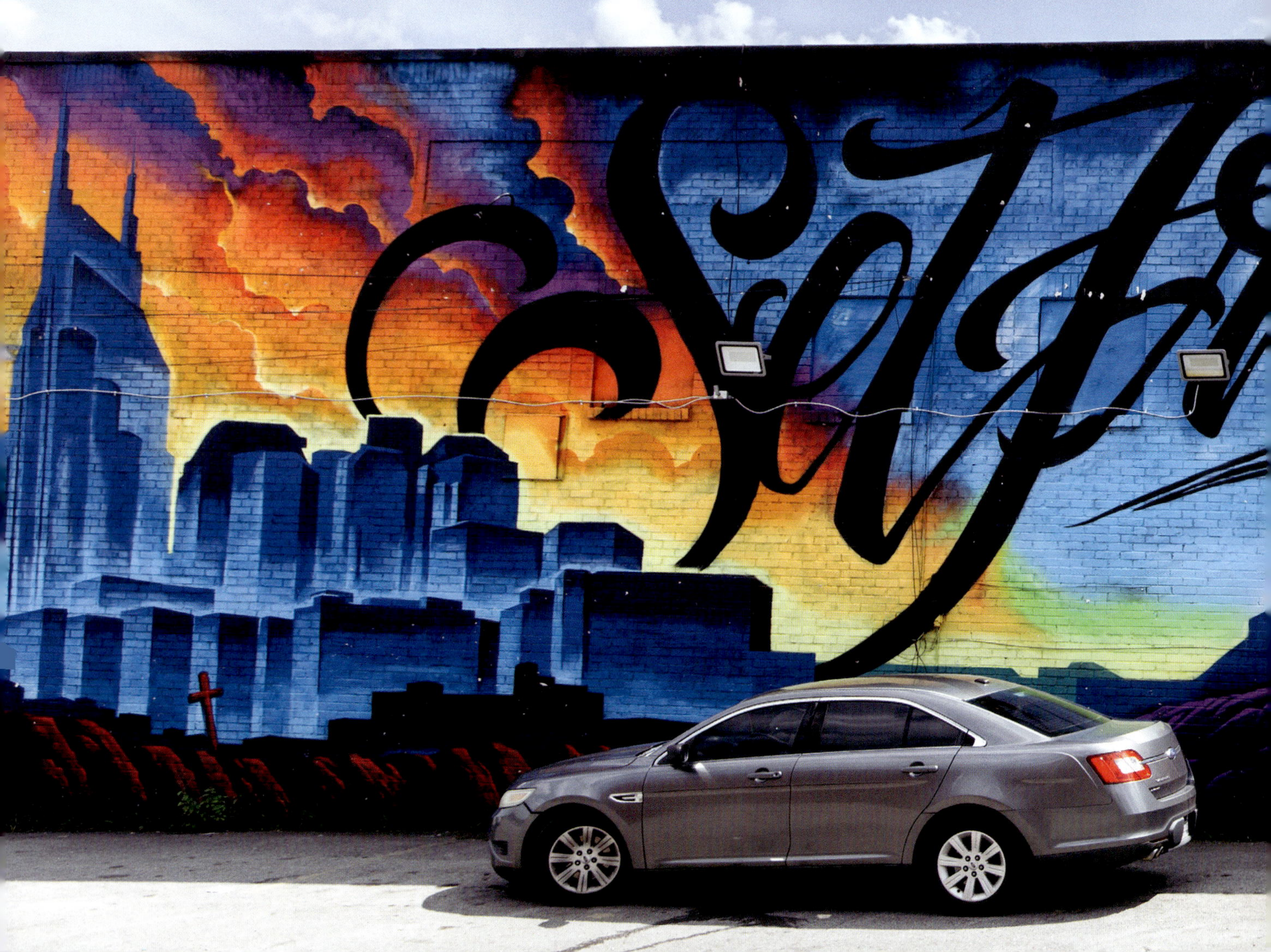

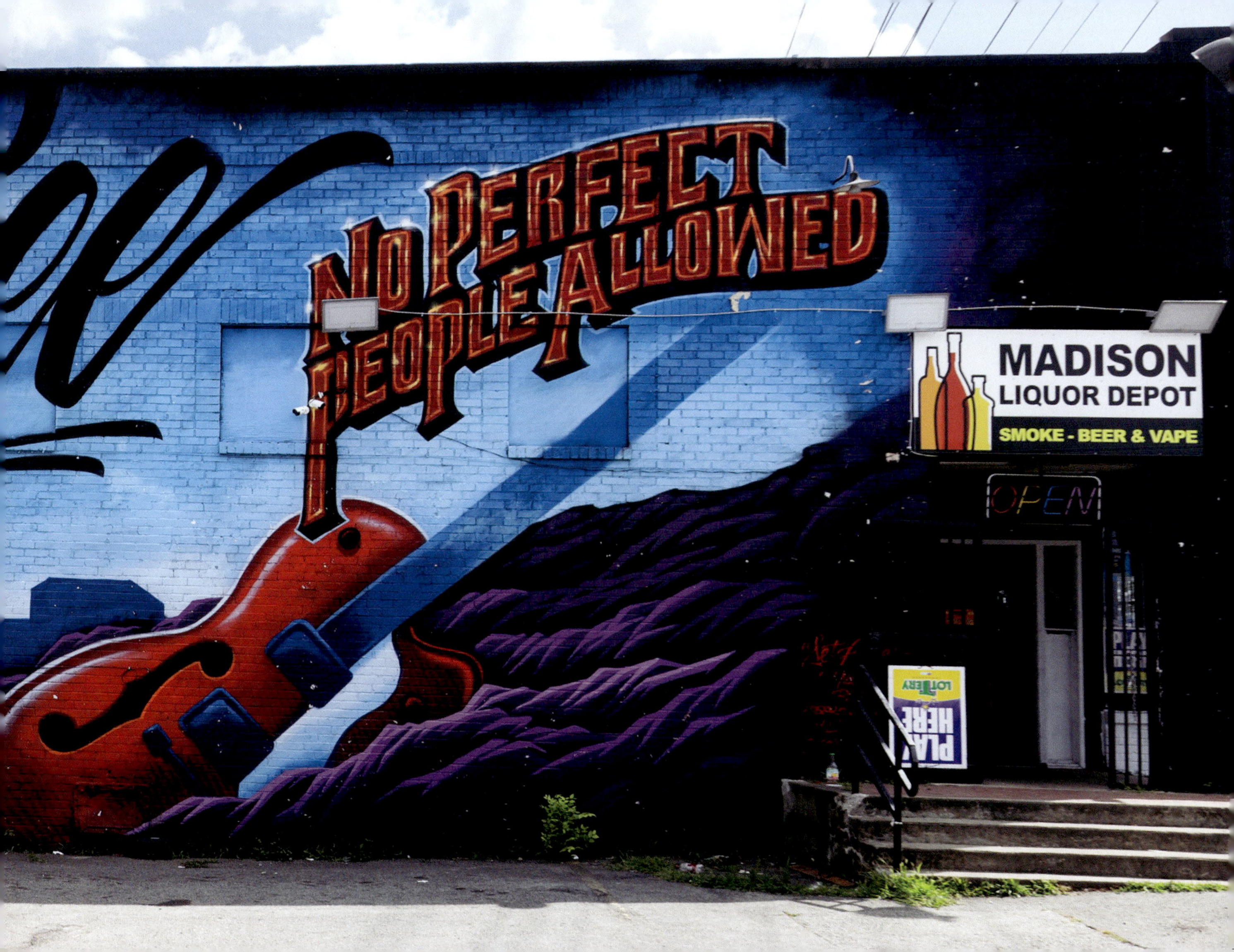
NO PERFECT
PEOPLE ALLOWED
MADISON
LIQUOR DEPOT
SMOKE - BEER & VAPE
OPEN

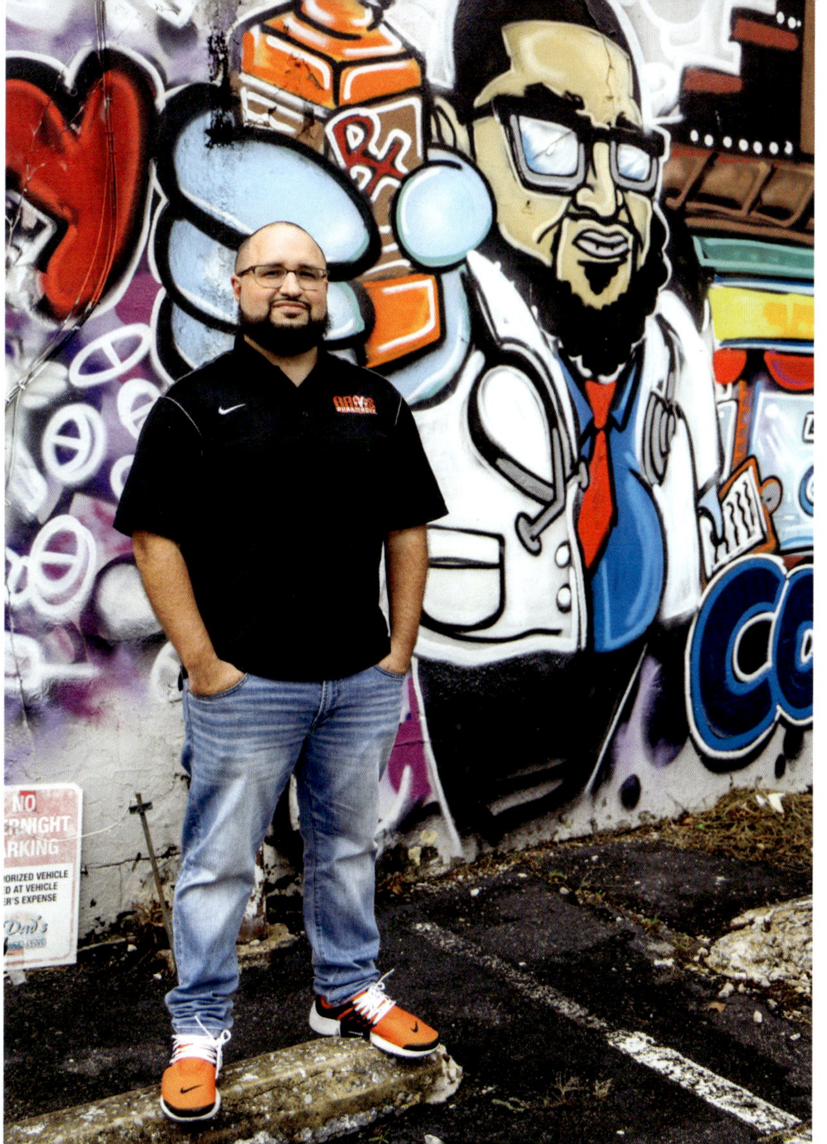

Travis Sparks,

owner of Rams Pharmacy, stands in front of his store's mural. The pharmacy's name is a nod to the old Madison High School mascot, the Rams.

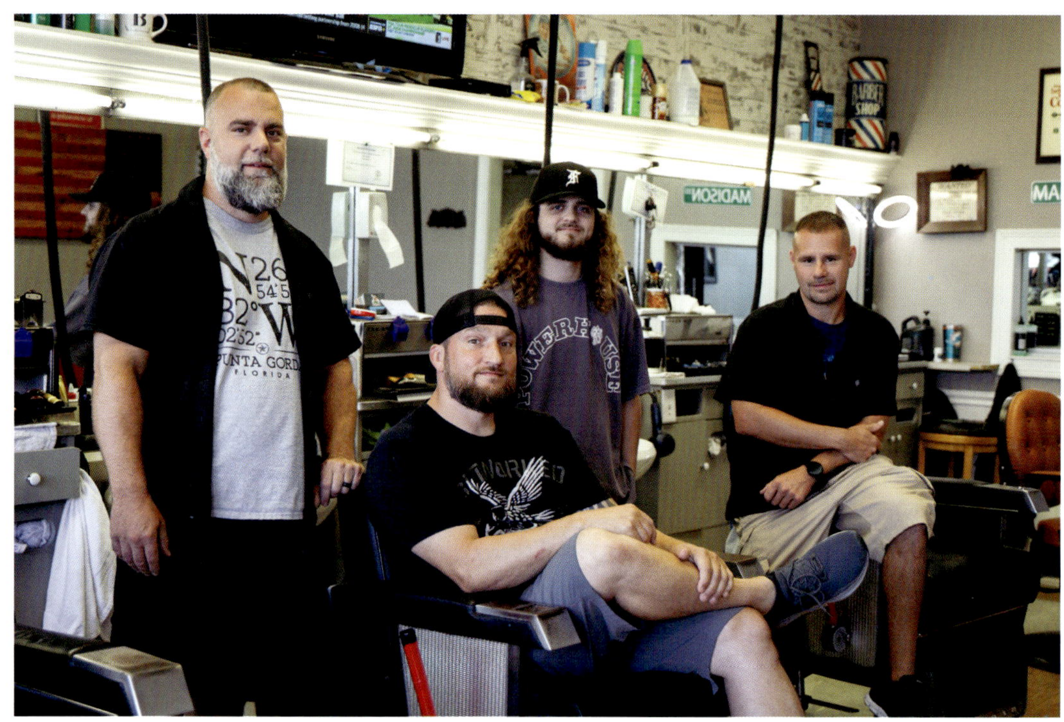

Brad, owner of **Brad's Barber Shop**, with his crew, Victor, Bradley Jr., and Chad. His barbershop has been a staple in Madison for more than twenty-five years.

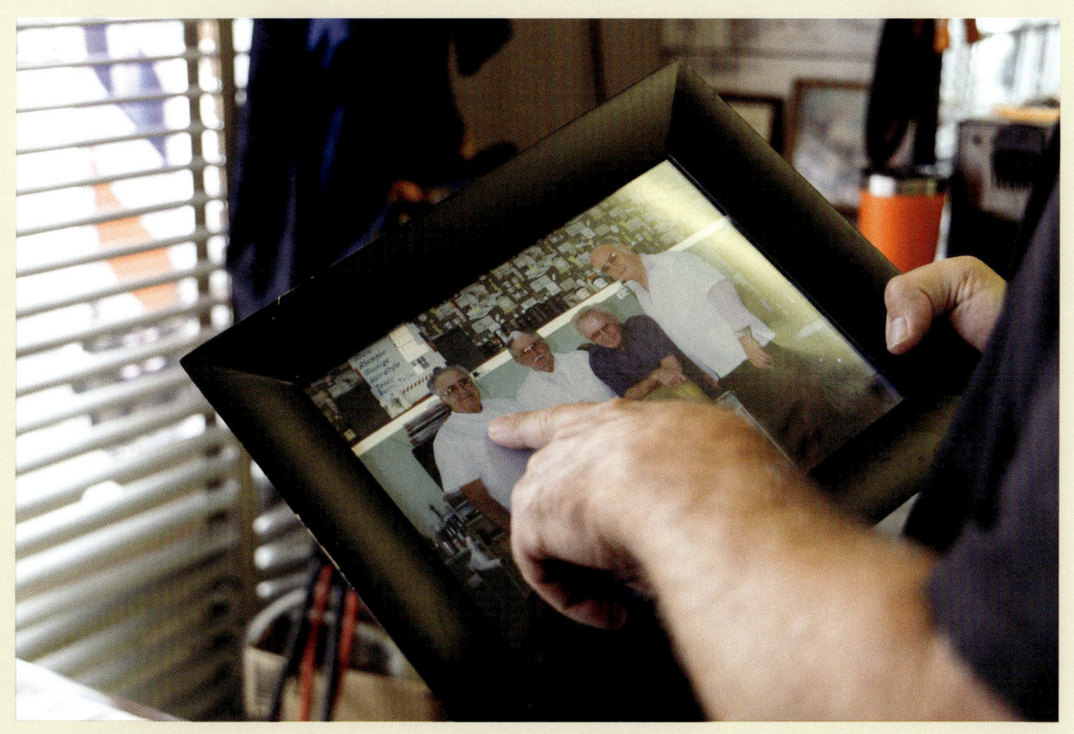

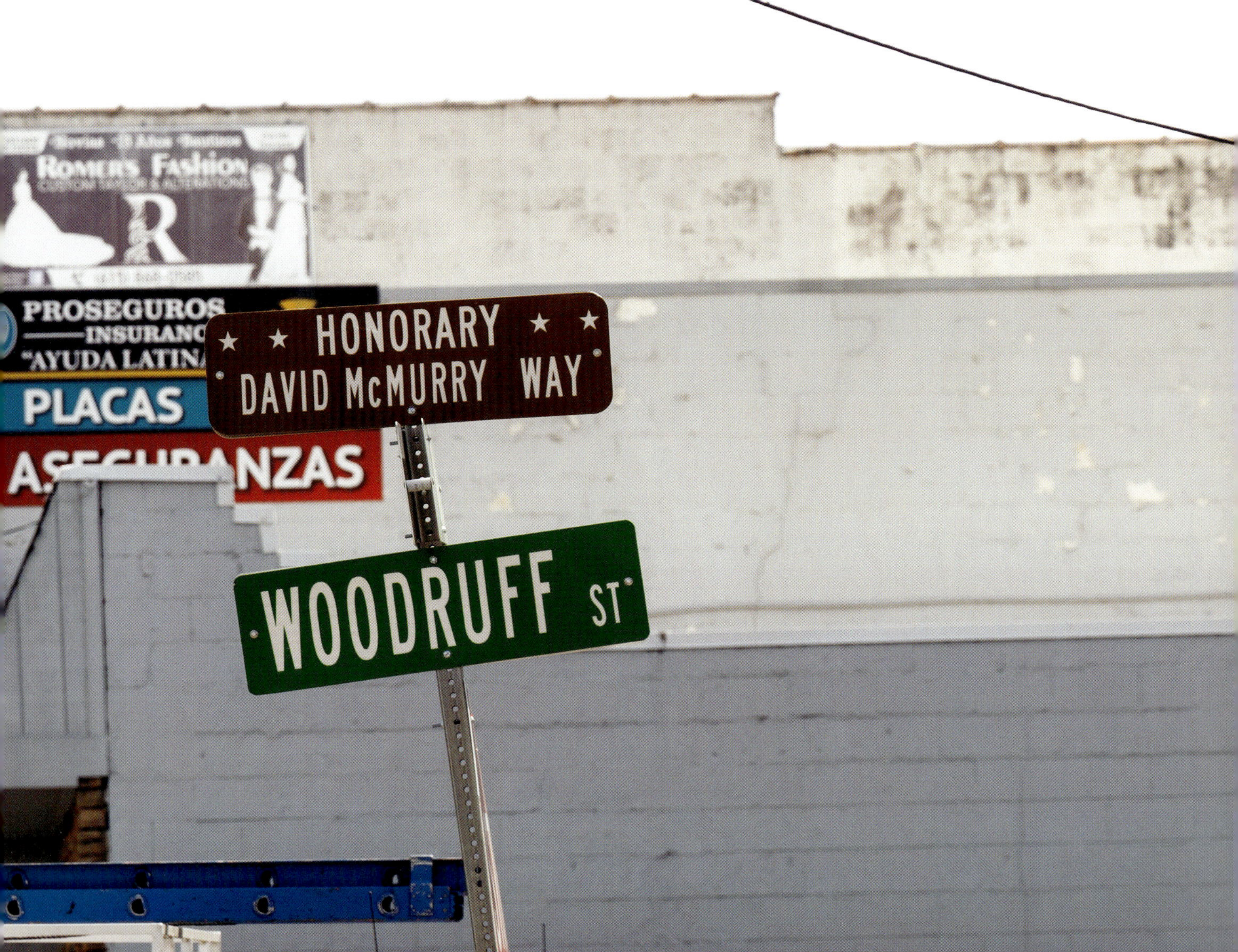
ROMERS FASHION
R
PROSEGUROS
INSURANC
"AYUDA LATINA
PLACAS
HONORARY
DAVID McMURRY WAY
WOODRUFF ST

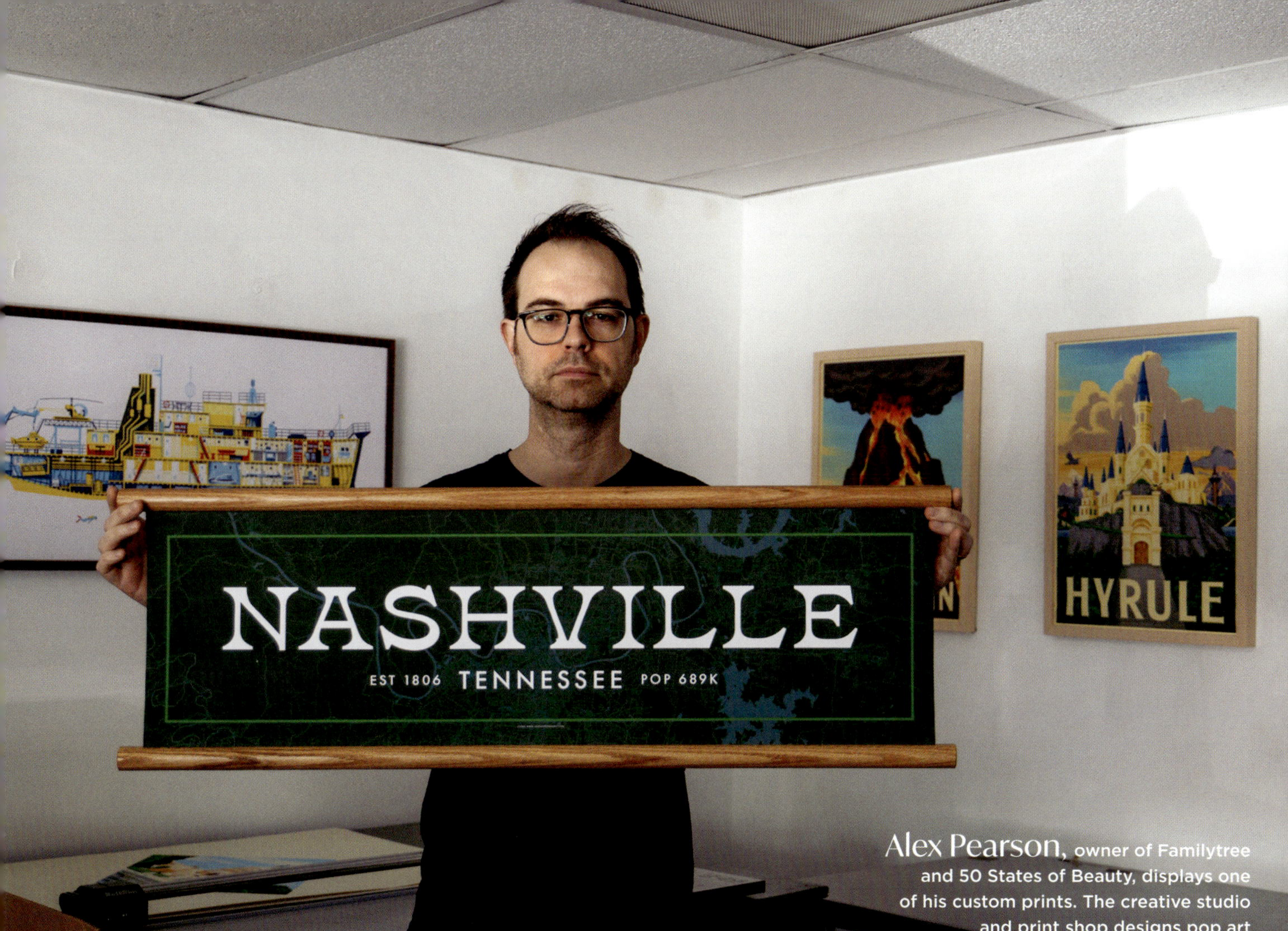

Alex Pearson, owner of Familytree and 50 States of Beauty, displays one of his custom prints. The creative studio and print shop designs pop art prints inspired by things they love.

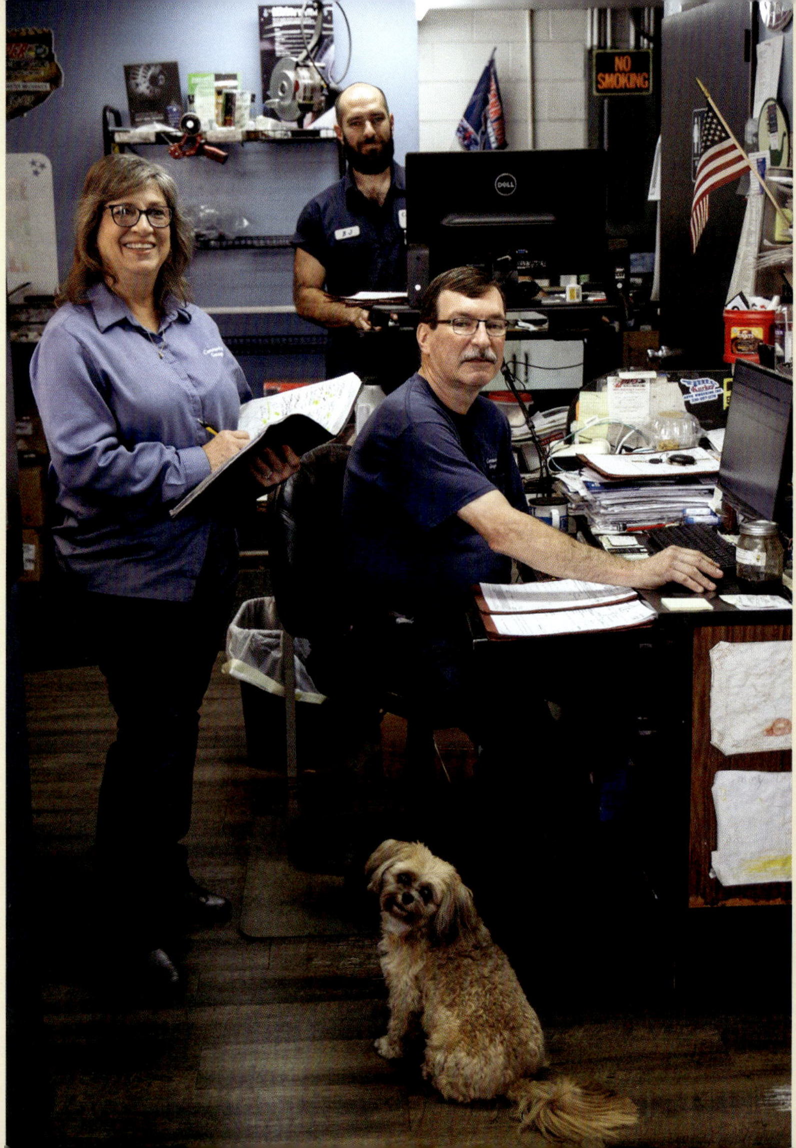

Community Garage owners **Carol and Brian Howald, B. J. Howald,** their son, and shop mascot Dusty inside the garage. The faith-based, community-minded company is proud of its reputation for excellent service.

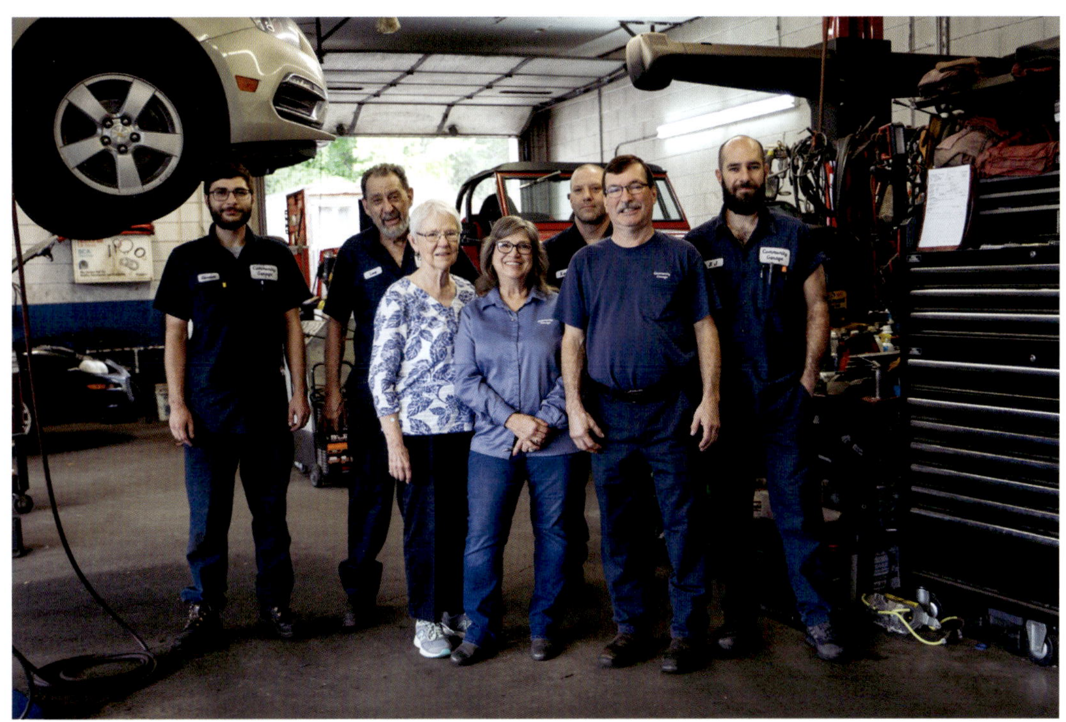
Community
Garage

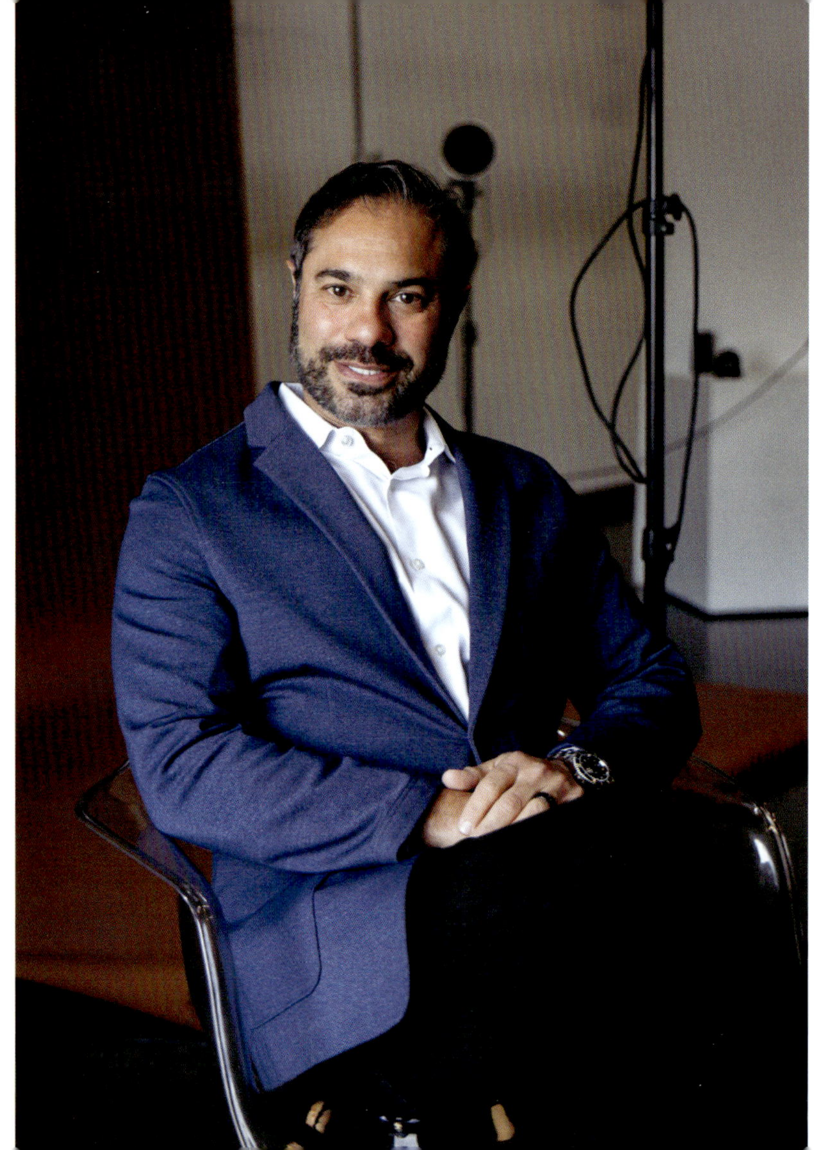

Cyrus Vatandoost, president and CEO of Nossi College of Art and Design, sits inside one of the campus's state-of-the-art studios.

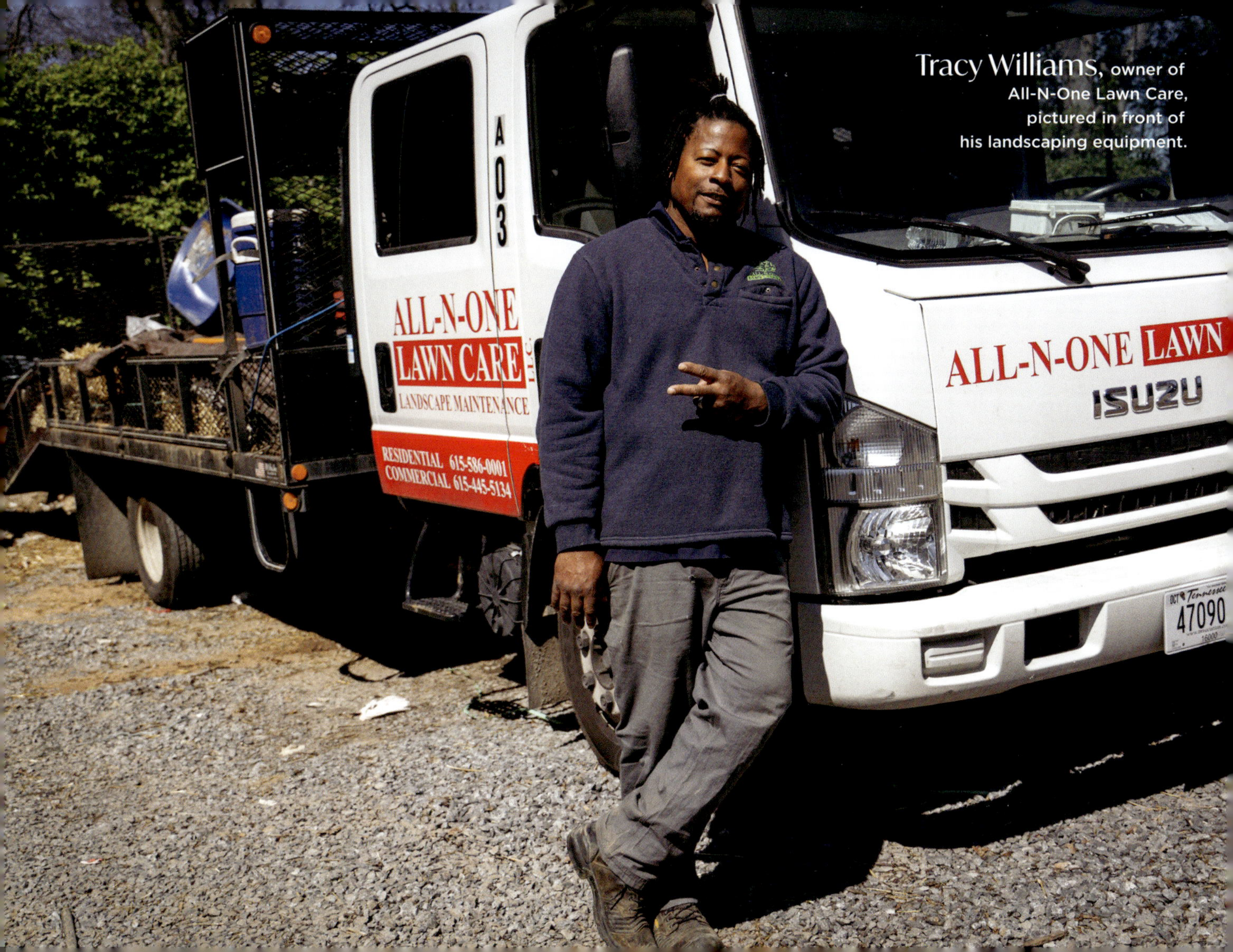

Tracy Williams, owner of All-N-One Lawn Care, pictured in front of his landscaping equipment.

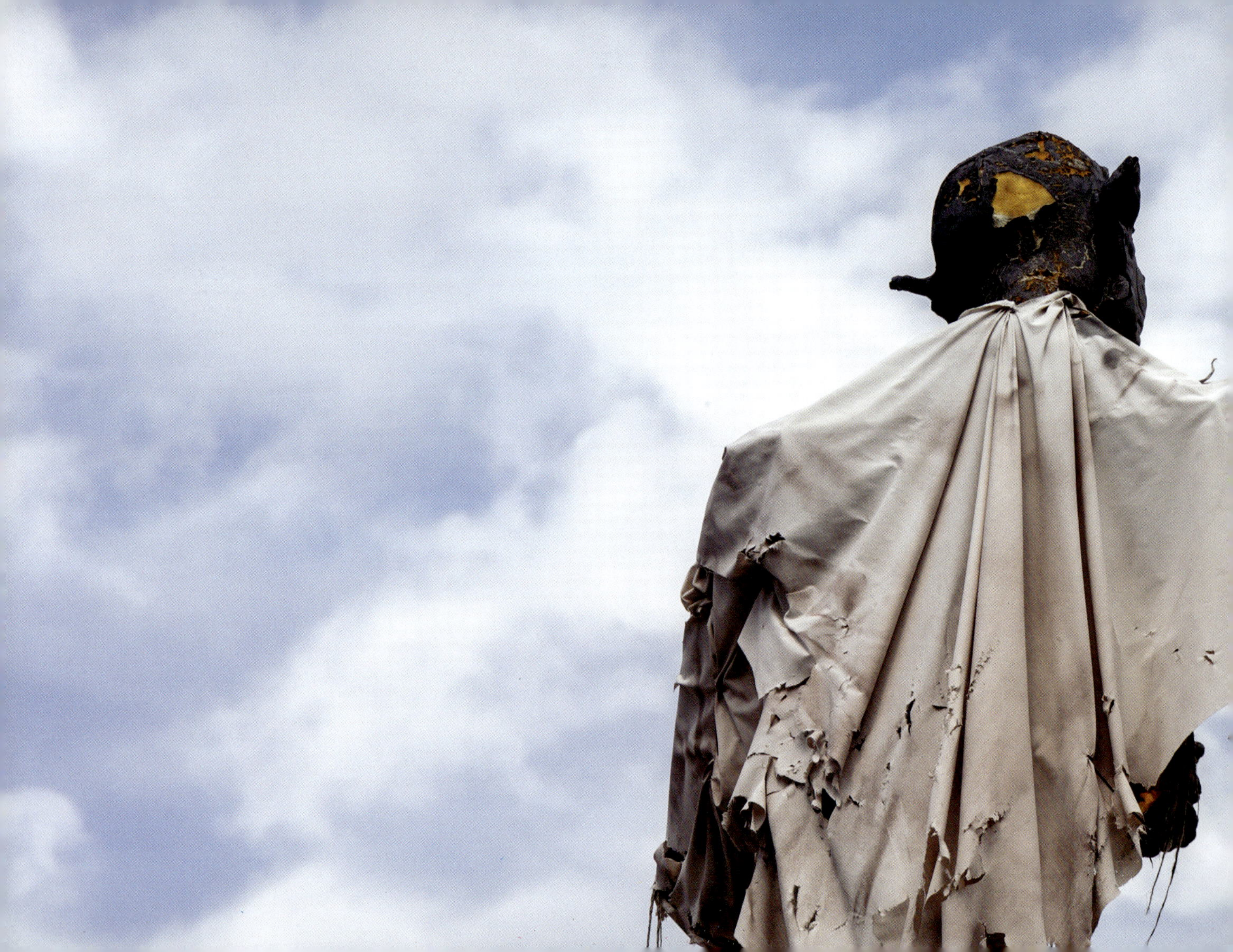

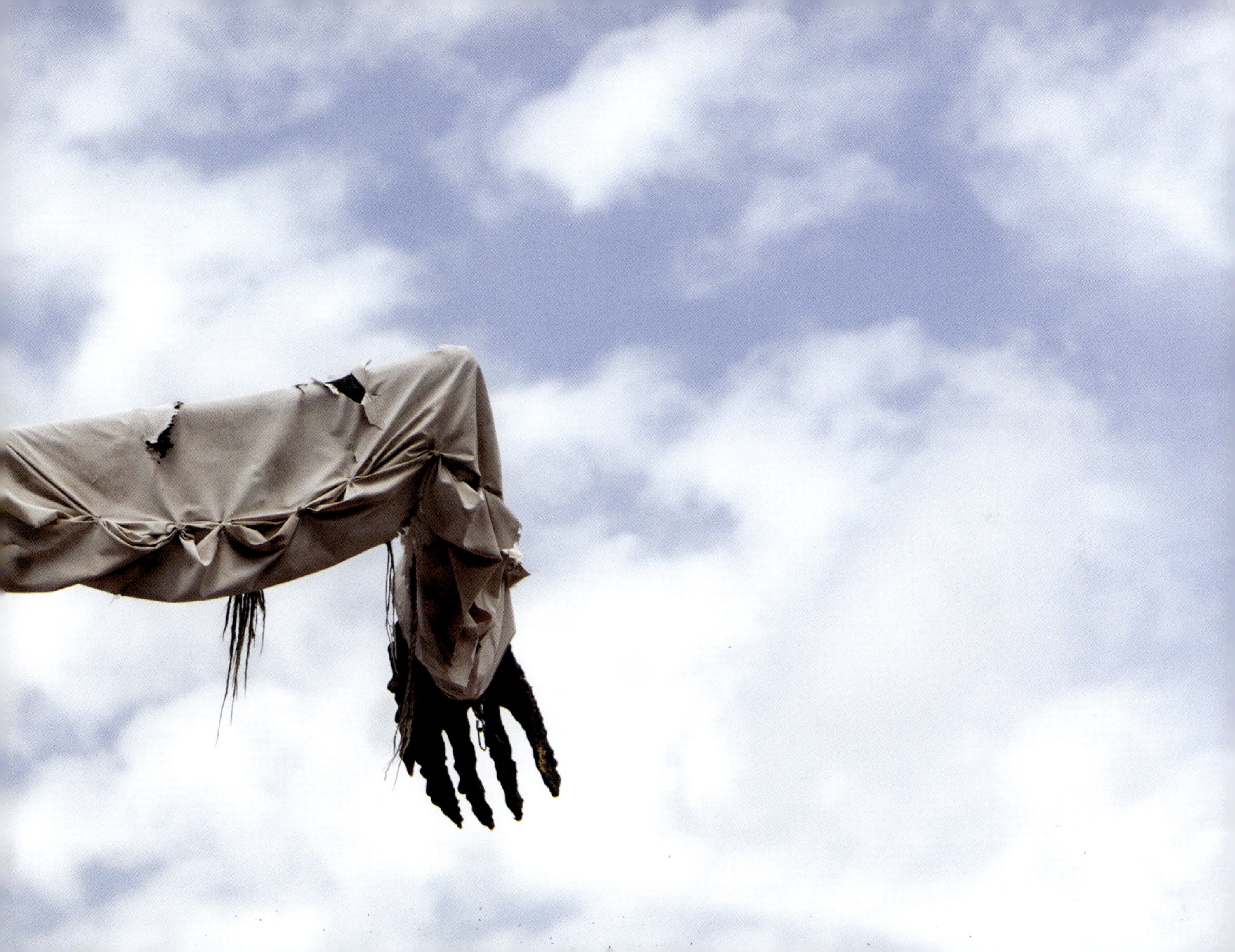

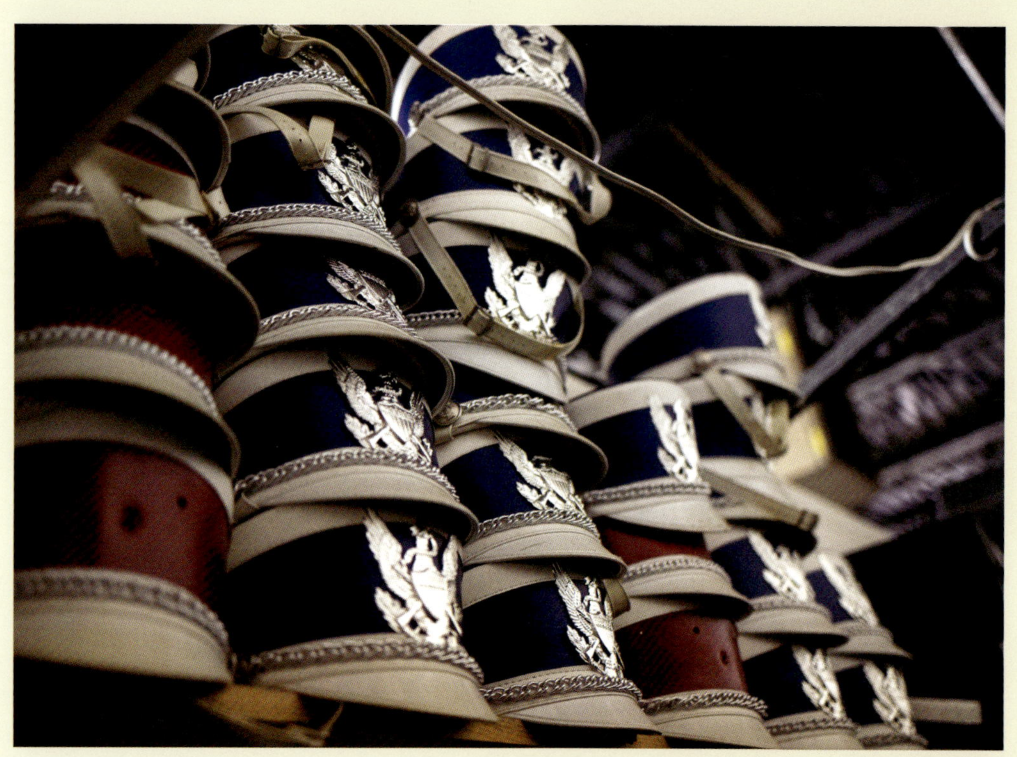

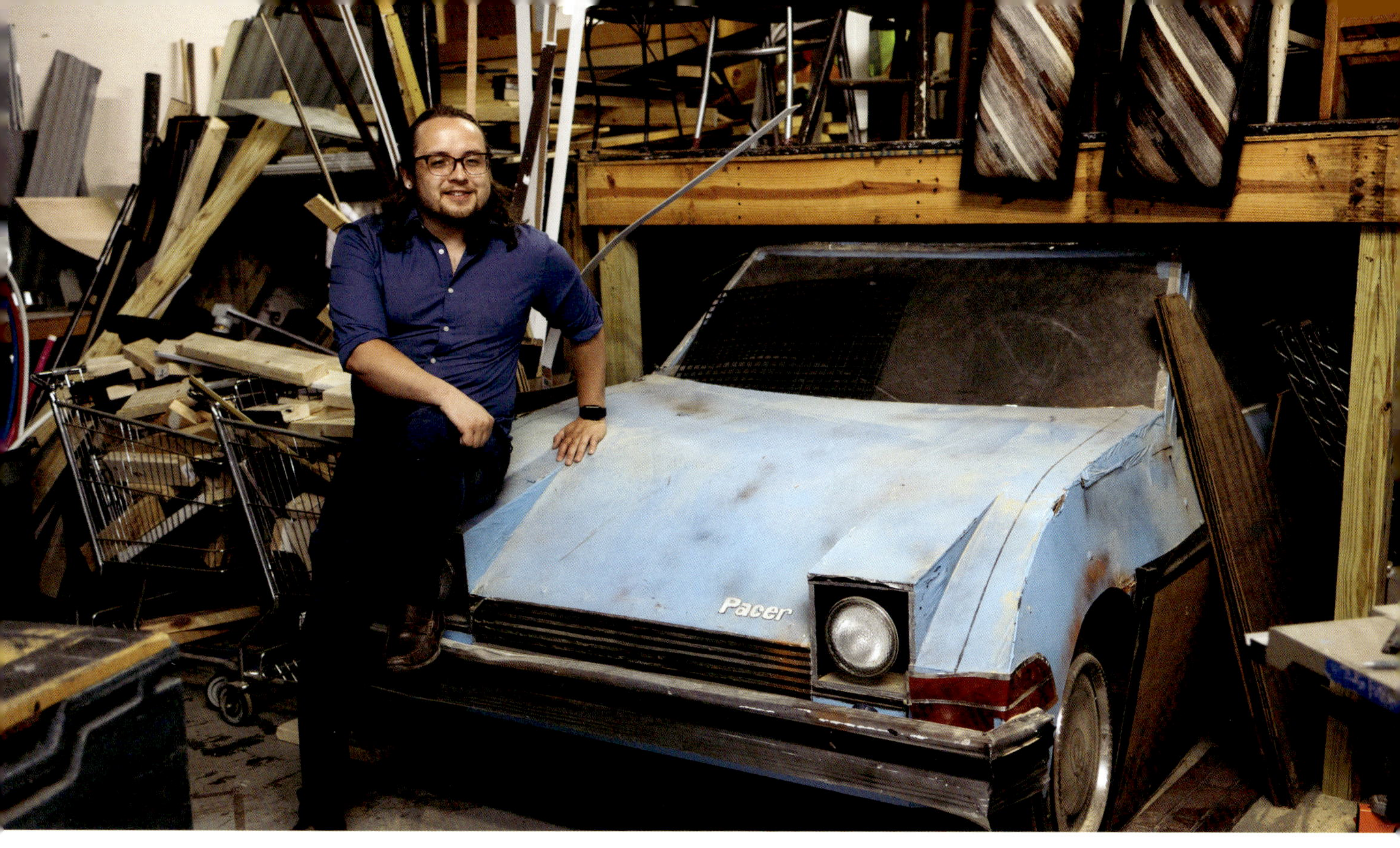

Clint Randolph, actor and director, sits among the props in the Circle Players rehearsal space. Circle Players is one of Tennessee's oldest community theater companies.

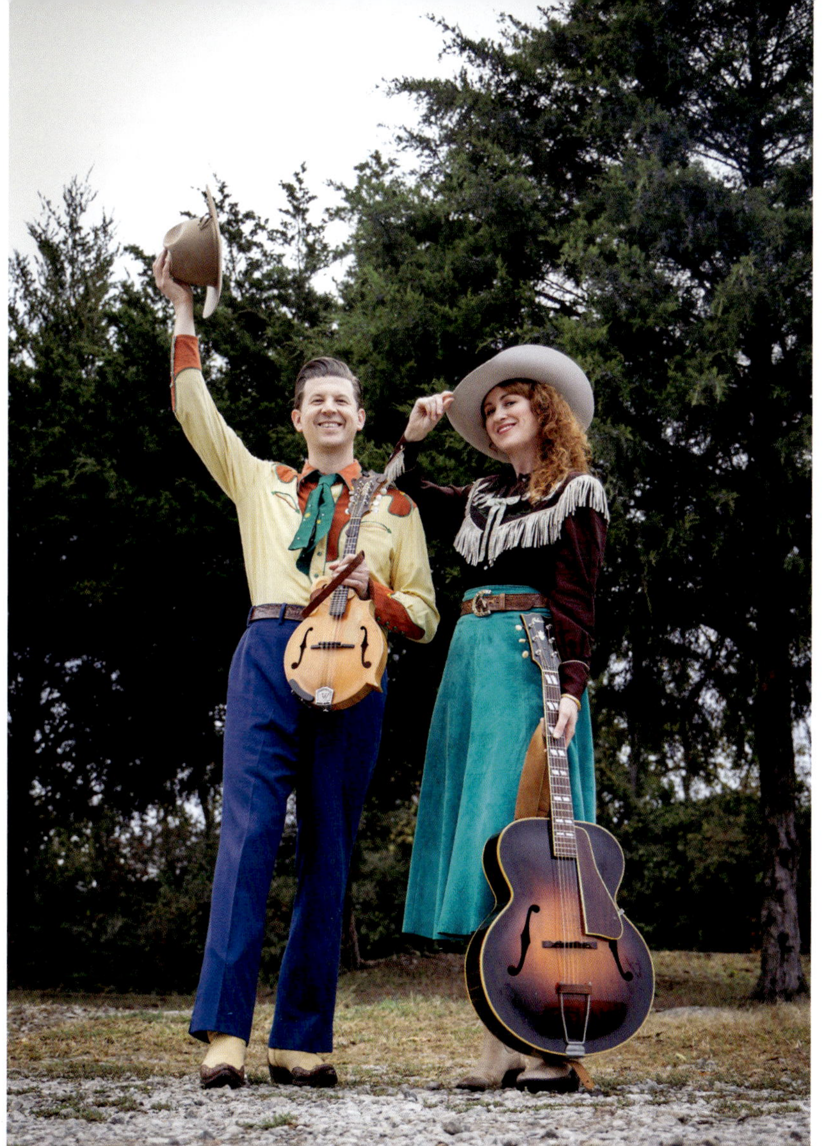

Husband and wife **Keenan Wade and Grace Adele,** the duo known as The Farmer and Adele. They perform at the Amqui Station Farmers Market.

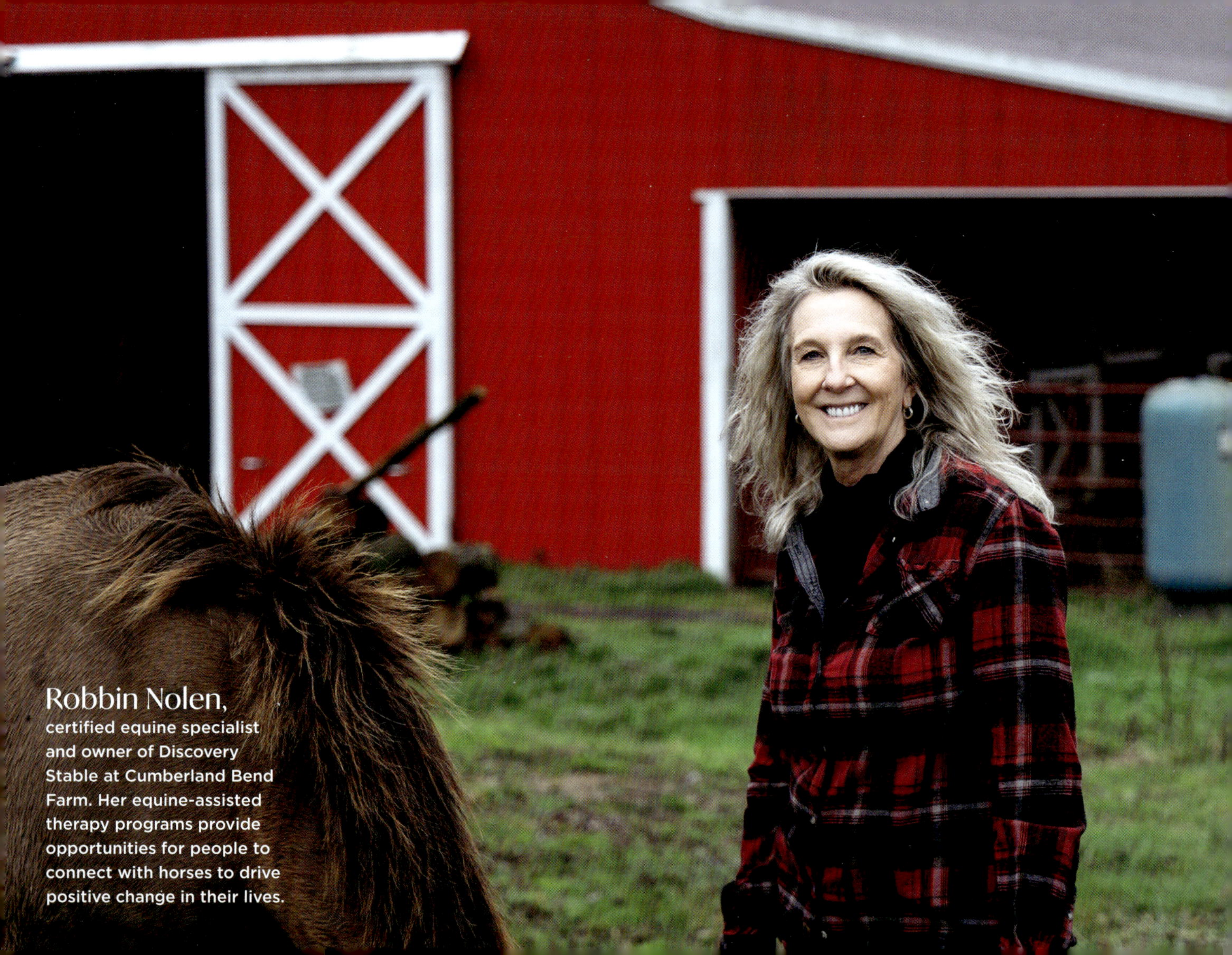

Robbin Nolen, certified equine specialist and owner of Discovery Stable at Cumberland Bend Farm. Her equine-assisted therapy programs provide opportunities for people to connect with horses to drive positive change in their lives.

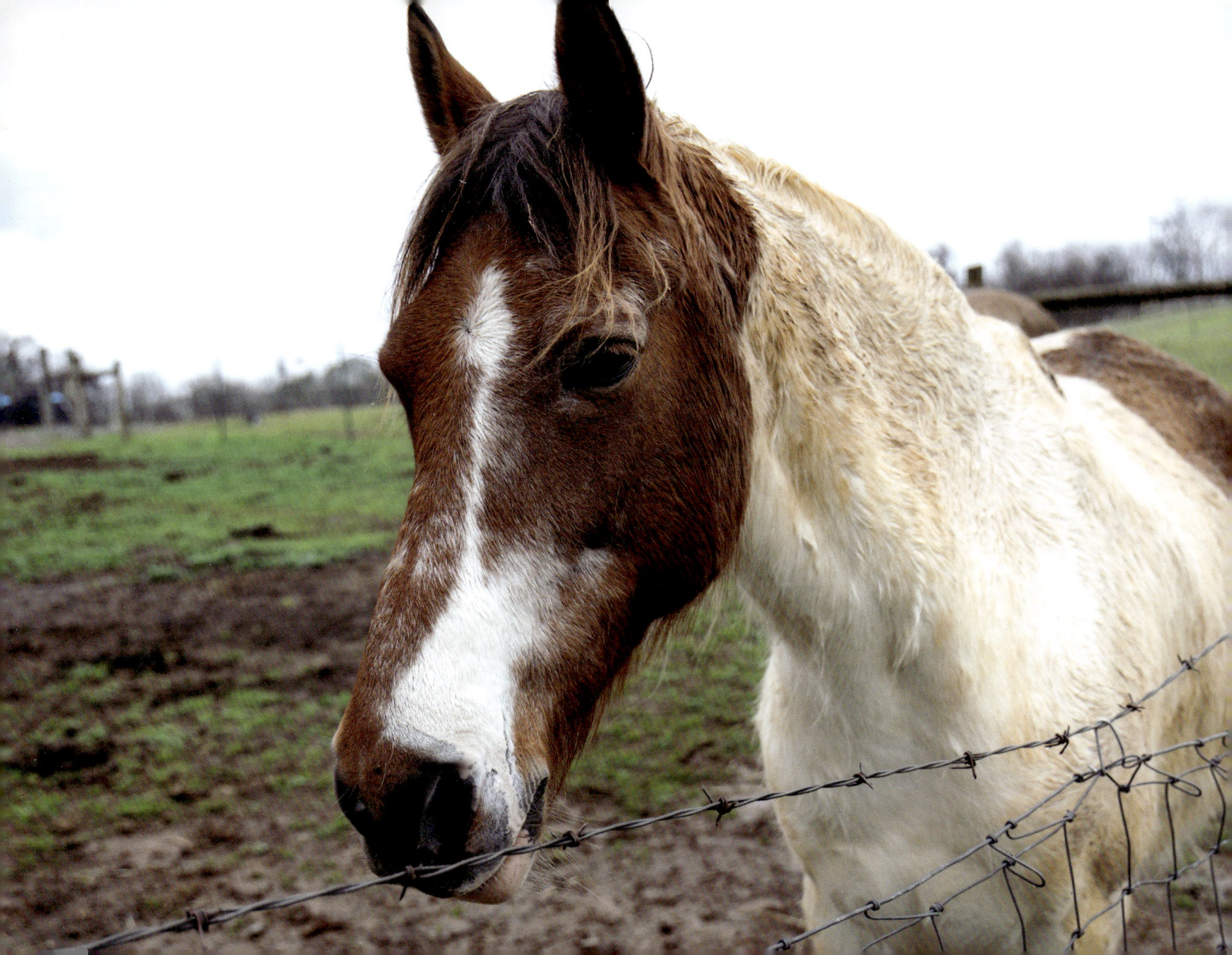

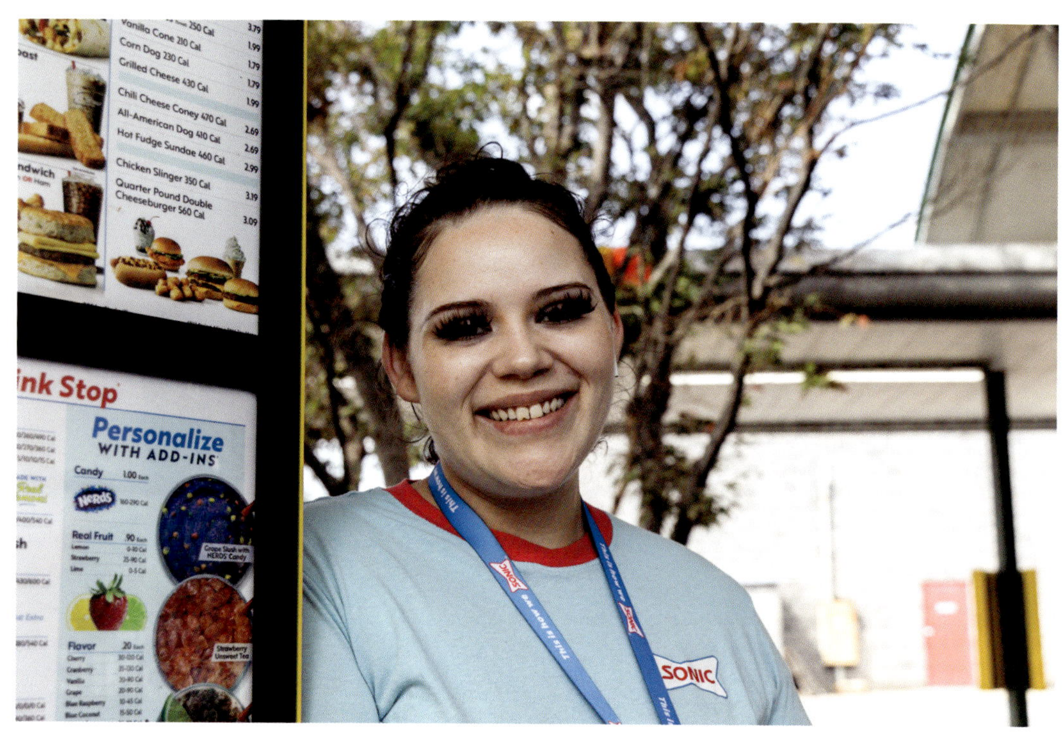

Autumn, Sonic carhop, serves customers at the Gallatin Pike restaurant.

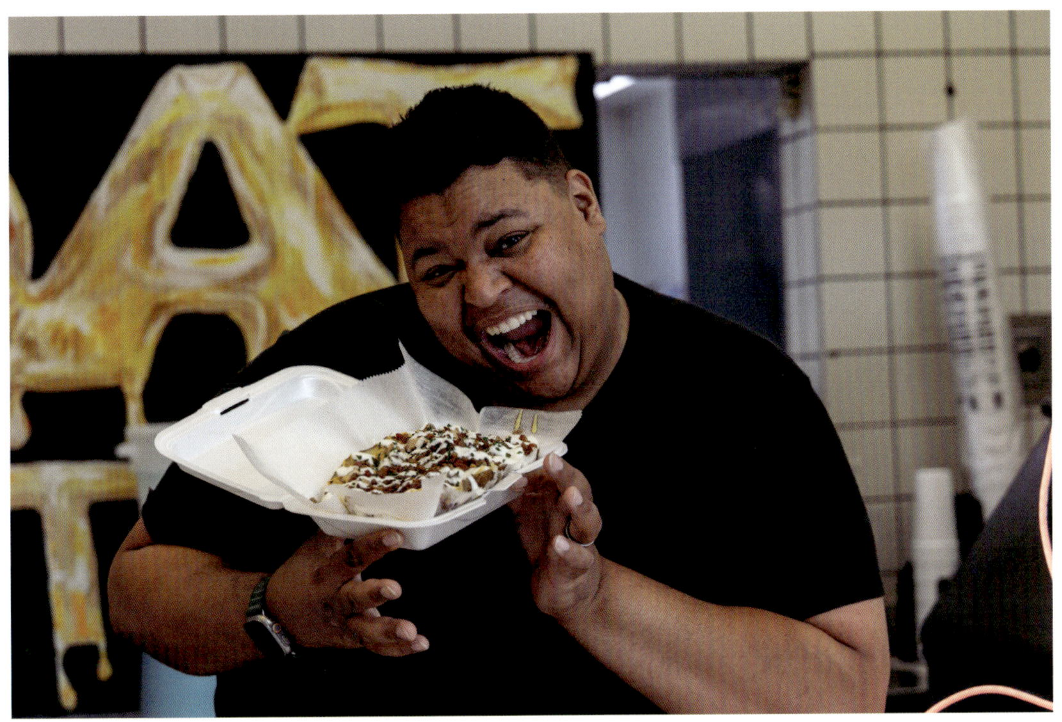

Michael Harvey, owner of One Spunky Spud restaurant, self-titled Grand Master of Potatoes, and TikTok personality, serves up lunch behind the counter of his restaurant inside the Rivergate Mall food court.

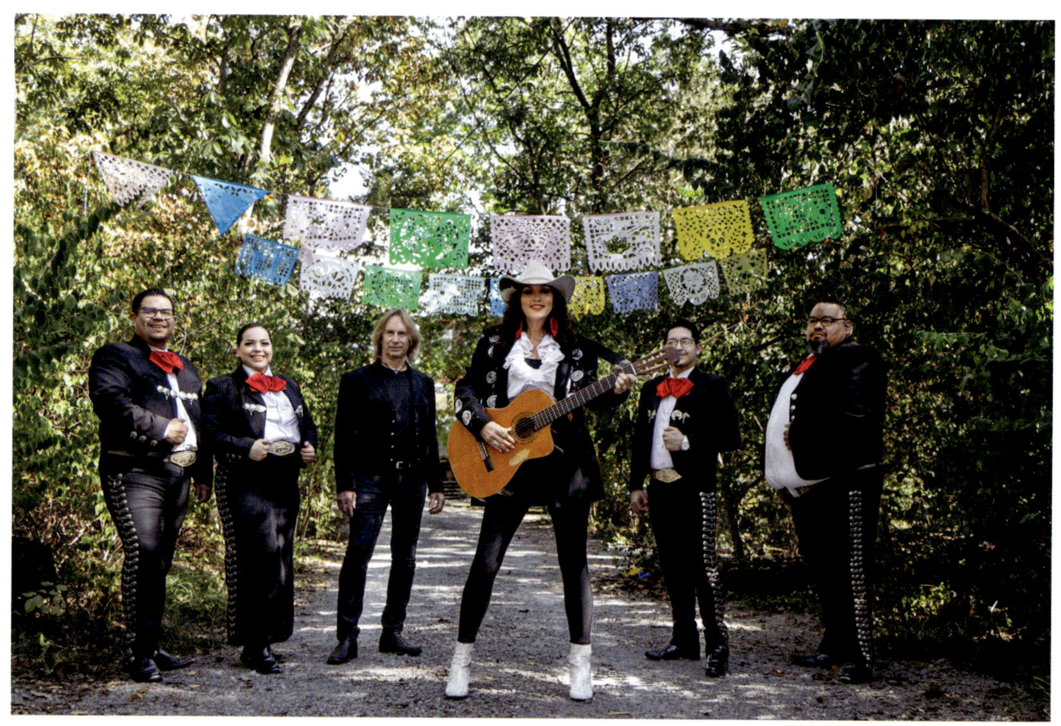

Singer-songwriter **Stephanie Urbina Jones** poses outside her riverfront home with her band, The Honky Tonk Mariachi. She playfully refers to her style as "country music with chili peppers."

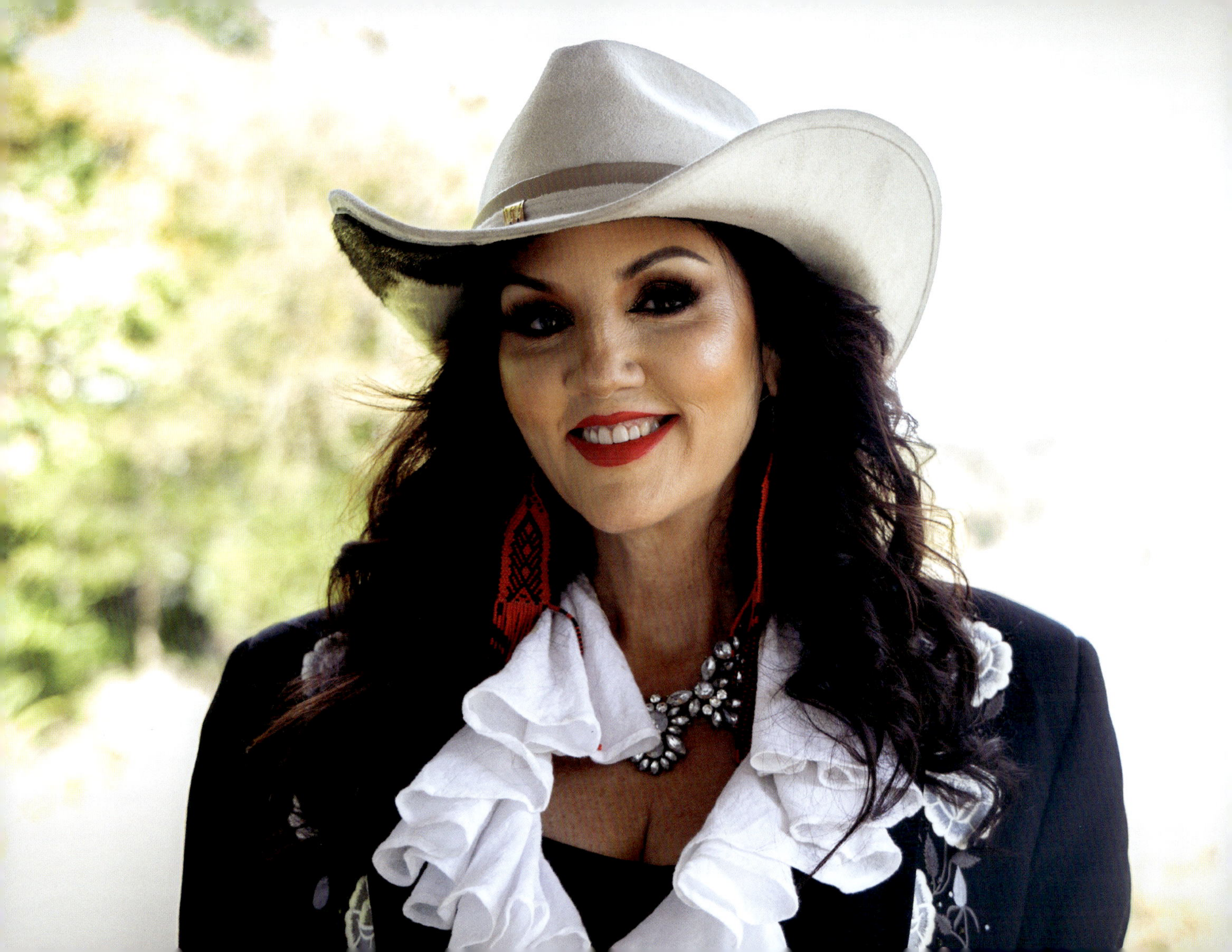

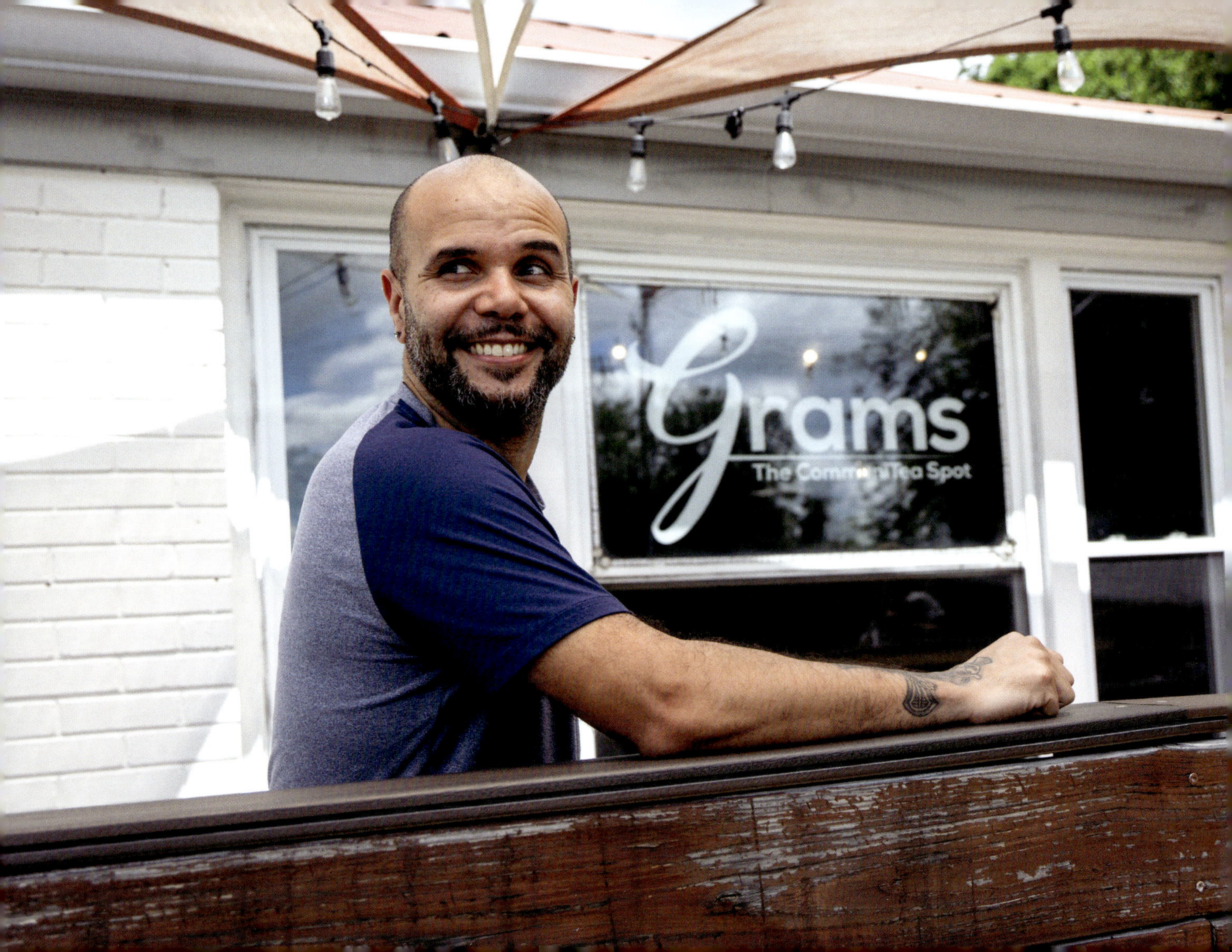
Grams

Edward Gray, owner of Gram's Coffee and Tea, stands outside the cafe. He prides himself on serving the "CommuniTea."

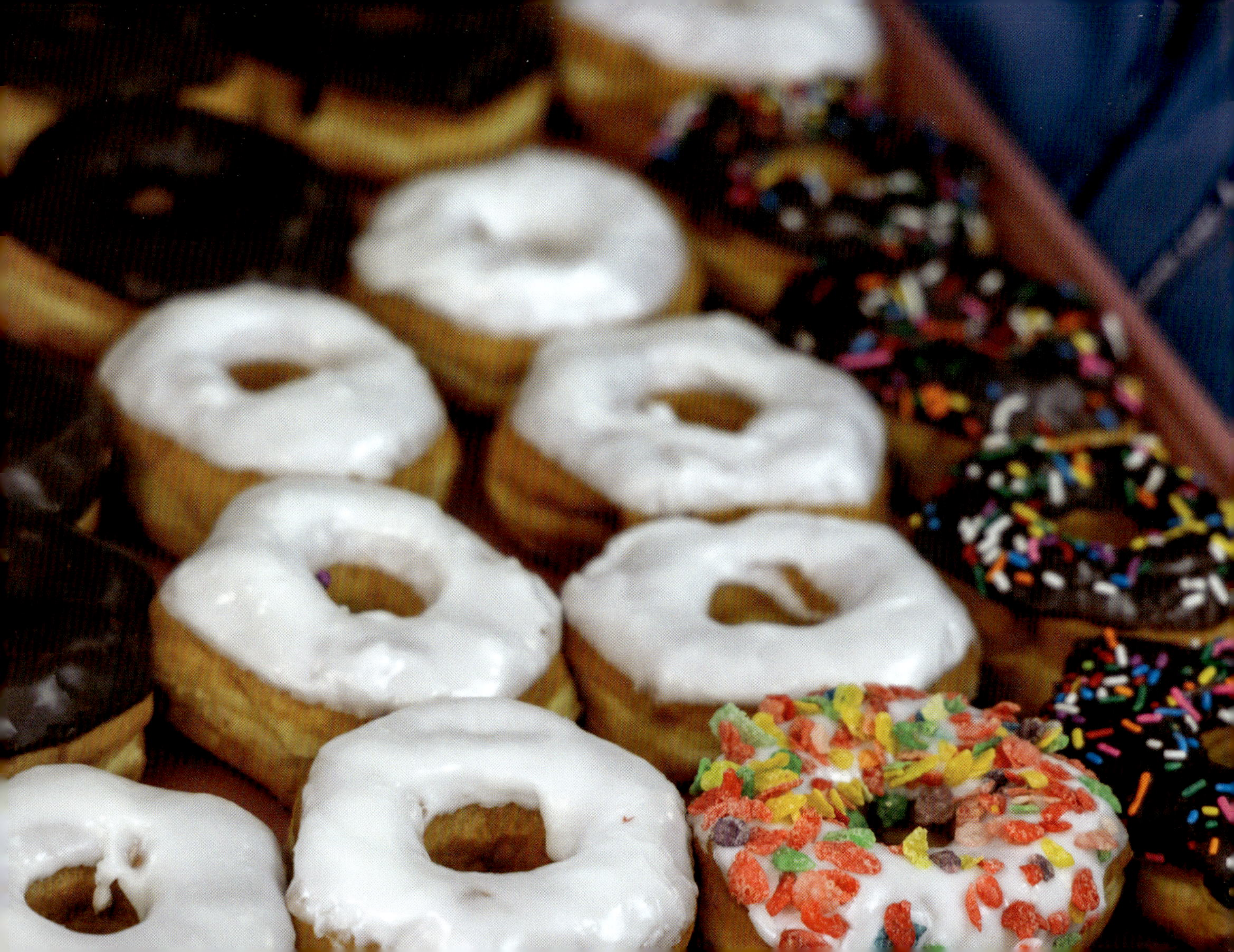

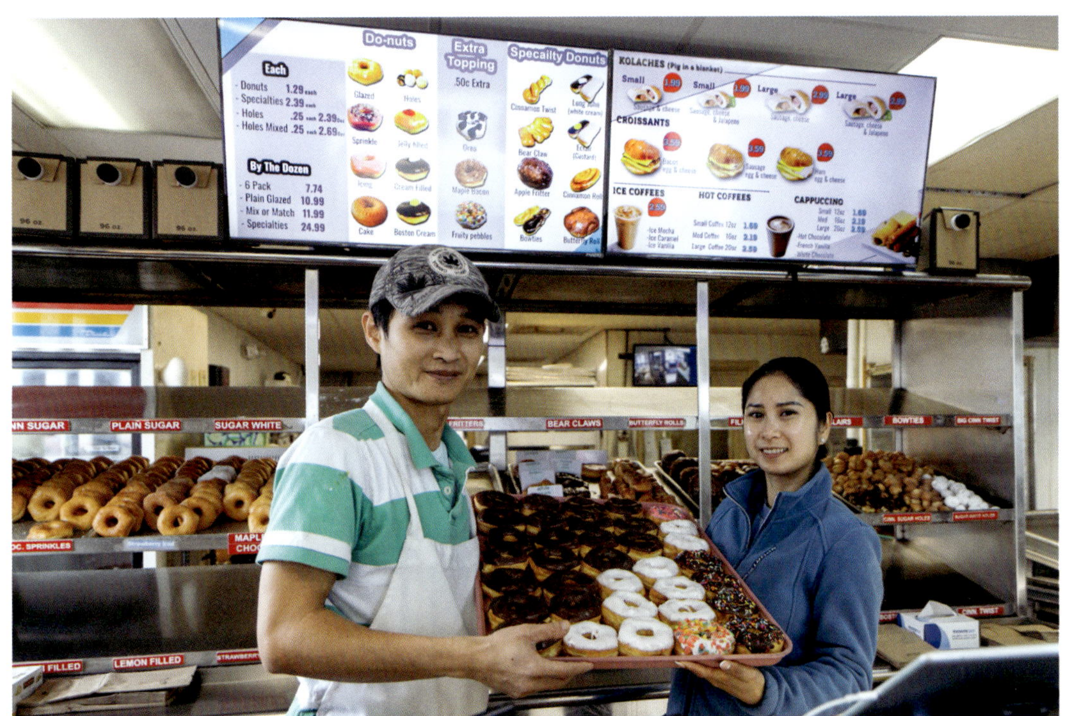

Sitha and Mab Lin,

owners of McGaugh's Donuts, proudly display a fresh batch of donuts.

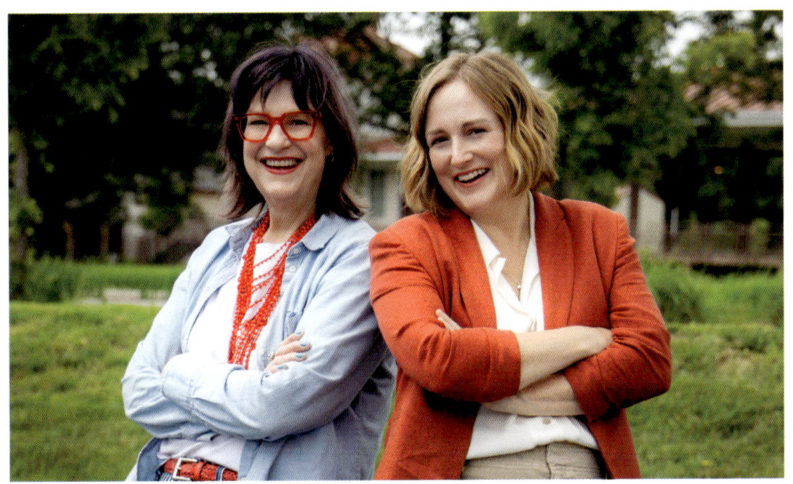

Authors' Biographies

STACIE HUCKEBA is an award-winning, internationally recognized photographer, writer, public speaker, and filmmaker. Most recently the director of photography for Dolly Parton's *New York Times*–bestseller, *Behind the Seams, My Life in Rhinestones,* Huckeba's pictures have graced the cover of *Marie Claire,* as well as the pages of *Rolling Stone, USA Today, The Wall Street Journal,* and others.

LAURA JO AMARAL is a Madison resident passionate about building community. A lover of books and supporter of original art, she started Lucky Jo Publishing to create beautiful art books. She lives in Neelys Bend with her husband and two daughters. One can find her nearly every day hiking Peeler Park, the crown jewel of Madison, Tennessee.

Together, Stacie and I would like to thank the following:

Chuck Beard and the team at Metro Arts for their Thrive grant investment in us and many other worthy Nashville artists.

Betsy Phillips and everyone at Vanderbilt University Press for believing in this book and making it so beautiful.

Carlene Carter for not only writing the heartfelt foreword, but for always giving back to the Madison community.

Katie Harford Hogue and John Hogue at John Hartford Enterprises for blessing this project by allowing us the use of John Hartford's lyrics.

Acknowledgments

First and foremost, my biggest thanks and an enormous debt of gratitude goes to Stacie Huckeba. I was shooting for the moon when I asked her to collaborate on this project and beyond grateful she said yes. Her ability to capture beautiful portraits of our neighbors just as adeptly as her celebrity clients is one of her true gifts as a photographer. • Sincere thanks to my husband Justin for his support and encouragement to create this book from the first moment I mentioned the idea was rattling around in my head. Watching him pursue his own creative projects so heart forward instilled in me a belief that I could also create art. • Extra special thanks to my daughters, Rosemary and Julia, for their enthusiasm and teenage stamp of approval on this project. If this book sparks their own creative journeys, it will have accomplished something well beyond my original expectations. —**LAURA**

I wish to express my deepest gratitude to Laura Amaral for inviting me to be part of this remarkable project. It has been an honor to work beside her in bringing this book to life. Her tireless dedication and commitment to our community and neighborhood are a true reflection of her character—as a friend, a mother, and a neighbor. I am proud to know her and to have contributed to this beautiful publication alongside her. • I want to dedicate this work to my "Granny," Bernice Huckeba, who from a young age taught me the meaning of "neighbors." From the time I could walk, she instilled in me the importance of seeing neighbors as far more than the people who live nearby—they are the heart of your shared community, the ones who stand with you in times of need, and those for whom you do the same. Her care of and friendship with those around her taught me to see beyond buildings and storefronts into homes, networks, and enduring relationships. She would be proud of my neighborhood here in Madison and she would have loved this book. —**STACIE**